Campaign Decision-Making

Campaign Decision-Making:

The Presidential Election of 1964

Karl A. Lamb

Cowell College, University of California, Santa Cruz

Paul A. Smith

Harpur College, State University of New York at Binghamton

Wadsworth Publishing Company, Inc.
Belmont, California

© 1968 by Wadsworth Publishing Company, Inc., Belmont,
California. All rights reserved. No part of this book may be
reproduced in any form, by mimeograph or any other means,
without permission in writing from the publisher.

L. C. Cat. Card No.: 68-27553
Printed in the United States of America

Preface

The 1964 Presidential election shattered generalizations enshrined in the dusty notes of a thousand political science lectures, just as it challenged the assumptions of a host of journalists. Yet the march of political events since the campaign of 1964 has caused its surprises to fade in memory, leaving unresolved the problems of their interpretation.

How does one explain the 1964 election? To dismiss it as an aberration—as an event in American politics so out of the ordinary that we shall not see its like again—is to settle for too little. Such an interpretation makes it easy to conclude that there is little to be learned from what took place and that the old rules of political campaigns are still valid.

The authors of this study do not suggest that the quest for total explanation can be fulfilled in the study of politics; but we do feel that the 1964 election, examined within an appropriate theoretical framework, has a relevance which extends beyond its boundaries of time and circumstance. This relevance concerns the nature of political decisions and the structure and strategies of political decision-making. The application of decision theory to the events of 1964 advances our understanding of that campaign; and it also provides us with an opportunity to review the organization of political parties and to understand political decision-making in situations other than campaigning. Our reexamination of the 1964 campaign permits us to conclude that one particular method for making and coordinating political decisions is most effective within the American political system.

This conclusion is uniquely that of the authors; we can blame it on no one else. It is supported, however, by evidence from a variety of sources. Not the least of these was our direct experience in the Republican and Democratic campaigns. The authors served as Faculty Fellows with the two National Committees from 1964 to 1965, in a program sponsored jointly by the Committees and the National Center for Education in Politics.

Faculty Fellows do not, in the order of things, sit in the seats of the mighty. Nevertheless, we were "inside" to a degree sufficient to observe decisions and decision-makers in a way that is not available to outside commentators or to the public. Early in the campaign we noted patterns of decision-making which seemed quite at odds with common assumptions about how political decisions should be organized and made. As events unfolded, we were able to sharpen the focus of our attention and to ask decision-makers about their decisions—in some cases during the heat of the campaign, in others during the relative tranquillity following defeat in one camp and victory in the other. During this latter period, we completed an extended series of systematic interviews with the campaign leaders of both parties. These interviews, which covered every major campaign operation, were designed to test explicit hypotheses about political decision-making. In many instances we have drawn direct quotations from this interview material; yet in most cases we do not identify our respondents. In the uncertain world of politics our appreciation to those men and women who shared their knowledge and candid appraisals with us is best expressed by protecting their anonymity.

Our data, then, have been gained through direct observation, informal discussions, and systematic interviews. As the second chapter makes clear, we place heavy emphasis upon the use and development of theory, but we claim little originality in theoretical invention. Decision-making theory is now well advanced, especially in the study of organizations. We have built upon many recent contributions to such theory, and our claim to originality comes from our application of that theory to the politics of presidential campaigns, a realm not previously explored from this particular vantage point. Our debt to the theoreticians of decision-making is acknowledged in the notes and references of Chapters 2 and 14.

We owe a particular debt to Professor Charles E. Lindblom, an originator of the decision-making theory that we have found most pertinent to our analysis. Professor Lindblom read an early version of the present manuscript and helped us to understand its existing flaws and potential virtues. We have not, however, sought his blessing for the revised version. Political scientists Charles O. Jones, John H. Kessel, and Henry Kariel have also reacted to all or part of the manuscript, and we thank them for their suggestions and hold them blameless for those we accepted as well as for those we did not.

We are deeply grateful to the NCEP and its vigorous, understanding director, Bernard C. Hennessy, for making our experiences possible. Special thanks, too, are more than deserved by Miss Maureen Drummy of the NCEP staff, who handled numerous details of Fellowship administration with wit and dispatch. Despite the vagaries of political finance, the checks always arrived on time.

We also must express our deep appreciation to those Democratic leaders who also read and commented upon early drafts of relevant chapters and to the Republican leaders who commented so freely upon a case study of the Goldwater campaign staff. What remains in no way implies their approval or disapproval. For reviewing our description of Richard Nixon's campaign of 1960, we wish to thank Robert H. Finch, presently Lieutenant Governor of California.

In ways too subtle to measure, many of our students have also contributed to this book; but the research of three graduate students at American University, Ellen E. Goss, Larry G. Hoffman, and Shirley V. Robson, was of specific and tangible help. The work of Mr. Hoffman was particularly outstanding and deserves both our recognition and our gratitude.

In its very nature, a transcontinental collaboration is prey to logistical difficulties. These were eased by the availablity of air mail and the Xerox machine, but our cooperation might never have come to fruition without the initiative of Alex Kugushev, now the Wadsworth mathematics editor; and the encouragement of our editor, Robert Gormley, whose belief in and support for our book helped us to weather a variety of storms. We are also grateful for the assistance of Mrs. Elizabeth K. Bauer and James Arntz of the Wadsworth editorial staff. Our principal West Coast typist, Charlotte Cassidy, was dependable, accurate, and patient, as were Rebecca Dilts and Mrs. Katherine Farish, who helped in emergencies. Our East Coast typists were too numerous and too varying in their competence to be recognized individually, but they were most helpful in riveting our attention to the typographical details of the manuscript. At all times, including those of despair, our East Coast departmental secretary, Mrs. Marion J. R. Berry, stood ready to perform heroics of salvage and support.

To the surprise of no one, the authors brought contrasting partisan, conceptual, and stylistic commitments to their work. We have disagreed; yet our disagreements have always been overcome. This book may be the only bipartisan result of the Goldwater-Johnson clash. In the long process of decision and revision, theorizing and criticizing, the book has become in every sense a joint venture. The use of the first person plural is no editorial pose; nearly every sentence has been so frequently questioned, pared, and transmuted that individual responsibility can no longer be established. Together, we accept sole responsibility for what follows.

Finally, and with more than customary fervor, we thank our wives, Sally Lamb and Joyce Smith. They shared the misadventures of our periods of participation-observation; suffered the longer agonies of our writing about it; endured pregnancies; protected writer-fathers from the curiosity and importunings of young children; soothed the aspiring creators in moments of irritation; and did not let theory interfere with the making of effective decisions.

Santa Cruz, California   Karl A. Lamb

Binghamton, New York   Paul A. Smith

Contents

Part 2 *Senator Goldwater's Comprehensive Organization*

Part 3 President Johnson and the Use of Incrementalism

Part 4 Conclusions

To Our Parents
Lawrence and Floribel K. Lamb
Herbert and Helene Smith

Part 1

Decision-Making Methods

1

Politics and Decisions: 1964

Outside the Cow Palace, civil rights and antiwar demonstrators marched on. Their signs were insistent, but their strident chants fell to a murmur. The crowd had long since found places inside, and national attention was focused through the eye of television on the speakers' platform. Richard Nixon finished his introduction. After an instant of silence, the sound exploded. The band struck up; red, white, and blue balloons tumbled down from the rafters; delegates and galleries joined in the chant: "We want Barry!" Barry Goldwater walked into the glaring spotlights to accept the presidential nomination of the Republican Party.

The acceptance speech would mark an end and a beginning. Within the rules of American politics, National Conventions are recognized breaking points—times at which the game changes, new strategies are formulated, and disparate organizational units are gathered under a single command. Thus far, Goldwater's supporters had worked among the ranks of party activists to win Convention delegates. Now they had to win the support of a larger, more diverse electorate. When Goldwater submitted his qualifications to the registered Republican voters in the state primaries, his record was mediocre. But his narrow victory in the California primary ended the hopes of Nelson Rockefeller, and the last-minute campaign of William Scranton died noisily as the Convention opened. It was the end of the battle within the party. The battle with a different opposition—the contest to win the allegiance of the general public—lay ahead.

That Goldwater should be standing on this platform was a shock to seasoned politicians of both parties. As the spring of 1964 lengthened into summer, top Democratic leaders still found it hard to believe that the Republicans would nominate the Senator from Arizona. They were convinced that Goldwater was the one Republican candidate most likely to increase their own margin of victory. One of them explained, "All of us wanted Goldwater, but we didn't think they'd be crazy enough to nominate him." Said another, "After Kennedy's death, Goldwater was never really considered. He would be too easy to beat . . .   Until California, no one [of us] thought it would be Goldwater."

The cardinal assumption of American nominating conventions is that the candidate who emerges embodies his party's best chance to win the election. The Goldwater organization operated with smooth efficiency in San Francisco. Could it produce a campaign of similar quality which would make inroads into the Democratic voting habits of the American public? To Democratic leaders, at least, Goldwater's acceptance speech was vastly reassuring. "We couldn't believe our good fortune," one of them recalled, thinking back to the events of the Cow Palace. Disregarding the long accepted rule that the final act of a candidate at the national convention must be to bind up the wounds within the party and unify it in his support, Goldwater's speech vented some of his bitterness toward those who had opposed him. "Any one who joins us in all sincerity, we welcome," he said. "Those who don't care for our cause, we don't expect to enter our ranks in any case." Thrusting at what he considered the unfair tactics of his recently silenced opponents, he declared, "let our Republicanism . . . not be made fuzzy and futile by unthinking and stupid labels . . . . *Extremism in the defense of liberty is no vice. And let me remind you also that moderation in the pursuit of justice is no virtue.*"

Hoping to produce an eloquent conservative statement which would, in passing, demolish what they considered a phony issue, Goldwater and his advisers had not considered how the logic of the speech would be interrupted by sustained cheering, or how much damage could be done by quoting the two sentences on "extremism" out of context. They seemed unprepared for the statement's adverse effect on public opinion or for its destructive impact upon already shattered party harmony. Surely they knew that the same politicians and reporters who had made the word "extremism" into an emotional symbol would be listening critically to the acceptance speech. Was the oversight attributable to political amateurism?

This possibility was contradicted by the smooth professional touch of the Senator's Convention operation. The Goldwater organization had connected every delegation in the Cow Palace to the command post in a trailer outside the arena through a highly sophisticated communications network. The resulting feedback and control provided concerted action by the Goldwater delegates which effectively stifled opposition efforts to influence the course of the Convention. But there was no way to control the behavior of the galleries. Their cheers and boos were unrestrained, and their naked emotions reinforced the image of uncompromising ideological commitment which commentators suggested was the essence of the acceptance speech.

Thus Goldwater's actions appeared as a peculiar blend of blundering and proficiency. These actions fascinated reporters, delighted Democrats, and left Republicans in various states of uncertainty and apprehension. But the Convention had made its decision. Barry Goldwater and William Miller headed the Republican ticket for 1964.

The Impact of Campaign Decisions

Long-standing tradition holds that the challenger, following his first address to the people as the nominee, will take a brief holiday to recover from the labors of winning the nomination before he plunges anew into the campaign maelstrom. Barry Goldwater took his political ease on the yacht *Sundance* off the California coast. During or after this holiday, the new candidate recruits the rest of his personal campaign team, evaluates his political resources, and puts the finishing touches on his strategic plan for maximum mobilization of those resources on election day. Meanwhile, influential party members look to the candidate's headquarters for cues. Lines of communication must be established and plans made. Local leaders seek to determine the willingness of campaign managers to adapt schedule and content to local needs.

Countless decisions are required in a campaign. How were these to be made? By whom? Was there to be an "overall strategy"? If so, who was to make this strategy? What sort of research or information would be sought to sustain it? How comprehensive and detailed was it to be? How flexible? How were the many ideas for running the campaign to be integrated, and the inevitable disagreements to be resolved? And what were the channels of access to those at the top?

There is nothing original about these questions. They are faced by every candidate, though more intensely, perhaps, as the constituency expands and the office becomes more elevated. They are questions of process and method. Frequently obscured by the compelling and dramatic nature of the substantive "issues" dramatized for the voters, they are seldom articulated for public consumption. These questions are answered in private by the candidate and his staff. Most of the answers are not communicated to the public, and many are imperfectly communicated to the rest of the campaign organization. Yet such questions are always present and always answered. They were present in July 1964, as Barry Goldwater received his party's nomination and turned to prepare for the campaign ahead. Goldwater and his close advisers answered them in ways that gave the 1964 election campaign both a form and substance of unusual interest. For example, Goldwater's first appointment was Dean Burch, an obscure and youthful Arizona lawyer, as the new chairman of the Republican National Committee. Burch was an unknown quantity. His appointment offered no assurance that campaign decisions would be reached in familiar ways.

Many analysts of the election have expressed concern for the merits of these decisions, for the ideologies of the men who made them, and for the campaign's impact upon the Republican Party and two-party politics in the United States. A longer view suggests that journalistic prophecies of the demise of the two-party system were exaggerated. By 1966, it was clear that Republicans could still win important elections. The Goldwater campaign did break the established rules of electoral politics—thus reaffirming their validity. But is the Republican campaign to be dismissed as an inexplicable aberration, as little more than a dramatic lesson of what happens when the rules are broken? To do so neither explains why the rules were broken nor advances our understanding of campaigns in general.

The major political events of 1964 are part of the historical record. Data are available concerning the decisions that were related to those events. Journalists and participants have described the inner workings of the Democratic and Republican campaigns.[1] The characteristics and outcomes of campaign strategies have been further analyzed from several points of view within political science.[2] This considerable body of research data need not be repeated; we shall refer to it and add to it. But most important, we shall propose a new mode of interpreting this evidence.

The present authors held positions in the national headquarters of the Republican and Democratic National Committees in 1964. We were able to observe some campaign events at first hand and to gain further knowledge through postelection interviews. As the campaigns progressed, we became increasingly aware of the apparent contrasts in their modes of decision-making. Gradually we concluded that, if properly analyzed, the 1964 campaigns could provide comparative empirical data sufficient to make crude but fruitful tests of hypotheses linking processes of decision with their political effects. Defining the differences in decisional procedures, and establishing the relationship of these procedures to other specified variables, would be crucial. We would have some analytic "control" over our variables, but far from enough to regard the situation as experimental. Unlike the chemist in his laboratory, we could not repeat the "experiment" with varying ingredients to determine the cause or causes of the observed result—Lyndon B. Johnson's 16-million vote margin over Barry Goldwater.

Even before the national conventions were held, the contrast between the Johnson and Goldwater decision-making styles was established. This contrast was more than a disagreement over the substance of policies; it was a difference in the method of organizing a process of campaign policy-making. It seemed to us that the developing body of theory in the social sciences concerned with the making of decisions could provide a useful analytical device. Viewed from this theoretical perspective, the contrasting presidential campaigns could both illuminate the nature of decision-making in a political context and provide a test for different approaches to it. If the variance between Democratic and Republican campaign strategies and styles of organization could be linked to different forms of decision-making, then styles of decision could be designated as one of the forces contributing to the outcome of elections—provided that campaigns themselves affect these outcomes.

The idea that "campaigns really don't make any difference" occurs from time to time in the pronouncements of political experts, who are often defeated politicians. Recently reported research suggests that a "congratulation-rationalization effect" operates to give political victors an inflated perception of the voters' intelligence and of the importance of their personal campaign efforts, while the losers console themselves by downgrading the usefulness of electioneering.[3] Any desire to excuse personal responsibility for the campaign loss can be supported by citations from the massive and carefully documented studies of voting behavior. The focus of these studies has been on the social, economic, and partisan-identification correlates of voter choice. Such factors emphasize the political predispositions of the electorate, and these fairly permanent characteristics of the voting population are only marginally influenced by the events of particular campaigns. As a result, the impact of events occurring within the time-span of the campaign have received scant attention, at least in recent years.[4]

But there is a growing body of literature which suggests that, when judged by their impact upon the outcome of particular elections, campaigns do make a difference.[5] How much difference and in what circumstances are obviously complex questions, but they are being investigated with increasing sophistication. In his last book, the late V. O. Key, Jr., subjected the notion that electoral outcomes are determined by the voters' social and economic characteristics to a fresh analysis. He found that even when there is marked dissatisfaction with the current trend of political events, the opposition party must be perceived as an acceptable alternative; "the minority must not clearly threaten basic policies that have won majority acceptance."[6] After examining opinion survey evidence regarding the presidential elections from 1936 to 1960, Key depicts Eisenhower's victory in 1952 as a classic instance of voters perceiving the party out of power as a "usable minority." Refusing to renew the depression-born image of the Republicans as hostile to social reform, Eisenhower's campaign permitted voters to act upon their dissatisfaction with Democratic management of the Korean War.[7] John Kessel has performed a specific analysis of the 1964 election. Using data gathered periodically by the Survey Research Center, Kessel traces the impact of specific phases of the campaign upon voting intentions, particularly as external events made particular themes more salient to increased numbers of voters.[8] Additional arguments for the existence of campaign effects in 1964, which include actions aimed at gaining nomination, have been offered by scholars at the Survey Research Center.[9]

We offer no final answer to the question of the impact of political campaigns on voting behavior. We cannot imagine a campaign that would have assured a victory for Goldwater in 1964. An improbable combination of Goldwater triumphs and Johnson blunders would have been required to overcome Goldwater's handicaps. Widespread dissatisfaction with Johnson's administration simply did not exist. Lyndon Johnson had established a record of positive accomplishment, fulfilling the sense of loss and need created by Kennedy's assassination. And Senator Goldwater had established, long before his nomination, a public image which many voters were unwilling to associate with the presidential office. Nevertheless, we are convinced that the 1964 campaigns had a significant impact on the magnitude of the outcome— particularly when the "campaign" is defined as the process which leads to the party nomination as well as that which precedes the general election. We can imagine a Goldwater campaign that would have cost less than the actual 500 seats lost by Republican state legislators.

It is the central hypothesis of this book that the manner in which political decisions are organized and made has definite political consequences. We are initially concerned with how policy is made rather than with the wisdom of that policy, but we must find a connection between procedures and wisdom. This connection may seem to be evident; we think it is not. Let us suppose that election campaigns, as classic arenas of political action, can be distinguished by the character of their decision-making processes. In given political circumstances, it may be further supposed, certain processes will work better than others.

Yet how does one evaluate a process of decision? Perhaps by the decisions themselves. But the value of decisions, that is, the quality of their consequences, is often elusive and hard to measure. This may explain why these consequences are often taken for granted if the process of decision is of a certain type. For example, are not campaigns with command decisions and unified directives emanating from a central authority clearly superior to those in which various operations fend for themselves, and scattered decision-makers exercise individual judgment? The apparent simplicity of such a question rests on at least two assumptions. One, that the critical standards of "correct" campaign decision-making are obvious, and the other, that the relationship between these elements and election results is equally well known. We suggest that neither assumption is justified but that both were accepted by major campaign leaders in 1964. After all, competitive electoral politics is an old game in America. Can we assume that the rules of this game—even if stated in the form of political folklore—incorporate an effective understanding of how best to organize a process of decision for electoral purposes?

Conflicting Images of Effective Decision-Making

Practicing politicians are not likely to spend free hours theorizing upon the abstract problem of the best method of making decisions. But the memoirs of working politicians, the accounts of political reporters, and the conclusions of scholarly researchers suggest that many politicians have a sound instinct in these matters. Notions of decision-making are often embedded in analyses of "organization," "planning," or "strategy." The nature of these insights tends to obscure the fact that their content is usually contradictory. Any given campaign seems to produce exactly opposite descriptions of the styles of decision and coordination that are most appropriate and most effective.

Disagreements concerning the best kind of campaign organization were apparent in our own interviews. A middle-range executive of the Goldwater campaign stated:

> When I saw the organization chart for the Republican Party, I thought that Goldwater would win. The organizational plans and preliminary meetings were the best I had ever seen in the many times I had worked with the Republican National Committee on presidential campaigns. This was the first time since Hoover that the presidential candidate was working through the Republican National Committee. Here was the chance to use an organization to overcome our lack of numbers. His failure to work with the organization caused Nixon to lose.

Campaigns are carried on through organizations, and it is no surprise that they should produce their own kind of organization man. He has a vision of central direction and the smooth coordination of political energies. This point of view has been clearly expressed by Stephen C. Shadegg, manager of Goldwater's campaigns for the United States Senate:

> The campaign must have unity. The campaign must move steadily forward from its starting position to its objective of victory. Any delay or deviation from the basic strategic plan will waste precious time and money . . . The manager who has selected the strategy, after consultation with the candidate and his crew of experts, must be in a position of authority to implement that strategy. [10]

But other respondents found that, regardless of their attractiveness, centralized decisions and a clear chain of command could not be achieved in a campaign organization. A member of Goldwater's 1964 inner circle was asked, "What kinds of organizational decisions were made after consulting Goldwater?" He answered:

> In the kaleidoscope that is a presidential campaign, it's hard to remember which decisions resulted from that kind of consultation and which did not . . . We found that running a campaign is not at all like running a business.

His words were echoed by a veteran Democratic campaign leader, who was asked a similar question about the 1964 Democratic experience:

> I've been through so many campaigns that I don't marvel that they're not perfect but that they're as good as they are. This is the way they work. You can't run a campaign like a military organization.

If business and military structures are inappropriate for a presidential campaign, what kind of decisional process is appropriate? If the participants cannot agree, perhaps leading journalists can provide an answer. Since the 1960 campaign of John F. Kennedy is generally regarded as a highly effective one, competent journalistic reports should tell us how the "right" decisions are made.

As an example, let us consider Theodore White's description of John Kennedy's decision to telephone Mrs. Martin Luther King to assure her of his concern about her husband's imprisonment in Atlanta:

> The crisis was instantly recognized by all concerned with the Kennedy campaign . . . The suggestion for meeting it was born to . . . Harris Wofford. Wofford's idea was as simple as it was human—that the candidate telephone directly to Mrs. King . . . Desperately Wofford tried to reach his own chief, Sargent Shriver, head of the Civil Rights Section of the Kennedy campaign, so that Shriver might break through to the candidate barnstorming somewhere in the Middle West. Early [the next] morning, Wofford was able to locate Shriver . . . Moving fast, Shriver reached the candidate at . . . Chicago's International Airport as the latter was preparing to leave for a day of barnstorming in Michigan.
> The candidate's reaction to Wofford's suggestion . . . was impulsive, direct, and immediate. From his room at the Inn, without consulting anyone, [he placed the call] .[11]

There is no indication that this decision was made after a thorough consideration of alternatives. The idea reached Kennedy through an informal, haphazard process, which had not been devised beforehand. It was judged a noteworthy success, but the entire episode was unplanned. In military and business organizations, tactical suggestions do not usually pass from lower to higher echelons. Yet here a suggestion, which reached the candidate almost by chance from a lower echelon, became the basis for action. However, brilliantly exploited, the decision was not the product of careful, comprehensive calculation. White continues:

> Decisions now not only followed crisply and unfalteringly in sequence, but where decision pointed, the organization followed—and the various parts of the organization had all passed through their break-in period, had been road-tested, and purred in the comforting hum of human machinery intermeshing with . . . complete efficiency. . . .
> The machinery purred across the country . . . it purred in New York . . . it stuttered a bit in California; but purred silkily south of the Mason-Dixon line, where Lyndon B. Johnson oiled it with essence of magnolia.[12]

White seems to feel that a campaign can function like a military organization, at least in its final stages. He visualizes an ideal organization in which decisions are made at some central point, on the basis of clearly understood purposes and carefully explored alternative courses of action, and then coordinated and executed with speed and precision. But the vision is fleeting; reality tends to contradict it.

Our own respondents, reflecting on their previous experience, did not agree with White's perception of the smooth functioning of the Kennedy campaign in its closing weeks. They described continuing internal disagreements, off-the-cuff decisions, and organizational mixups. Looking back from a four-year perspective, they remembered trying to cope with all the reasons why people would not vote for Kennedy—"He was inexperienced, or not old enough, or of the wrong religion." They remembered that his campaign "had all the conflicts and sore spots to heal," and that these drained time and energy to the very end.

They remembered, too, the exhaustion and improvisation that overtook them:

It was chaos!

In 1960 there was next to no plan . . .

It was tough. In the last week or ten days of that campaign we were on a treadmill.

Theodore White does not offer a consistent description of procedures used to make effective campaign decisions. He uses a military model, implying centralized decision-making, an elaborate assignment of personnel to specialized functions, and unquestioned discipline. Presidential campaigns seldom enjoy these characteristics, and they are rarely present in White's description.

Finally, we turn to the literature of political science, which abounds in both descriptive and normative accounts of campaign decisions. But again the contrast is pronounced. On one hand, there is the legacy of the urban machine, evoking an image of powerful, hierarchical organizations immediately responsive to the commands of the "boss" and his lieutenants. Dayton McKean gives us a picture of how decisions are made in this political world:

With the thinking being done by the leader and with decisions being reached by him, there must be discipline, and strict discipline, of subordinates. It would be inconsistent for the boss to be the law and for his legislators or his city commissioners to vote as they pleased; they must vote as they are told, and they must do so unanimously—they must present a united front.

Complete obedience is necessary from the bottom to the top; officials are not supposed to have ideas on public policies, but to take orders.[13]

A similar picture of coherent decision-making emerges from this description of campaign planning found in an introductory text in American party politics.

Behind every speech, rally, and campaign piece go careful thought and planning. The planning and execution of a political campaign involve: (1) preparation of a master design or overall strategy, (2) selection of issues and the working out of strategy, (3) activation of the existing organization and the creation of new and subsidiary agencies, (4) counteroffensives, (5) campaign techniques, (6) campaign publicity, and (7) finance.[14]

Another political scientist prescribes centralized and authoritative decision-making for all party workers and managers when writing a *Handbook of Practical Politics*. He quotes the campaign manuals of both the Republican and Democratic National Committees to support his claim that there is general agreement concerning the need for strict lines of campaign authority, and he concludes:

Many campaigns are run with the loosest and most haphazard campaign structure imaginable, without either clear lines of authority or clear understandings of reponsibility. But such haphazard organization and structure brings only haphazard results . . . As a practical matter . . . every function should be delegated clearly and specifically to someone, preferably in writing, with a clear line of authority and a perfectly clear understanding of responsibility . . . Centralized control . . . must always be maintained.[15]

Thus we are told that if centralized control is abandoned, the result of the campaign will be imperiled. Yet this prescription is prefaced by the suggestion that many campaigns fall far short of the ideal. Do these campaigns fail? A partial answer is supplied by Professor Murray Levin, who reaches the following conclusion after studying Edward Kennedy's senatorial campaign of 1962:

The image of the political campaign as a highly efficient operation, directed by an expert staff, is rarely true-to-life. Most campaigns resemble a comedy of errors in which the victor prospers primarily because he has committed fewer strategic blunders than his opponent . . . Political strategy is formulated on the basis of accurate information, misinformation, rules of thumb, hunches, and the availability of scarce resources.[16]

V. O. Key expressed the same point in describing presidential campaigns:

A Presidential campaign may be thought to be the work of a tightly knit organization spread over the entire country and directed by cunning men wise in the ways of managing the multitude. In truth, the campaign organization is a jerry-built and makeshift structure manned largely by temporary and volunteer workers who labor long hours amidst confusion and uncertainty. Assignments of responsibility and lines of authority are likely to be hazy. The army of campaign workers is loosely articulated and some of its regiments may be sulky, if not actually insubordinate . . . Often the outlines of a campaign strategy are scarcely visible amidst the confusion of the campaign, and, indeed, campaigns often rest on only the sketchiest of plans. The preparation of a reasoned and comprehensive strategy requires more of a disposition to think through the campaign in its broadest outlines than often exists around a national headquarters.[17]

It would appear that political scientists are in no greater agreement than politicians and journalists about how effective campaign decisions should be made—or even how they are made. To our knowledge, only one major book dealing with party politics has a section explicitly devoted to decision-making.[18] Its portrayal of political party decision-making in Detroit is far removed from the centralized process called for in several of the preceding quotations. In sum, we have found conflicting points of view about how decisions can best be made. These views have been obscured by concepts of authority and function and lacking in clear evidence to support their evaluations. Thus both normative and descriptive treatments of decision-making in political campaigns are contradictory and inconclusive.

Requirements for Further Analysis

What has been gained by this preliminary quest for a model of campaign decision-making? We began by asking if particular processes of choice are sufficiently understood to be linked with particular campaign outcomes. The answer must be negative. There is no doubt that men like James Farley, Leonard Hall, Edward Flynn, and Robert Kennedy have been wise enough to mount effective, even spectacular—and certainly winning—campaigns. But what procedures have been used to insure the making of effective decisions? There is a marked tendency to ascribe effectiveness to centralized and authoritative decision-making, and to identify this with "good organization"; yet this style is perceived as an ideal that is seldom attained in the real world. We have found criticisms of this ideal which imply that some other style of decision-making might be more suited to the circumstances of political campaigning in America.

This is a beginning. To organize a presidential campaign requires countless decisions. If we ask what guidelines were available to Barry Goldwater and Lyndon Johnson as they and their advisers sought to provide for these decisions, we seem to find only a scanty collection of familiar notions, many of them contradictory and ambiguous. Even when the 1960 Kennedy campaign is taken as an example, precisely what worked and what did not is debatable. Indeed, the need to isolate decision-making styles in order to examine their effectiveness seems hardly recognized. Recognition is a prerequisite to systematic enquiry.

Do mistaken interpretations of decision-making in the 1960 campaign help to explain the contradictions we found in the actions of Goldwater and his staff at the 1964 Convention? Were they attempting to reach decisions according to the details of an explicit procedure? Did this procedure increase the likelihood of political error? Or were the Senator and his staff insensitive to the way in which decisions should be reached, caring only about their substance? And what was Lyndon Johnson's approach? Did he consciously employ a distinct procedure for making decisions during the campaign? Can it be distinguished from that used by Goldwater? Can it be related to the scope of Democratic victory?

Until we can clearly describe different methods of decision-making and establish their relationship to political results, little progress can be made in answering such questions. It will be the task of the next chapter to construct formal models which are related to the contrasting patterns of decision-making in the Goldwater and Johnson campaigns. These models must enable us to identify the procedures used in reaching decisions and link these procedures to the quality of the decisions. This linkage should be sufficiently firm so that we can suggest that different procedures would, in given circumstances, have produced different political results. The models thus will provide tools of analysis which will be applied to the two presidential campaigns in the chapters that follow.

The present chapter bears ample witness to the difficulties of identifying and evaluating a process of decision. While we do not claim to produce the definitive explanation of what happened in 1964, our analysis should do much to illuminate the nature of decision-making in campaign politics. If we can determine that Lyndon Johnson and his staff consistently used a different mode of reaching decisions than did the Goldwater organization, and that the Johnson method regularly proved more effective for the reasons predicted through analyzing our models, we shall be able to assert with some confidence that decision-making methods did indeed influence the magnitude of the electoral outcome in 1964. We may then be able to commend certain aspects of the Goldwater and Johnson styles to the further attention of both politicians and scholars.

Notes on Chapter 1

[1]Robert J. Donovan, *The Future of the Republican Party* (New York: New American Library, 1964); Robert D. Novak, *The Agony of the G.O.P. 1964* (New York: Macmillan, 1965); Richard H. Rovere, *The Goldwater Caper* (New York: Harcourt, 1965); Stephen Shadegg, *What Happened to Goldwater?* (New York: Holt, 1965); Theodore H. White, *The Making of the President 1964* (New York: Atheneum, 1965); Karl Hess, *In a Cause that Will Triumph* (Garden City, N.Y.: Doubleday, 1967); Harold Faber,

ed., *The Road to the White House* (New York: McGraw-Hill, 1965); and George F. Guilder and Bruce K. Chapman, *The Party That Lost Its Head* (New York: Knopf, 1966).

[2]Nelson W. Polsby and Aaron Wildavsky, *Presidential Elections: Strategies of American Electoral Politics* (New York: Scribner's, 1964); Ithiel de Sola Pool *et al.*, "A Postscript on the 1964 Election," *The American Behavioral Scientist*, 8 (May 1965), 39-44; *Election '64: A Ripon Society Report* (Cambridge: Ripon Society, 1965); *The 1964 Elections* (Washington: Republican National Committee, 1965); and John H. Kessel, "The Impact of Strategy: The 1964 Presidential Campaign" (Paper prepared for the 1966 Annual Meeting of the American Political Science Association, New York City, September 6-10).

[3]John W. Kingdon, "Politicians' Beliefs About Voters," *American Political Science Review*, 61 (March 1967), 137-145.

[4]The pioneer study of voting behavior utilizing panel surveys was conducted in Erie County, New York, during the presidential election campaign of 1940: P. F. Lazarsfeld, B. R. Berelson, and Hazel Gaudet, *The People's Choice*, 2nd ed. (New York: Columbia University Press, 1948). Growing from studies of consumer choice, the study was designed on the assumption that the selection of candidates would resemble the choice of competing brands on a market shelf; thus the content of the mass media and the events of the campaign would be of great significance. The findings were quite the reverse. The level of voter information and interest were found to be quite low; the influence of party preference ("brand loyalty") to be quite high.

A similar major survey was carried out in Elmira, New York, during the election of 1948: B. R. Berelson, P. F. Lazarsfeld, and W. N. McPhee, *Voting* (Chicago: University of Chicago Press, 1954). The conception of party identification, a relatively permanent attribute of individual attitude patterns, has been developed, refined, and used as the basis for research by the University of Michigan Survey Research Center in Angus Campbell, Gerald Gurin, and W. E. Miller, *The Voter Decides* (Evanston, Ill.: Row, Peterson, 1954); Campbell, P. E. Converse, Miller, and Donald E. Stokes, *The American Voter* (New York: Wiley, 1960); and Campbell, Converse *et al.*, *Elections and the Political Order* (New York: Wiley, 1966). The Michigan survey data has been utilized by many other scholars. Notable among them is Heinz Eulau, *Class and Party in the Eisenhower Years* (New York: Free Press, 1962).

Concurrently with the publication of these major works, the last 20 years have seen the proliferation of voting studies in the periodical literature. Studies of voting behavior in the 1964 election, most of which tend to emphasize sociological factors, include Philip E. Converse *et al.*, "Electoral Myth and Reality: The 1964 Election," *American Political Science Review*, 59 (June 1965), 321-336; Leon D. Epstein and Austin Ranney, "Who Voted for Goldwater: The Wisconsin Case," *Political Science Quarterly*, 81 (March 1966), 82-94; Thomas W. Benham, "Polling for a Presidential Campaign," *Public Opinion Quarterly*, 29 (Fall 1965); 357-367; Louis Harris, "The Election of 1964," reprinted in Donald G. Herzberg and Gerald M. Pomper, eds., *American Party Politics* (New York: Holt, 1966), pp. 404-409; and Donald E. Stokes, "Some Dynamic Elements of Contests for the Presidency," *American Political Science Review*, 60 (March 1966), 19-28.

[5]Although the pioneer students of voting behavior found that the campaign had considerably less impact on voter choice than anticipated, they found a measurable influence. See Berelson *et al., Voting*, Chapters 10, 11, and 12. Studies which assess the impact of campaigns by focusing on the campaigns themselves, rather than the individual voter, include Stanley Kelley, Jr., *Political Campaigning* (Washington: The Brookings Institution, 1960); Kelley, *Professional Public Relations and Political Power* (Baltimore: Johns Hopkins University Press, 1956); Murray B. Levin, *The Alienated Voter* (New York: Holt, 1960); Levin, *Kennedy Campaigning* (Boston: Beacon,

1966); and *The New Methodology: A Study of Political Strategy and Tactics* (Washington, D.C.: American Institute for Political Communication, 1967).

[6]V.O. Key, Jr. (with the assistance of Milton C. Cummings, Jr.), *The Responsible Electorate* (Cambridge, Mass.: Harvard University Press, 1966), p. 77.

[7]Key, pp. 67-79.

[8]Kessel, "The Impact of Strategy."

[9]Converse *et al.*, "Electoral Myth and Reality," p. 321.

[10]Stephen C. Shadegg, *How to Win an Election* (New York: Taplinger, 1964), pp. 30-31.

[11]*The Making of the President 1960* (New York: Pocket Books, 1961), p. 386.

[12]*The Making of the President 1960*, p. 387.

[13]Dayton D. McKean, *The Boss* (Boston: Houghton Mifflin, 1940), p. 271. There are countless descriptions of "machine politics" in American literature, varying widely in style, indignation, and analytic form. A good review of this writing is found in Austin Ranney and Willmore Kendall, *Democracy and the American Party System* (New York: Harcourt, 1956), pp. 249-259. Several representative machines are described in William M. Reddig, *Tom's Town* (Philadelphia: Lippincott, 1947), and J. T. Salter, *Boss Rule: Portraits in City Politics* (New York: McGraw-Hill, 1935).

[14]Hugh A. Bone, *American Politics and the Party System* (New York: McGraw-Hill, 1965), p. 342.

[15]Paul P. Van Riper, *Handbook of Practical Politics* (New York: Harper, 1967), pp. 137-138.

[16]Levin, *Kennedy Campaigning*, pp. 115-116.

[17]V. O. Key, Jr., *Politics, Parties, and Pressure Groups*, 5th ed. (New York: Crowell, 1964), pp. 457, 463.

[18]Samuel J. Eldersveld, *Political Parties* (Chicago: Rand McNally, 1964), Ch. 15.

2

Models of Campaign Decision-Making

To assert that particular policy decisions of the 1964 presidential campaigns occasioned unusually keen interest is an understatement. Barry Goldwater's actions at the Republican National Convention and the impact of those actions on party harmony and public opinion are a case in point; for much that was criticized in Goldwater's later campaign seemed foreshadowed in San Francisco. But little attention has been paid to the process of decision within the Goldwater organization which determined the behavior of the candidate and his staff at the Convention. This is understandable, for the results of these decisions were more obvious, and more amenable to analysis, than the process used in reaching them.

We hold, however, that the results at San Francisco followed from a pattern of decision-making by Goldwater, his advisers, and his staff that was well established by Convention time. Both the content of those decisions and the organizational structure in which they occurred were based on an analysis of previous Republican campaigns and an effort to avoid their presumed errors. Goldwater's actions at San Francisco were deliberate; they were not accidental. They were not made out of ignorance of the nature of American party politics. Rather, they were based on conclusions reached by men of varying degrees of political experience who felt that the usual approach of the Republican party to the national electorate should be drastically modified.

This assertion seems remarkable, since the Republicans departed radically from the accepted "rules" of presidential campaign politics. These rules are so well accepted that many observers could not believe that Goldwater would break them, until his actions at the Convention resolved all lingering doubts. There is nothing mysterious about them. They are part of both conventional wisdom and systematic analysis. They specify that presidential elections are won through diverse and moderate appeals at the center, where party membership overlaps and party identification may be transitory. They advise that the minority party should select a candidate who has not been identified with the less popular positions associated with his party. His nomination will blur those group attachments and ideological associations which reinforce party identification in the minds of the voters. By "cross-cutting" established allegiances, he will have a better chance of victory.[1]

But Senator Goldwater presented himself to the electorate as a militant conservative. He sharpened the very party differences which Republican candidates since at least 1940 had attempted to soothe and obscure. Recognizing his vulnerability, Democrats cast Goldwater as the "heavy" in the electoral drama—a candidate at once alarming and absurd. The result was decisive. The validity of the rules was reaffirmed.[2]

This convergence of systematic theory, predictive hypotheses, conventional wisdom, and empirical results left political analysts happily satisfied with their explanations of voting behavior. But their writings made few attempts at explaining Senator Goldwater's behavior. The one-sided outcome only reemphasized the surprises of 1964. Why did the Republicans choose "a minority candidate within a minority party"?[3] Why, before, after, and during the Convention, did this candidate persist in breaking so many established rules of the campaign game? What process led Barry Goldwater and his organization to formulate so many decisions that can only be regarded as political mistakes? And was Goldwater's experience unique, or is there reason to expect that other candidates, undeterred by Goldwater's example, may arrive at similar conclusions and make similar decisions?

It is our contention that, in large measure, the answers to these questions may be arrived at by applying decision theory to the events of 1964. Since the boundaries of this theory enclose a rich variety of types, let us review some major aspects of the intellectual framework we shall be using.

The Decision-Making Framework for Political Analysis

Decision-making is not an esoteric aspect of human behavior in politics. Herbert A. Simon emphasizes this point:

In talking about decision-making, I am dealing not with some highly special aspect of the political process, but with its central core. Voting, legislating, adjudicating, and administering have always been conceived of as decision-making processes. The tools of political analysis—legal, historical, and behavioral—have always been adapted to the analysis of decision. The use of a decision-making framework for political research is not novel; it represents continuing development along paths that stretch back to the beginnings of political science.[4]

When broadly conceived, the decision-making process encompasses much of what has traditionally been regarded as political action. The decisions studied must be significant—a vote, a judicial opinion, an executive order, or a military command. Decisions gain this significance from being made in the context of an organization or process in which the decision has an impact—an election, a court of law, a government bureaucracy, or an infantry company. Thus decision-making analysis is concerned with discernible political events, rather than with attitudes, identifications, or effects. Furthermore, while the focus of analysis can be either upon a single decision (such as the intervention in Korea[5]) or upon a series of decisions (such as a presidential campaign), it is assumed that a continuous stream of human behavior is taking place.

To gain significance, the event called "a decision" must be preceded and followed by others. A decision is not a single act;[6] rather, it is part of a process of action. This process takes place within a relevant environment of rules, values, and physical restraints which draws the attention of the decision-maker to the problem requiring solution. Sometimes this environment is a formal organization; often it is not. In either case, it influences the range of alternative possibilities that will be considered; and from what perspective and in what manner these alternatives will be judged. Thus, following Simon, it might be useful to think of the process of decision as consisting of at least three separable components: the focus of attention, the search for alternatives, and the choice itself.[7]

Each of these components may be treated separately in order to describe or to judge a process of decision. Taken together, with data stretching over a span of time, they constitute a definable pattern, one which may encompass both decision-making and the character of the organization in which decisions take place.

By the *focus of attention* we mean the range of items perceived by the decision-maker as requiring choice. Items may be added to his "agenda for decision" through his own initiative, the action of other elements in the organization, or external events. The construction of this hypothetical agenda by the top decision-maker (in our example, the presidential candidate) reveals the essence of his approach to his task. Some matters are considered to be of such importance that they must be decided long in advance, before they can be raised within the organization or by external events; some matters are assigned to subordinates; and others are left to the habitual workings of the organization. The focus of attention reflects an ordering of political values in the mind of the decision-maker.

Once the matter to be decided has been defined, the *search for alternatives* may be complicated and exhaustive. On the other hand, it may be telescoped to the vanishing point. The circumstances in which the question to be decided arises and the style of the decision-maker are crucial. The use of staff assistants, the processing of information, the communication demanded and received from other elements in the organization, and the influence of various advisers are all variables which become relevant at this point. Perhaps the most important consideration is the adaptability and flexibility of the decision-maker, together with his concept of how decisions ought to be made.

The *act of choosing* is the least significant component of the decisional process in terms of time consumed. The focus of attention determines which matters are perceived as requiring decision, eliminating a range of matters which other decision-makers (or critics writing after the fact) may consider of central importance. The search for alternatives will proceed according to the convictions of the decision-maker as to what kinds of information or sources of inspiration are necessary, useful, and relevant. These first two components may, in fact, reduce the alternatives so completely that the decision-maker is hardly aware of the possibility of choice. The answer he gives to the question posed seems inevitable—so inevitable that he may express annoyance at subordinates who doubted what his decision would be.

By separating the process of decision into these three phases, the complexity of the process is both emphasized and clarified. To think of a decision as a single event occurring at a point in time is deceptive. The focus of attention of a given decision-maker is determined by his own nature and political attitudes and modified by the organizational environment in which he works. His experience and temperament may dictate a limited concern for any but the most obvious alternative. One of Barry Goldwater's closest associates told us:

A physicist who knows the laws of gravity is not going to step off a roof. Goldwater believed in certain things. This made his decisions easy. There was never anything hard for Goldwater in making decisions.

Thus the Republican candidate's basic orientation to his political world had a direct impact upon the universe of alternatives he would consider and the manner in which he would choose among them. The three phases of decision were intimately related, the character of one leading to that of the others.

When the analysis shifts from a single decision-maker to the entire campaign organization, it becomes obvious that the intersecting components of the decision process will generate matching structures of authority and function. Together, these serve to answer certain questions: Who will have the ear of the candidate? Will those who urge particular types of alternatives be excluded in the jockeying for influence? At what point can authoritative choice be made? Is authority so specifically delegated that no intermediary can intervene in the affairs of a colleague when he feels a mistake is being made? Can disagreements only be resolved by referring them to the next higher echelon? Are the personnel of the next higher echelon readily available, or are they embroiled in their own problems? Is influence so distributed that the focus of decision of the organization is broadened, giving the representatives of many points of view access to the relevant decision-makers?

Our beginning chapter quoted several descriptions of the way decisions are and should be made in campaigns. The central tendencies of these quotations seemed to reveal two distinct conceptions of campaign decision-making. The most admired of these held that decisions should be made at a central point, communicated in an orderly way, and executed by specialists. The second conception held that, like it or not, campaigns are decentralized, disorderly, and confused. It is now time to refine these conflicting notions in order to construct formal models which may help us explain the events of 1964.

The Comprehensive Model of Rational Decision-Making

The first model is based upon the ideals of centralized decision-making and hierarchical organization so frequently praised. It is a pattern of complete rationality, closely analogous to the classical "economic man" operating in an "ideal type" bureaucracy. Its rules may be applied to both the intellectual practices of the individual decision-maker and the process of ordering collective decisions by organized groups of individuals.[8]

This model requires that each decision-maker have a clear perception of his goals, including their relative value or rank; an equally clear understanding of the scope and purposes of his own and others' decision-making authority; and full knowledge of the relationship of his decisions to a sequence of goals to be attained. Thus his focus of attention is clearly defined, and the decision-maker has no reason to concern himself with the areas for which other leaders are responsible. He proceeds by identifying all courses of action that might be used to achieve his goals. Each alternative is weighed by making a careful study of its consequences, including how these consequences relate to his entire range of values. Therefore, the search for alternatives is exhaustive. The decision-maker then selects that alternative which is "best," that is, which will achieve his given aims at the lowest cost (to other values). The actual choice is relatively easy, because it is based on a complete survey of the possibilities.

For collective decisions, the model calls for a hierarchical structure of authority. At the top are a small number of decision-makers who agree explicitly on the definition and ranking of goals. They decide policy questions and coordinate the decisions and actions of all those who implement policy decisions. Ordinarily, this requires functional specialization, unbroken lines of authority, and complete internal communication.[9]

As a campaign operation, such a system of political choice would produce a frictionless exploitation of available resources so that the best possible combination of appeals is addressed to the electorate under the most favorable circumstances. The candidate and a few very close, like-minded associates, at the pinnacle of a pyramid-like campaign organization, would be the decision-makers. Their decisions would produce the best political moves, and the maximum coordination of those moves. The election might not be won, but the candidate would receive all the votes it would be possible for him to garner in the given circumstances. If both candidates achieve this ideal of rational decision-making, the campaign would become an imposing edifice of perfect moves, with the outcomes presumably calculable.

As used here, "rational" means a certain procedure and implies a certain context for making choices, whether on the part of an individual candidate or of a campaign organization. An essential feature of the context is the theoretical ability to consider all possible alternative goals and means, together with their consequences. The procedure is distinguished by the discovery and evaluation of these alternatives, and the selection of the best according to clearly defined values or purposes. Even when purposes are accepted as "given"—winning the election, for example—the available information, and the process of search and assessment must be comprehensive, just as the resulting decision must be accepted and carried out in every part of the organization. Therefore we have chosen to follow a number of other authors in calling our first model the Comprehensive Ideal.[10]

Several points need to be made about this model at once. First, it is clearly "normative" rather than "descriptive."[11] That is, instead of saying what campaign decision-makers do, or can do, it tells us what they should do in order to assure organizational efficiency. And it promises that results will be achieved smoothly, with just the right strategies devised on high and applied with unfailing precision to remove conflicts of interest and uncertainty among potential supporters. Comprehensive decision-making promises that more votes will be garnered by a campaign organization unified on the basis of agreement concerning goals and marked by well-defined, hierarchical, and orderly relationships.

Second, we are aware of very few serious politicians who have attempted to convert the model's specifications into political reality. This might be surprising. Given its premises, even a costly and imperfect effort to follow the model could lead to significant political rewards. One possible explanation for such neglect would be that the Comprehensive Ideal has never really been considered. This possibility seems remote in view of the notions of "good organization" that were expressed by the campaign participants, journalists, and scholars quoted in our first chapter. Their apparent failure to comprehend, or even care about, the logical structure of the Ideal did not prevent them from accepting its operational assumptions and guidelines.

Which leads us to a third point. The ideal of comprehensive, rational decision-making, even if not formally conceived, remains strong and widely respected in both practical and academic circles. Despite the herculean burdens it places upon the politician, evidence abounds for the continuing appeal of "rationality" in political decision-making. The *New York Times* summarized the views of a prominent practicing politician, Robert F. Kennedy, on how he would decide which candidate to endorse for the 1966 Democratic nomination in New York:

Before making a choice, he said, he would have to consider whether one man would "make a distinctly better Governor" than the others, what kinds of campaigns the various candidates might make against Governor Rockefeller, the amount of support that a particular candidate would have across the state, and whether the candidate "could unite the various factions or splinter them." .... He did not know whether [these standards] could be found "in such a combination that it would make me decide I should endorse a candidate."[12]

With a set of political ends in mind, Kennedy proposed an exhaustive consideration of alternative means (candidates) to achieve them. The pattern of anticipated decision-making exhibited many characteristics of the Comprehensive Ideal. It was a tall order, and Kennedy never did endorse a candidate.

Statements such as Kennedy's do not necessarily imply a belief that a fully rational decision-making process is about to be consummated. Indeed, there seldom are grounds for supposing that the speakers have a Comprehensive model of rational choice explicitly in mind. What such statements do show is that major features of the model continue to dominate the self-conscious expressions of working politicians and political observers trying to describe how proper decision-making should be carried on. Many are resigned to the fact that the Ideal will remain forever beyond their grasp, yet their admiration persists.

The few party leaders we interviewed who offered criticisms of the Comprehensive Ideal proposed no alternative mode of decision-making and organization. Rather, they limited themselves to concrete instances of what would be more "realistic," "practical," or "like we have always done it before." From this perspective, attacks on particular examples of political decision-making have left our Comprehensive model largely unscathed. As a normative ideal it remains generally cherished and rarely questioned. And the procedures used to make actual campaign decisions ordinarily have been justified either by proud claims for how closely (under the circumstances) the Ideal has been approximated, or by vague and deprecating references to those who have taken it too literally.

The gradual accumulation of better empirical data has led to a modified conception of what decision-makers actually do, and this, in turn, has cast serious doubt upon the operational validity of the Comprehensive model. There is an abundance of both intuitive and systematic evidence "that the range of things a human being takes into account when he is making a complex decision is not enormous, and that the thought processes he goes through are not terribly involved or sophisticated."[13] These findings suggest that decision-makers may be fundamentally incapable of meeting the requirements of the model. To make an initial test of the operational validity of Comprehensiveness under given conditions, three kinds of questions may be asked.

First, what is the scope of anticipated decisions? How diverse are the policy areas which must be considered? How many people will be immediately affected? And how important are the changes which the decisions will bring about? The scope of decisions assigning headquarters office space is smaller than of those distributing aid to congressional candidates. In the latter case, more persons are affected, they pose more diverse situations to be considered, and more alternative choices will be urged upon the decision-makers. Furthermore, the candidates are likely to be more influential and to attach more importance to what is decided, and it is plausible to suppose that the help the party gives them will have more numerous and important consequences than on decisions about the physical placement of the campaign staff. Thus, campaign leaders are likely to delegate the authority for room assignments to an office manager. The office manager may, of course, systematically favor members of one party faction over another, thereby stimulating conflict within the staff which was not intended by the candidate and which angers other leaders.

Factors measured by the number and influence of persons and alternatives, the amount of resulting change, and the importance (value) of this change, delineate the scope of the decisions. If the example just cited is typical, however, leading decision-makers must be prepared to intervene in decisions of small scope as well as of large. There will be cases in which the scope of one set of decisions is not demonstrably larger than that of another. Moreover, how does one "prove" that the consequences of certain decisions are greater than the consequences of others? Despite these difficulties of determination, we think that, as a practical matter, there is sufficient agreement to make the question of scope meaningful for our purposes.[14] Taken together, the decisions required in a presidential campaign will be large in scope. This means that leading decision-makers must develop broad foci of attention, consider numerous alternatives, and make complex choices.

Second, how much information is available to support the search for alternatives? Is the information upon which the decisions must be based characterized by certainty, risk, or uncertainty? Certainty exists if each alternative is known, and known to lead invariably to a specific outcome; risk, if each alternative leads to one of a set of possible specific outcomes, each occurring with a known probability; and uncertainty, if only some alternatives are known, each of which has possible specific outcomes, the probabilities of which are completely unknown or not even meaningful.[15] Less formally, uncertainty is any lack of sure knowledge about real or hypothetical conditions or events.[16] More certain knowlege is available, for example, about how and where to install telephones in the campaign headquarters than about how and where to get the support of state party leaders. Much uncertainty exists in any presidential campaign. There are obvious limitations upon the search for alternatives and upon the confidence with which one alternative may be chosen from a list of possible solutions.

The third group of questions concerns the capabilities of the decision-makers. How much of the available information can actually reach them?

And what proportion of this information are they able to use or "process" in making their decisions? To answer these questions, many specific characteristics of the decision-makers are important: their training and experience, their emotional and intellectual resources, their available time, their staff and data-processing facilities, and so forth. In presidential campaigns, the most highly trained decision-makers, equipped with the most formidable processing aids, would be taxed by the range of relevant information and the existence of "noise." And campaigns have not been noted for training or equipping their decision-makers to increase their capabilities.

The answers to these types of questions enable us to specify different kinds of decision-making situations. The focus of attention of the decision-makers must be broad. A substantial amount of uncertainty inhibits the search for alternatives, and the highly variable capabilities of decision-makers will affect the way they focus their attention, search for alternatives, and make their choices. Whatever its logical elegance, the Comprehensive Ideal would seem impractical in presidential campaigns. It would appear to be well suited to situations in which highly trained decision-makers, with ample time and facilities, are called upon to reach decisions within the scope of their training and on the basis of almost complete information. The scope of the decisions would be small, the information abundant, and the decision-making capabilities great. Where should a federal highway or flood-control project be constructed? What changes in Selective Service eligibility requirements will bring 100,000 more men into the armed forces? How should a new tax law be drafted to achieve certain revenue purposes? In these areas of technical expertise and professional training, situations conducive to Comprehensive decision-making are approximated in the real world, and the model is a useful device for guiding and assessing the quality of the actions taken.[17]

Up to this point our discussion of the Comprehensive Ideal has emphasized its practical limitations. We have suggested that these limitations are serious enough to undermine the operational validity of the model in campaign politics. Yet it still may be argued that Comprehensiveness is not defective; it is just difficult because of particular circumstances of decision. To meet this argument, we must turn to more formal criticisms of the model, most of which are found in the very disciplines which originally gave it form: economics, philosophy, mathematics, and theoretical approaches to organization.[18] In drawing upon this work, we found certain studies unusually relevant. Those of Charles E. Lindblom have proved especially useful.[19] The thrust of these criticisms goes beyond saying that it is hard to be Comprehensive in making political choices. Rather, they suggest that attempting to achieve the model's specifications will result in less effective decisions than would otherwise be reached. The intrinsic defects of the Comprehensive Ideal for a political campaign may be summarized as follows:

Permanent agreement on goals is unlikely. The assumption of a single or unified set of goals or purposes is not and cannot be valid in campaign politics. Indeed, other researchers have found that such an assumption lacks validity even in what would seem to be more appropriate situations, such as those prevailing within business firms.[20] One might suppose that a political party would be unified around the goal of winning, but this proposition does not cope with the subgoals and values involved in an actual campaign. These are not only multiple; they are subject to change. Individual members of the organization will differ among themselves about the value of a project, as Goldwater disagreed with F. Clifton White concerning the film *Choice* or Lyndon Johnson's media advisers quarreled with his party leaders over the "daisy girl" television spot. Members will change their minds about the importance of projects, and will think of new projects (which then must be assigned a priority) as the campaign advances. Conflicts of ambition or personality will generate differences in program evaluation. Sources outside the organization, including the opposition, the press, or an action of some foreign government (such as Red China's first nuclear bomb explosion), will raise issues which in turn introduce new values or require a reordering of existing priorities. Finally, the pluralistic distribution of power in party organizations works to frustrate attempts to impose a particular set of projects or goals from on high.[21]

A serious effort to achieve the value conditions prescribed in the model therefore threatens either greater conflict over goals, or a situation in which the decision-makers dangerously misperceive reality. This latter possibility is emphasized by the finding of Kenneth Arrow that under circumstances of multiple, competing values, decision-makers cannot learn from the electorate the precise ordering of values preferred by "the people."[22]

Complete information is unavailable. The assumptions of complete information and exhaustive evaluation of alternatives by decision-makers are adaptable neither to the actual number of alternative possibilities nor to man's limited problem-solving capacities. We have observed the impossible burdens of detection and reasoning the Comprehensive Ideal places upon the political decision-maker. The dimensions of these are merely reemphasized by the alternatives which must be considered in determinate situations, such as chess.[23] But politics is not a determinate game. The number of possible alternatives which might be considered in a campaign situation is beyond calculation, and the consequences of each are infinite. The decision-maker would be forced either into no decisions at all or arbitrary choices based on inadequate information. If, at some point, the decision-maker concluded that his planning allowed for all possibilities and narrowed his focus of attention, he might well exclude information that threatened the assumptions of his plan.

The prototype of the Comprehensive style is found in military organizations, and military history provides the classic demonstrations of this fault of Comprehensive decision-making. One occurred in the opening month of the First World War. The Schlieffen Plan, developed by the German General Staff during two decades of Comprehensive planning, required the immediate invasion of Belgium and promised the encirclement of Paris and the defeat of France in exactly 39 days. Plan Seventeen, developed by the French General Staff, provided for an attack through the "lost" province of Alsace, a march to the Rhine, and equally early victory over Germany. Both France and Germany believed that their plans allowed for every contingency, and both were put into operation.

Germany badly underestimated the effect on world opinion of the violation of Belgian neutrality, the strength of Belgian resistance, and the ability of French troops exhausted by retreat to turn and fight again. German General von Kluck stated that this last possibility "was not studied in our war academy." The French badly underestimated the number of armed men Germany could put into the field. Preoccupied with the need for an offensive on their right, French generals discounted reports of massive German advances on their left, although the reports were brought by French aviators. The clash of the two plans resulted in the crushing tragedy of a war of attrition which brought such massive and meaningless destruction that the world stage was set for the conflict of 1939-1945; but Comprehensive planning remained the favored military mode.

Another example is pertinent. In 1942, the Japanese naval fleet sailed toward Midway Island, expecting that its capture would lure the American fleet out of Pearl Harbor into a fatal ambush. Success of the plan depended on secrecy, so the plan itself stated that the Japanese naval code was secure. The code had in fact been broken by American intelligence officers, and the American fleet sailed out to ambush the ambushers, destroying effective Japanese naval power in the Battle of Midway.[24]

Ends and means cannot be separated. The assumed separation between fact and value or means and ends does not exist in the real world of politics. Given the major goal of winning the election, various means are assessed by different decision-makers according to their own perceptions of effectiveness. Means are many and diverse: television broadcasts, minority group organizations, speaking tours, voter registration drives, the adoption and presentation of issue positions. Very few of such means are value-free in themselves. The registration director, for example, will place a high value on signing up new voters, arguing that an expanded electorate is essential for victory. The "advance men" will see nothing more important than well-arranged appearances of the candidate, and will be outraged by any lack of money, facilities, or materials which hampers their work. The foreign policy expert will claim that a particular policy statement requires immediate attention, its publication holding the key to needed public support. Means, therefore, take on, in varying degrees, the value aspects of ends.

In addition, the availability and use of means affect the desirability of ends. Assignments of priority rarely stay firm. As decisions are made and projects (means) are put into operation, they produce changes in the campaign situation calling for new appraisals of sub-goals. ("The candidate drew a huge crowd in Atlanta. Maybe we should have more tours in the South"; or, "Those books criticizing Johnson are getting wide circulation; we'd better get out more publicity attacking them.") In the face of this intimate relationship between means and ends, the Comprehensive model could in theory collapse under the sheer weight of decisions regarding the order of values. More likely, harried decision-makers will make an arbitrary selection which ignores or underestimates major values that are widely accepted. The immediate consequences will be a loss of public support and aggravated conflicts within the campaign organization.

Costs of decision are disregarded. The lack of provision for decision-making costs is another serious flaw in the Comprehensive model when it is applied to political campaigns. Any decisions are costly to make.[25] But in a campaign, information, money, time, and social agreement are particularly scarce resources. Comprehensive analyses take enormous amounts of each. So pronounced are these costs of decision that a campaign determined to follow the Comprehensive model would be in danger of making no substantial decisions at all. Furthermore, decision costs are multiplied in a geometric ratio by the sequential character of campaign planning. Each decision in a sequence would have to be based on the calculated effects of the preceding decisions. Thus Comprehensive strategy can hardly be devised before the start of the formal campaign, when resources, at least of time, might be more abundant. Finance and social agreement may also be less costly in the early stages of a campaign, especially one that promises to succeed.

The likelihood of victory is inversely related to the costs of decision. An increasing "cost gap" develops between obviously winning and obviously losing campaigns. In a losing campaign the Comprehensive model is in grave danger of being "priced out of the market."

The preceding four criticisms do not exhaust the shortcomings of the Comprehensive Ideal.[26] We have stressed weaknesses arising from insufficient information and intrinsic uncertainty. It is worth adding that a hypothetical world of perfect knowledge harbors even more theoretical horrors. In a brief, incisive analysis, Anthony Downs has shown that under given conditions of rationality and complete information no government can be reelected, a majority cannot be ascertained, leadership has no purpose, and democracy becomes inoperative.[27]

The Incremental Model

Our second model of political decision-making bears a distinct resemblance to the less than "ideal" campaign practices outlined in Chapter 1. An analysis of these descriptions allows us to construct a model which avoids the defects of Comprehensiveness while retaining a concern for systematic design and rational choice. The model is expressly normative. It draws heavily upon the fully developed "strategy" of decision-making called "Disjointed Incrementalism" by its principal authors, David Braybrook and Charles Lindblom.[28] With appropriate modifications, we adopt this "strategy" as the basis for our second model, Incrementalism.

Incrementalism is composed of a set of statements which specify the decision-maker's focus of attention, his procedures for consideration and choice, and the empirical characteristics of his resulting decisions, together with descriptions of the organizational structure in which this kind of decision-making takes place. There is a defined set of identifiable elements and relationships, with additional relationships implied; and all of these rest upon a set of explicit assumptions.* These features meet at least the

---

*In passing we note that Incrementalism shares these and other features with allied models derived from inductive modifications of the Comprehensive Ideal, representative of which is the model of "bounded rationality" developed by Herbert A. Simon in his *Administrative Behavior* (1957), esp. pp. ix-xxxix, and *Models of Man*, esp. pp. 198 ff. and 241-260. This model works very well in certain administrative situations, but it suffers from some of the same difficulties as the Comprehensive Ideal in the arena of politics. The richness and veriety of Simon's work, and its continuing expansion into broader applications, is not captured by such a brief reference.

minimum requirements of the term "model."[29] In our judgment, Incrementalism is better suited to the world of political campaigns.

We should add that "Incrementalism" is now a commonly used concept in social analysis, and it is important to bear in mind that in our usage the term refers to more than just increments. Our reference is always to a coherent set of statements bound together by a theoretic approach to decision-making under conditions of uncertainty.

Attributes of the Incremental Model may be grouped under two major headings:[30]

1. Individual decision-makers follow a systematic set of rules to simplify their choices and reduce their costs.

They accept as given certain major goals (such as winning the election or at least getting as many votes as possible) and make little effort to rank goals or values, or to separate ends from means. Indeed, ends and means are usually considered simultaneously. This avoids the irrelevance of a laborious ordering of goals which is discovered to be incongruous with available means. Ordinarily, only those objectives attainable by reasonably available means are considered at all.

Campaign planners normally review only those means (and goals) used before. Campaign issues, strategies, or techniques that are novel, remote, poorly understood, or whose consequences constitute sharp changes from the *status quo*, are usually avoided. Decision-making is thus concentrated within the most well-explored areas of the political world.

Campaign leaders take up only the most pressing problems, delegating and ignoring those which are not urgent. As a result, attention is concentrated upon finding remedies for compelling ills of the campaign or, indeed, of the body politic. Little effort is made to conceive of comprehensive organizational or social reforms not already begun. The campaign is thus constructed in a series of limited, related, and remedial steps that are expected to continue. Speeches are neither written nor scheduled far in advance. Party organization is "patched up" rather than basically remodeled, and it is taken for granted that large problems can, at the moment, only be mitigated or temporarily resolved.

Decision-makers avoid the use of rigid peremptory rules prescribing a hierarchy of goals or projects or devices. Instead, "themes" are developed which bring into play generally recognized "important considerations." These tend to blur rather than sharpen issues. They go something like this: needy population groups should be helped, but the government should not be spendthrift; or, communism should be vigorously opposed, but war should be avoided. As the campaign progresses, themes are combined and recombined, and new ones formulated to match emerging issues and their accompanying "facts."

Finally, campaign leaders make choices among alternative themes and projects on the basis of "distributive" tests, that is, census-type data about individual persons or groups aided or deprived by the alternatives. Indeed, themes often are expressed in distributive form. For example, better education is needed and X policy will build N more schools than will Y policy; or, X campaign strategy will suit N more voters (or party leaders, etc.) than will Y strategy. These distributive tests do not give definitive answers to the decision-maker, since one alternative rarely is altogether superior to every other, and census-type evidence is seldom conclusive. But such tests avoid disastrous mistakes by preventing gross deprivations of substantial segments of the population and provide rough notions of the audience likely to be attentive to a particular appeal. The decision-maker searches for that combination of themes which will win the support of the greatest number of voters.

2. *Collective decisions are coordinated through bargaining and mutual adjustment in a decentralized and flexible organizational structure.*

The campaign organization is designed around the individual decision-making patterns described above. Organizational decisions are made in piecemeal fashion at many points in the formal structure of authority. Projects and operations are multiplied, as are points of decision and decision-makers. Just as the campaign strategy and organization are constructed in a series of Incremental steps, responsibilities tend to proliferate and overlap. Self-assignment of functions is common. Hierarchies of decision tend to be fluid. Ends or goals are not left exclusively to leaders, while subordinates consider only means or techniques. Diverse goals, strategies, and tactics can be inserted for consideration, and collective choices are ordinarily the product of reconstruction and revision of various decision-makers. Campaign decision-making thus takes on a "disjointed" aspect, with multiple positions of power and confused lines of authority.

Decisions gain visible direction not through well-defined channels of command, but from vigorous statements (within Incremental limits) by the candidate and his aggressive efforts to control campaign operations personally. This produces a seeming contradiction, since the requirements of the model (e.g., proliferating programs, distributed power, few hard and fast rules of choice, and easing the work of decision) make direct personal control impossible. The contradiction, though more apparent than real, is not resolved; the model prescribes a condition of tension between the rules of decision-making and of candidate leadership. A presidential campaign is intended above all to draw public attention to the candidate. His words and actions give the campaign meaning. His word is *the* word; it defines issues and gives significance to the many operations of the campaign. No subordinate wields meaningful authority except in this name. This absorbs a certain amount of uncertainty by placing recognized limits upon the process of bargaining and by simplifying the criteria of choice for subordinate decision-makers. But the candidate decides Incrementally; he is sensitive to the interests of other leaders and attentive to their advice.

Decisions are coordinated through mutual adjustment, an endless process of bargaining and compromise. Since there are many decision-makers, with different values, interests, and resources, each must gain cooperation and help from others in order to develop his part of the campaign. This interaction and mutual accommodation produces a significant amount of decision coordination; it also insures a broad focus of attention for the decision-makers taken together. The candidate and his principal aides are not troubled by a multiplicity of semi-independent operations and interpersonal competition and bargaining, so long as they are able to intervene directly at chosen points of decision. A great range of problems will be left to others, who understand that their usefulness and success depend upon how much they can do without bothering the candidate and upsetting the flow of his personal activity. Given the Incremental orientation of each decision-maker, and the fact that no "large" decisions can be reached without considerable pulling and hauling among a number of decision-makers, major blunders are rare, and the candidate's intervention is almost always remedial and Incremental.

In summary, the Incremental model has the following elements:

1. A concentration on immediate needs and on alternatives that are only marginally different from existing policies or conditions, goals or means.

2. A reduction of decision-making costs through simplification, omission, and postponement.

3. The adjustment of ends to means, of goals to resources, with little differentiation between the two.

4. Serial analysis and evaluation, and a stress upon immediate remedies rather than great reforms.

5. The use of distributive tests to evaluate goals and means, issues and programs.

6. Evaluation guided by broad, often overlapping themes rather than explicit, unyielding rules, resulting in frequent reconstructions of arguments and analyses.

7. The fragmentation and dispersion of authority and decision, with analysis and evaluation being highly diversified, leaving few alternatives, values, or techniques unexamined.

8. Coordination through mutual adjustment between decision-makers at every level, with decisions at one point characteristically being challenged and "corrected" at others, in order to fit the needs of the candidate.

Instead of clearly perceived goals and the exhaustive evaluation of all ways of achieving them before the "best" ones are chosen and put into effect, we have decision-making that is Incremental, exploratory, means-oriented, serial, remedial, fragmented, and given shape both by mutual adjustment and by active intervention by the candidate. Instead of coherence, discipline, and order, there is the appearance of untidiness, and disorder.

The effects of Incrementalism upon the three phases of the decision process are in sharp contrast to those of Comprehensiveness. While Comprehensive decision-making makes the phases easy to distinguish by separating ends from means and clearly delegating authority, Incrementalism may render the boundaries quite obscure. If we hold the phases analytically separate, the Incremental decision-maker may be expected to exhibit a relatively narrow focus of attention, consider few alternatives, and make simple choices. Collective decision-making, however, will encompass diverse and therefore broad foci of attention, the consideration of numerous alternatives, and an extended process of persuasion and compromise. But precisely where "the act of choice" occurs may be impossible to determine, since it can be composed of innumerable choices by various individuals at different times. Thus a decision of an Incremental campaign is likely to "emerge," rather than seem to be a single event.

Although additional aspects of the two models will become apparent as they are applied to the 1964 campaigns, their principal elements are now before us. While Incrementalism lacks the formal neatness of the Comprehensive Ideal, it has a systematic and normative structure of its own. In place of the Comprehensive promise of "best" decisions, Incrementalism tells the decision-maker what to do when he must act with less than complete information at his command. Thus it claims superiority in most political circumstances, including those of presidential campaigns. It postulates that decision-makers face an uncertain world, have limited capabilities of "absorbing" uncertainty, and will be under both internal and external pressures to act. It provides guidelines for meeting these conditions, and promises that the resulting decisions will be more appropriate, and thus beneficial, than those guided by either Comprehensiveness or chance. These promises are based on an explicit, systematic analysis relating structures of investigation and choice to resources of information and the characteristics of desirable decisions.

Compared to Comprehensiveness, the Incremental model makes significantly fewer demands on decision-makers for analysis and evaluation. Its operational difficulties are accordingly much less. Just as with Comprehensiveness, however, there may be a number of basic weaknesses in the model which are inherent in its theoretic structure. We shall mention five.

First, the structure of the Incremental model is neither very firm nor very sharply delineated. Its operating rules give decision-makers a considerable range of choice within which quite different decisions may "fit." It may thus be too crude to provide effective guidelines for determining how "ideal" their procedures are. Fortunately, remedial action is assured to correct any errors of judgment, so this "weakness" may, in fact, serve to locate the most competent decision-makers.

Second, the focus of Incrementalism on the familiar, the precedented and the practical might build in a bias against the discovery of novel opportunities, particularly those emerging from dramatic new conceptualizations of political circumstances. This is not to say that Incrementalism is inhospitable to innovation, but rather that its procedures do not demand new modes of understanding.

Third, the Incremental orientation to pressing issues, and to remedial and serial resolutions of these issues, diverts attention from "larger" problems that emerge slowly from a long line of Incremental decisions each of which seemed correct in itself. The same weakness may be found in its concentration on means rather than goals. To take an obvious example, Incremental additions to the total resources committed in a limited war ("escalation") may stimulate a broadening of the boundaries of the conflict into a major war, contrary to the wishes of both antagonists. It must be added that Incrementalism makes provision for the difficulties of the second and third weaknesses through dispersion of decision-making. Nonetheless, its rather loose operational guidelines and its comparative indifference to long-term consequences are more or less serious weaknesses.

Fourth, a focus on distributive measures of both wisdom and need can cause Incremental decision-makers to ignore ideas and demands of deserving individuals or minorities. The Incremental Ideal would detect these cases in the course of multiplying and dispersing decision-makers, but short of the Ideal, the chance of this weakness becomes much greater. American politics has had sufficient instances of such "invisible" minorities—migrant laborers, Indians, and the very poor—to lend credibility to the problem.[31]

Fifth, to operate successfully, Incrementalism implies that mutual adjustment is possible. Differences of goals and values are assumed, but where these are irreconcilable the promise of coordination will be frustrated. The model has great adaptability to situations of social conflict, but if this conflict is generalized, opposing decision-makers may find it impossible to find areas of bargaining and adjustment even though the overt procedures are followed. Of course, it can be argued that the cure is simply more Incrementalism.

These weaknesses that appear implicit in the Incremental model are not so clear-cut as those of the Comprehensive Ideal. For the most part, they involve a series of lapses, not by one, but by a set of decision-makers. Characteristically, they also take effect in an extended series of decisions over time. Even to the extent that these weaknesses are "real," they might not be felt in the course of an election campaign. How, then, are we to test the strengths and weaknesses of our two models?

Comprehensiveness vs. Incrementalism: Testing Their Effectiveness

The task before us is to find evidence of the use of our two methods of decision-making, and of their relative effectiveness, in the presidential campaigns of Barry Goldwater and Lyndon Johnson. Each model demands consistent patterns of behavior from a large number of individuals over a measurable span of time. We cannot expect them to occur in their "pure" form with every detail neatly in place, in the actual world of campaign politics. Furthermore, the two models are not designed to encompass *all* campaign decision-making. Countless motivations, strategies, and patterns of choice can be found in the repertoire of those involved in a national election. The real world is far richer than our models, and we shall make no attempt to fit every campaign decision of 1964 into one or the other of them.

We have hypothesized a relationship between different methods of campaign decision-making and resulting political consequences. The specifications of formal models is the first step in testing this hypothesis, for they focus our attention on relevant evidence and help to overcome the basic problem of recognition we confronted in Chapter 1. From our analysis of the Comprehensive and Incremental models we further hypothesize that Incrementalism will produce better political outcomes than Comprehensiveness.

But how can we evaluate either the direct impact of a decision-making procedure or the value of individual decisions? Campaign decisions are obviously
sequential; it is difficult to select a single decision (such as the insertion of the
phrase concerning "extremism" in Goldwater's acceptance speech) and prove
that, in the existing circumstances, it could have been made differently by the
same set of individuals. In this case, Goldwater's earlier selection of advisers
and speechwriters (and the exclusion of other persons from the formulation
of the acceptance speech) may be considered crucial, for their focus of attention and consideration of alternatives determined the decision.

We have presented decision-making not as a discrete event, but as a process,
a stream of behavior marked by certain personal styles and organizational
forms. We shall seek to demonstrate that each campaign developed characteristic patterns of decision. Our initial observations suggest that the Goldwater
pattern developed important similarities to the model of the Comprehensive
Ideal, while the Johnson paradigm usually paralleled the Incremental model.
The next step is to associate these contrasting decisional processes with political consequences.

In the chapters that follow, we shall link the Incremental and Comprehensive modes of decision used in 1964 with several types of political effects.
The first type will be the response of other political leaders. We assume that
during most of the campaign period, presidential candidates desire support
from party members and leaders who control resources of money, organization, and prestige. We further assume that this support will be beneficial. In
American politics these leaders are diverse, ranging from officers of business
and labor groups, to state and local party officials, to individual public figures, such as former Presidents Eisenhower or Truman. When they do not
respond favorably to the manner or substance of campaign decisions, conflicts will appear which require the diversion of campaign energies.

The second type of political consequence will be the demonstrated competence and morale (or their lack) of the campaign staff. This is more difficult
to measure, but we assume that a certain amount of political benefit is
derived from smooth travel schedules, well-written speeches, the timely distribution of materials, and staffers who do not create issues unintended by the
candidate. The connection between this "internal" result of decision-making
and later election returns will be hard to demonstrate; yet such staff performance can be tied quite successfully to the response of other leaders.

It also can be connected to a third type of political effect, the actual
output of campaign decisions. This is a tricky measure, since it attempts to

separate the timing and frequency of decisions from their "quality." Despite this difficulty, there will be cases where the decision-making process can be associated with the output of choices or actions that informed observers agree were obviously needed—the preparation of a speech, the organization of a program, a news release, a response to an attack, and so forth.

The fourth type of political result will be found in published assessments of the candidate and his campaign by political journalists and observers. Here we assume that the campaign accounts and images that are propagated through the mass media have some influence upon the behavior of voters and politicians.[32] We think that the standards of what is and is not a "good press," especially in specific circumstances, such as the two national conventions, are sufficiently clear to serve as partial bases of evaluation.

The fifth type of political consequence will involve actual voting behavior. We have already indicated that linkages between procedures of campaign decision and subsequent electoral acts cannot be "proved." With this understanding, we propose that in particular instances, some evidence of such a relationship may be discovered in public opinion surveys, especially of candidate and party images held by the electorate. Nevertheless, because of the multitude of variables that might intervene between a particular campaign decision and a particular set of public images, this political relationship will be relied upon in only a few rather clear-cut instances.

From the structure of our two models, we infer that the campaign leader who strives for Comprehensiveness will either find his decisions difficult to reach or be led to narrow his focus of attention to exclude data which his original plan did not encompass. In any case, his decisions will be hard to enforce. Occasionally he may originate a brilliant project. The mistakes he makes will be large and noticeable, and his campaign will be marked by severe problems of discipline, sharp internal conflict, and missed opportunities. The Incremental leader will make decisions more rapidly and easily, and they will generate little attention. Rarely will they comprise an original program. His campaign will appear disorderly but not divisive, and almost no discernible political opportunities will be altogether missed.

On the basis of its traditional and conceptually unchallenged appeal, we would expect that both the Republican and Democratic leadership consciously or unconsciously adhered to the Comprehensive Ideal as the 1964 campaign began. But we hypothesize that the Republican leaders were more firmly attached to Comprehensiveness, and that this placed them at a continuing disadvantage to their Democratic counterparts, who more readily abandoned it for Incrementalism. We are not asserting that Senator Gold-water would have won the election had he adhered to the Incremental model, or that other factors were not more important in affecting the vote. But we shall argue that the attachment of the Republican candidate and his close associates to the Comprehensive Ideal was an important—and analytically discernible—aspect of their general attitude toward American politics. And that attitude helped to bring crushing electoral defeat.

Notes on Chapter 2

[1] All the leading studies of American presidential elections argue for these propositions. The major deductive argument may be found in Anthony Downs, *An Economic Theory of Democracy* (New York: Harper, 1957), esp. Ch. 8. Representative analyses based on empirical evidence of electoral motivations are, Angus Campbell, *et al., The American Voter* (New York: Wiley, 1960), and *Elections and the Political Order* (New York: Wiley, 1966), esp. Chs. 2 and 12; John H. Kessel, "A Game Theory Analysis of Campaign Strategy," in M. Kent Jennings and L. Harmon Zeigler, eds., *The Electoral Process* (Englewood Cliffs, N.J.: Prentice-Hall, 1966), pp. 290-302; and Nelson W. Polsby and Aaron Wildavsky, *Presidential Elections: Strategies of American Electoral Politics* (New York: Scribner's, 1964).

[2] A. Campbell, *et al., Elections and the Political Order,* pp. 240-241; Philip E. Converse, *et al.,* "Electoral Myth and Reality: The 1964 Election," *American Political Science Review,* 59 (June 1965), 321-336; *Election '64: A Ripon Society Report* (Cambridge: Ripon Society, 1965); and Donald E. Stokes, "Some Dynamic Elements of Contests for the Presidency," *American Political Science Review,* 60 (March 1966), 19-28, and Milton C. Cummings, ed., *The National Elections of 1964* (Washington, D.C.: The Brookings Institution, 1966).

[3] Philip E. Converse, *et al.,* "Electoral Myth and Reality: The 1964 Election," *American Political Science Review,* 59 (June 1965), 326. The phrase appears first in Robert J. Donovan, *The Future of the Republican Party* (New York: New American Library, 1964), p. 31.

[4] Herbert A. Simon, "Political Research: The Decision-Making Framework," in David Easton, ed., *Varieties of Political Theory* (Englewood Cliffs, N.J.: Prentice-Hall, 1966), p. 15.

[5] Richard C. Snyder and Glenn D. Paige, "The United States Decision to Resist Aggression in Korea: The Application of an Analytic Scheme," *Administrative Science Quarterly,* 3 (December 1958), 341-378.

[6] Our conception is thus distinguished from that of more formal "mathematical" decision theory in which alternatives, payoffs, and procedures of choice are completely

delineated. Simon refers to this in "Political Research," p. 18 text and n. 6. Useful illustrations and discussions of such theory may be found in Martin Shubik, ed., *Game Theory and Related Approaches to Social Behavior* (New York: Wiley, 1964.)

[7]Simon, "Political Research," p. 24.

[8]See Chester I. Barnard, *The Functions of the Executive* (Cambridge: Harvard University Press, 1938), pp. 65-81; Rudolf Heberle, *Social Movements* (New York: Appleton-Century-Crofts, 1951), pp. 269-270; Herbert A. Simon, *et al., Public Administration* (New York: Knopf, 1950), pp. 85-87; Herbert A. Simon, *Administrative Behavior* (New York: Free Press, 1957), pp. 20-30; and, for an excellent application of these concepts to party organization, Austin Ranney and Willmore Kendall, *Democracy and the American Party System* (New York: Harcourt, 1956), pp. 213-217.

[9]The classic statement of rational organization is that of Max Weber, *The Theory of Social and Economic Organization*, ed. T. Parsons, tr. A. M. Henderson and T. Parsons (New York: Free Press, 1947), pp. 89 ff. For good selected references to the vast body of literature relevant to our rational model, see David Braybrooke and Charles E. Lindblom, *A Strategy of Decision* (New York: Free Press, 1963), pp. 9-16; Lindblom, *The Intelligence of Democracy* (New York: Free Press, 1965), Ch. 11 *et seq.*; Irwin D. J. Bross, *Design for Decision* (New York: Macmillan, 1953), pp. 18-28 and 264-266; Richard M. Cyert and James G. March, *A Behavioral Theory of the Firm* (Englewood Cliffs, N.J.: Prentice-Hall, 1963), pp. 16-19; Ward Edwards, "The Theory of Decision Making," *Psychological Bulletin*, 51, 5 (1954), 380-417; James G. March and Herbert A. Simon, *Organizations* (New York: Wiley, 1958), pp. 12-33; Simon, *Administrative Behavior*, pp. 20-30; and Carl J. Friedrich, ed., *Nomos VII: Rational Decision* (New York: Atherton Press, 1964).

[10]See Julian Feldman and Herschel E. Kanter, "Organizational Decision Making," in James G. March, ed., *Handbook of Organizations* (Chicago: Rand McNally, 1965), pp. 614-615. Braybrooke and Lindblom use the term "synoptic ideal" to describe the same model in *A Strategy of Decision*, pp. 37 ff; others have continued to use some phrase which includes the terms "rational" or "economic man," etc. See Herbert A. Simon, *Administrative Behavior*, pp. ix-xxxix, and "A Behavioral Model of Rational Choice," in *Models of Man* (New York: Wiley, 1958), pp. 241-260.

[11]For a review of these concepts in terms of the model presented, see Donald W. Taylor, "Decision Making and Problem Solving," in James G. March, ed., *Handbook of Organizations* (Chicago: Rand McNally, 1965), pp. 49-51.

[12]*The New York Times*, July 27, 1966, p. 23.

[13]Herbert A. Simon, "Political Research: The Decision-Making Framework," in Easton, ed., *Varieties of Political Theory*, p. 23. Anthony Downs reaches a similar, though more restricted, conclusion deductively in his analysis of bureaucracy, *Inside Bureaucracy* (Boston: Little, Brown, 1967), esp. Ch. 15.

[14]In a simplified form, Braybrooke and Lindblom treat this problem similarly. See *A Strategy of Decision*, pp. 62-64.

[15]R. Duncan Luce and Howard Raiffa, *Games and Decisions* (New York: Wiley, 1947), pp. 13 ff.

[16]Anthony Downs, *An Economic Theory of Democracy* (New York: Harper, 1957), p. 77. This definition can serve our purposes so long as conditions of risk need not be distinguished.

[17]*A Strategy of Decision*, pp. 78-79.

[18]This can be seen most readily in the papers by Julian Feldman and Herschel E. Kanter, "Organizational Decision Making," pp. 614-649, and Taylor, "Decision Making and Problem Solving," in James G. March, ed., *Handbook of Organizations.*

[19]Notably in (with David Braybrooke) *A Strategy of Decision* and *The Intelligence of Democracy.*

[20]Cyert and March, *Behavioral Theory of the Firm*, and Edmund P. Learned and Audrey T. Sproat, *Organization Theory and Policy* (Homewood, Ill.: Irwin, 1966), pp. 89-94. Anthony Downs presents an extremely interesting theoretic discussion of the problem in the context of formal organizations. See *Inside Bureaucracy*, p. 134 and Ch. 18.

[21]*A Strategy of Decision*, pp. 23-36, and Feldman and Kanter, "Organizational Decision Making," pp. 628-642.

[22]Kenneth Arrow, *Social Choice and Individual Values* (New York: Wiley, 1951). However, under the required conditions, the probability that Arrow's Paradox will occur might be lower than previously thought. See David Klahr, "A Computer Simulation of the Paradox of Voting," *American Political Science Review,* 60 (June 1966), 384-390.

[23]See for example, Alex Bernstein and Michael De V. Roberts, "Computer vs. Chess-Player," *Scientific American*, 198, 6 (1958), 96-105; or A. Newell, *et al.*, "Chess-Playing Programs and the Problem of Complexity," *IBM Journal of Research and Development*, 2 (1958), 320-335.

[24]This excursion into military history is not intended to start any feuds with military historians, unless it would be to suggest that the application of decision theory might assist in their enterprise. The examples cited here are drawn from Barbara Tuchman, *The Guns of August* (New York: Dell, 1963) and Walter Lord, *Incredible Victory* (New York: Harper, 1967).

[25]*A Strategy of Decision*, pp. 50-51, and *The Intelligence of Democracy*, pp. 139 ff. In "The United States Decision to Resist Aggression in Korea; The Application of an Analytic Scheme," *Administrative Science Quarterly,* 3 (December 1958), 341-378, Snyder and Paige show how decision costs of time, in particular, force a high degree of simplification into the process of choice. Also, see Downs, *Inside Bureaucracy*, Ch. 15.

[26]Friedrich, ed., *Nomos VII: Rational Decision*, esp. Chs. 4, 14, and 16.

[27]*An Economic Theory of Democracy*, pp. 55-95.

[28]*A Strategy of Decision,* esp. Ch. 5.

[29]The requirements of rigorous definition, specification, and generality are severe in the construction of models, but not unmanageable. For a general statement, see Bross, *Design for Decision*, Ch. 10; and also, James G. March, "The Power of Power," in David Easton, ed., *Varieties of Political Theory*, pp. 49 ff.

[30]For a basic development of these propositions, see *A Strategy of Decision*, esp. Chs. 8 and 9. Norman C. Thomas has considered the problem of classifying modes of decision-making, but emerges with different categories. See his *Rule 9: Politics, Administration, and Civil Rights* (New York: Random House, 1966), esp. pp. 7-17.

[31]Robert A. Dahl discusses this and other weaknesses of Incrementalism, within the context of comparative democratic systems, in *Political Oppositions in Western Democracies* (New Haven, Conn.: Yale University Press, 1966), pp. 392 ff.

[32]We recognize that this assumption remains moot. We think it is plausible, but taken as a major hypothesis, it has been difficult to test. This has been especially true as

published assessments become mixed. See the different conclusions of Kurt and Gladys Engel Lang, "The Mass Media and Voting," in Eugene Burdick and Arthur J. Brodbeck, *American Voting Behavior* (New York: Free Press, 1959), Ch. 12; Ithiel de Sola Pool, "T.V.: A New Dimension in Politics," *ibid.*, Ch. 13; Herbert A. Simon and Frederick Stern, "The Effects of Television upon Voting Behavior in Iowa in the 1952 Presidential Election," *American Political Science Review*, 49 (1955), 470-477; and Joseph T. Klapper, *The Effects of Mass Communication* (New York: Free Press, 1960), *passim*. For succinct, balanced summaries of the evidence for both television and press effects, see Bernard C. Hennessy, *Public Opinion* (Belmont, California: Wadsworth, 1965), Chs. 17 and 18.

Part 2

Senator Goldwater's
Comprehensive Organization

3

The Political Education of Barry Goldwater

In the cold light of dawn following election day, those who labored valiantly for the losing candidate traditionally pose anguished questions about the conduct of the campaign. In 1964, counting the ballots only intensified the public debate on that topic. Senator Goldwater's concession speech hinted that "more than 25,000,000 conservatives" couldn't be wrong. While liberal Republicans described Goldwater's candidacy as an effort to "control" the party, rather than offer a responsible alternative to President Johnson's Great Society, Goldwater partisans bitterly castigated Governor George Romney for encouraging ticket-splitting in Michigan. Within weeks, a majority of the Republican National Committeemen decided that the interests of the party would best be served through the resignation of Dean Burch, Goldwater's appointee as National Chairman.

This partial repudiation of the losing campaign made the recriminations more bitter. The collegiate Republican liberals of the Ripon Society labeled the campaign "one of the most inept and unprofessional campaigns in American history,"[1] because Goldwater and his advisers, pursuing a "dream of a political world without politics,"[2] sought a hidden conservative vote which experienced Republican politicians, not to mention journalists and pollsters, knew did not exist. Yet a survey of the Convention delegates who nominated

Goldwater revealed that a substantial majority felt that "Goldwater failed to discuss the conservative issues in depth." And nearly half of this group felt that "Barry Goldwater was somehow different"—his conservative views and even his political personality presumably modified by his managers—"from the Republican worker who had won their affection in the earlier years."[3] Thus Goldwater was damned from the left for being obstinately ideological and damned from the right for watering down his conservatism.

The shortcomings of such analyses have been summarized by Stephen Shadegg, the manager of Goldwater's senatorial campaigns.

The question of what happened to Barry Goldwater pleads for a precise, definitive answer. Those who were involved as partisan supporters of the Senator and those who opposed him would be pleased to find that one particular action or single statement overbalanced the scale in favor of Lyndon Johnson. In truth no such simple explanation can be advanced. In less complicated contests hindsight can sometimes illuminate the particular play, the brilliant offensive move, or the error in defense responsible for the final decision. In a political race the spectators are themselves participants; their mood and their assumptions must be considered.[4]

If the analysis of decision-making styles outlined in this volume can make any claim to validity, it should avoid just those pitfalls which Shadegg outlines. It should permit the consideration of the "mood and assumptions" of the participant-spectators in an objective manner. It should provide an explanation of "what happened to Goldwater" that includes the successes and shortcomings of both the Republican and Democratic campaigns within a single theoretical framework.

At the conclusion of Chapter 2, we suggested that the attachment of Barry Goldwater and his close associates to what we labeled the Comprehensive model of political decision-making was an important aspect of their general attitude toward American politics—an attitude which brought crushing electoral defeat. We must now trace the development of that attitude and its component beliefs concerning both political issues and organization. Barry Morris Goldwater, the "grandson of a Jewish peddler" who would become his party's 1964 standard-bearer, was born on January 1, 1909, and spent his boyhood in the desert town of Phoenix, Arizona. Phoenix was then a stable community which retained much of the flavor of the frontier era. Barry was the eldest son in the third generation of a successful pioneer family. His childhood was secure, untroubled by distant rumblings of conflict between nations or of social unrest in Eastern cities. One of his earliest memories is of the celebration of Arizona's achievement of statehood. Barry helped his brother found an athletic club, and, at age eleven, he owned one of the earliest radio sets in Arizona.

In high school, Goldwater was a keen sports competitor and was elected president of his freshman class, but his academic record was so undistinguished as to gravely distress his father. His secondary education was completed in three years at Staunton Military Academy in Virginia, where Goldwater adapted easily to the military regimen and rose to positions of student leadership. Studies at the University of Arizona were interrupted after one year, in part by family necessity—with the economic depression and the death of his father, the eldest son was needed in the family business—and partly by his lack of interest in further studies. "In 1929," explains Stephen Shadegg, "people in Arizona did not yet feel that a University education was essential."[5]

Beginning as a clerk and working in every department of the family's Phoenix store, Goldwater in 1937 was named president of the Goldwater department stores. He was married in 1934 and devoted his free energies to his family and the pursuit of his varied hobbies. He developed skill with the camera, producing some remarkably sensitive photographs; he became an enthusiastic explorer of the natural grandeur of Arizona, publishing equally sensitive accounts of his travels; he studied the history and customs of Arizona's Indians; and he learned to fly.

In frequent contact with his Uncle Morris, a founder of the conservative Arizona Democratic party and long-time mayor of Prescott, Goldwater became interested in public affairs. According to his biographer, Goldwater "began reading those books of political theory he had neglected during his school years: Burke, Jefferson, Plato, Madison, Locke, Hamilton—their words now took on a new meaning."[6] The only public result was a guest editorial, written by "former playboy" Goldwater for *The Phoenix Gazette*, which criticized New Deal spending policies and foreshadowed Goldwater's interest in the Republican party.

When World War II came, Goldwater was prevented by old athletic injuries from qualifying for combat flying, but he was able to serve as a gunnery instructor and later flew many missions as a ferry pilot, including several passages over the famous "Hump" of the Himalayas. In 1942, he piloted single-engine fighter planes across the North Atlantic, volunteer duty for which he was awarded the Air Medal. At the end of the war, he was a Lieutenant Colonel.

Goldwater seemed a model citizen-soldier of the twentieth century, developing technical skills as a peactime hobby which he gladly devoted to national needs in time of war. But the citizen-soldier is seldom able to compartmentalize the separate segments of his experience. Attitudes and habits acquired during military duty are likely to influence both the content and the style of decisions made by the citizen.

The Formation of a Political Style

Goldwater returned to a Phoenix on the verge of a fantastic postwar development. His portrait as a returning war veteran includes the conception of a man at peace with himself and with his Arizona, aware of the rewards for individual enterprise available in a boom economy, yet with a restless mind and a multiplicity of interests. His entrance into politics, as a member of a nonpartisan reform slate seeking election to the Phoenix City Council, seemed only the latest addition to his string of hobbies. When Goldwater yielded to the urging of friends that he make the race, which would mean withdrawing from some of his responsibilities in the family enterprise, a note of apology was dispatched to his brother. "It ain't for life," Goldwater wrote, "and it may be fun."[7]

Accounts differ as to the scope of Goldwater's accomplishments on the Phoenix Council and the seriousness of his purpose. By 1950, however, politics for Goldwater was clearly more than a passing fancy, and his dedication to Arizona's developing Republican party was complete. In that year, he managed the successful gubernatorial campaign of his friend, Howard Pyle. In 1952, Goldwater was himself elected a United States Senator from Arizona. Although he waged a vigorous campaign, Goldwater acknowledged the coattail power of Dwight D. Eisenhower. Political gratitude, simple patriotism, and military protocol combined to formulate Goldwater's attitude toward President Eisenhower: "a genuine, almost naive attitude of worship and respect."[8]

But Goldwater found himself increasingly in disagreement with Eisenhower Administration policies. The trend of those policies seemed contrary to beliefs about the proper role of government in relation to the individual citizen and to the economy which Goldwater had absorbed as a young Arizona businessman. This clash between Washington practices and Arizona certainties led Goldwater to reexamine his assumptions. Any conflict was resolved in favor of the Arizona-learned attitudes, but the process of reexamination molded

Goldwater's outlook in such a way that Theodore White would later describe him, in a famous and controversial phrase, as a "frustrated intellectual."[9] In White's view, Goldwater came late to the world of books and ideas, and he came without the formal education that would allow him to feel secure in his preparation for that world. The meaning White assigns to the phrase is unclear. It seems to describe Goldwater's acceptance of the validity of certain abstract concepts and his anger upon discovering that ideas he found self-evident were ignored or discounted by those in high places. The phrase must at least mean that Goldwater believes that the complexities and contradictions of the modern world can be made comprehensible by classifying diverse phenomena according to sound basic principles. The contrast between Goldwater and his 1964 opponent has nowhere been better summarized than by White who wrote, "where his conqueror, Lyndon B. Johnson, knows there are only pressures and directions, Goldwater is a man who believes there are certainties."[10]

But Goldwater's was not a search for the relative certainty of probabilities that results from the careful analysis of empirical data. Rather it was an inward, philosophical, and even moral quest. The guide to decisions on political issues became his own conscience, and the resulting policy recommendations were articulated in moral terms. Moral rightness, not administrative feasibility, became the most important consideration. Goldwater's concern was with the basic issue. Implementation of the decision would be the work of others. Again to quote Theodore White, "Goldwater's favorite style in politics is exhortation; he is a moralist, not an organizer. He preaches; he does not direct."[11]

One of Goldwater's longest-standing political convictions was his belief that the growth of the federal government must be limited in order to preserve individual freedom. On April 8, 1957, he attacked the spending levels of the Eisenhower administration on the Senate floor. This and similar articulations of his disagreement with the trends of governmental policy since 1932 won enthusiastic response from Republican audiences, and he soon found himself moving into a vacuum of leadership on the Republican right created by the deaths of Senators Robert A. Taft of Ohio and Eugene Milliken of Colorado. But his style was not that of Milliken and Taft, who were careful strategists of the legislative process. Goldwater's element was the banquet table and speaker's rostrum. His political attitudes were expressed with complete frankness, in succinct phrases that sharpened the impact of whatever attitude he held at the moment. A growing number of admirers felt that Goldwater was one figure in public life who would never change his political views to improve his chances of winning an election.

Goldwater's developing political style was summarized in the title of his first popular book, *The Conscience of a Conservative*, published in 1960. Making the conservative conscience the standard for political decisions seemed to preclude the traditional conception of politics as the art of compromise. It also precluded the manipulation of men by temporarily pandering to their desires or ambitions. In selecting staff assistants and advisers, Goldwater was not prepared to use men while the association seemed of mutual advantage, and then ask them to depart. Rather, he required that they share his vision of the conservative conscience. A former political associate wrote:

In the world of politics where today's friend and supporter is tomorrow's opponent, Goldwater has always put loyalty above every other consideration ... A review of the men he has chosen to be his administrative assistants and political advisers suggests that he always sought people personally loyal to him and willing to serve him without question or contradiction.[12]

Whether stated in terms of personal loyalty or a shared vision, the pattern fits the requirements of the Comprehensive model. The leaders at the top must agree on goals. No questioning of basic principles is permitted. When Barry Goldwater began to prepare for his presidential candidacy, he surrounded himself with a circle of close friends—men whose attitudes he knew and trusted because of long acquaintance. The phrase "Arizona Mafia" was misleading. His closest confidant, Denison Kitchel, was an Ivy Leaguer transplanted to Arizona; Goldwater's intellectual mentor, William Baroody, Sr., had long been a resident of New Hampshire; and United States Senators from Texas (John Tower), California (former Senator William Knowland), and New Hampshire (Norris Cotton) were drawn into the circle for consultation.

Having selected his loyal aides, Goldwater tended to delegate rather complete authority to them, as would a military commander. He had no patience for the kind of reaching down from on high into the recesses of the organization that characterized the political styles of Lyndon Johnson and John Kennedy. A professional political manager who worked at the Republican National Committee before and during the Goldwater campaign told us:

Goldwater is spasmodic, despising details. He just says to his workers that he has delegated authority to them and expects them to do their jobs, like [he was] hiring a man to buy clothes for men in his Phoenix store. He gives him the responsibility and does not want to be troubled with the details.

But such questions of organizational procedure were of little relevance when Barry Goldwater first appeared on the national scene. His appearance coincided with manifestations of new interest in political attitudes labeled "conservative." Expressed in the books of Russell Kirk, the acerbic essays of William Buckley, and the growth of campus student organizations, this new interest marked a reaction to the liberal consensus initiated by Franklin D. Roosevelt and implemented by Republican Eisenhower as well as by Democrat Truman. As Senator Goldwater held the highest office of any of the "new conservatives," he became a natural public spokesman. And he stimulated a response more passionate than any evoked by the dignified posture of Robert A. Taft. Invitations to speak to Republican audiences flooded in, and Goldwater demonstrated his ability to draw an affluent and responsive crowd. After his overwhelming reelection to the Senate in 1958, Goldwater's colleagues elected him Chairman of the Senatorial Campaign Committee, charged with raising funds to reelect Republican senators.

When the 1960 Republican Convention was held, Goldwater was firmly recognized as the leader of Republican conservatives. He articulated their outrage at the agreement between Richard Nixon and Nelson Rockefeller concerning platform language. Goldwater's name was placed in nomination by the Louisiana delegation, stimulating what many considered to be the noisiest and most nearly spontaneous demonstration of the Convention. Never having regarded his candidacy seriously, Goldwater appeared on the rostrum to withdraw it. "We have lost election after election in this country in the last several years," he said, "because conservative Republicans got mad and stayed home." Goldwater called upon his fellow partisans to unite behind the candidacy of Richard Nixon. Then came his famous exhortation: "Let's grow up, conservatives. Let's, if we want to take this Party back—and I think we can some day—let's get to work."[13]

Having laid down this challenge, Goldwater plunged into the thick of campaign activities. He spoke for Richard Nixon wherever he was invited. As Chairman of the Senate Republican Campaign Committee, he did his best to elect Republican senators. And from his vantage point on the fringes of the Nixon campaign, Goldwater confirmed his criticisms of previous Republican organizations.

A Republican state chairman who was close to Goldwater summarized the crystallization of his views:

[Goldwater] felt that it was a mistake for the Republicans to launch a campaign organization consisting of temporary citizens' groups that competed with the Republican National Committee. This problem was a residue of the 1952 Eisenhower-Taft fight, when Ike used citizen groups as his base of support. Goldwater found these annoying from 1952 to 1960 and saw the citizens' groups competing with the Republican National Committee [for scarce supplies of] money, literature, and influence in strategy making. This caused confusion. Goldwater saw one party acting as an umbrella ranging from Goldwater to Javits. He said this particular statement many times. He saw cutting down on this bifurcated party [as necessary] for saving money. He wanted to make the Republican National Committee the focal point or the center of the Republican Party. In 1960, he was outraged at the Nixon campaign, with its confusion of management and competition for funds. This he saw as a compounding of the problems of the 1956 campaign, which began with a number of splinter groups and developed more. In 1960, the Republican National Committee and [Leonard] Hall were unable to talk to Nixon, and the citizens' groups gave their own views. There was an $800,000 deficit which had to be paid off, and this took away money needed to fight the Democrats. . . . The only way to run a campaign is with the regulars, there is no business having an organization except to win. These are Goldwater's views, [and I share them]. I see Dewey's problems in 1948, Willkie's in 1940, Landon's in 1936 as due to this problem.

Given the desire of Nixon to appeal to a range of the electorate broader than voters who identify their own good fortune with that of the Republican Party, such aspects of Nixon's organizational structure as the formation of volunteer organizations made very good sense. Furthermore, aspects of the Nixon campaign were thoroughly Incremental. Lines of authority in his staff were fluid and imprecise. The closest document to an organization chart was the list of telephone extension numbers. Nixon retained personal authority in nearly every aspect of the campaign effort.

Nixon's attempt to use his conference with Nelson Rockefeller to pressure the 1960 platform writers into inserting more liberal language had all the earmarks of an Incremental operation. The requirement of the model that candidates be able to intervene personally in the concerns of the organization was almost caricatured by the circumstances. The Vice President was absent from Chicago as the platform drafting began. When rumblings of discontent issued from Governor Rockefeller's headquarters, Nixon flew directly to the conference in New York without informing his aides in Chicago of his destination or intent, so that they denied the reality of the event to inquiring reporters. The agreement was made final during a three-hour telephone conversation between Nixon and Rockefeller in New York and Platform Committee officials in Chicago. In many cases, the language already prepared for consideration by the Committee was endorsed by Rockefeller. Manipulation by Governor Rockefeller's public relations staff gave the impression that the agreement represented a capitulation by Nixon. Barry Goldwater labeled the outcome a "Republican Munich," and the resulting feud in the Platform Committee required all Nixon's skills to resolve.[14]

Having achieved a liberal statement (in the context of 1960) regarding civil rights, Mr. Nixon found that his campaign tours in the South brought out enthusiastic crowds, and he increased the concentration of his Southern efforts beyond their originally planned scope. If Nixon had gone on to win the election, this shift in emphasis would perhaps be described as a brilliantly Incremental decision. But the election was lost, and Nixon was described as unable to decide where he really stood on the issue of civil rights or which of two perhaps mutually exclusive elements of the electorate—Northern Negroes or Southern conservatives—he should attempt to add to his supporting coalition.[15]

Nixon was attempting to unite the most liberal and conservative wings of the Republican Party—identified with Nelson Rockefeller and Barry Goldwater, respectively—in order to hold together his own base of partisan support, while attempting to draw enough Democratic partisans away from John Kennedy to eke out a majority. Any campaign based on such a delicate balancing act was bound to seem a series of responses to unforeseen cues, failures to follow through on decisions once made, and even—the traditional epithet—proof of "willingness to abandon principle for expediency." It was a campaign certain to enrage Barry Goldwater.

The influences which shaped Goldwater's convictions concerning appropriate presidential campaign organization should now be clear. His experiences in the Army Air Force and as a small businessman, added to his secondary schooling at the Staunton Military Academy, disposed him favorably toward organizations of a Comprehensive style. His observations of the Nixon campaign filled in the specifics. He decided that a presidential campaign should be managed from the National Committee headquarters. Lines of command should extend to the state party headquarters, volunteer groups should be excluded, and finances should be managed in a businesslike manner. It was a vision of a strictly hierarchical, professional, and efficient organization, with policy determined in the clear and quiet air at the top of the pyramid.

But Goldwater's growing support among Republican partisans was not dependent upon his theories of campaign organization. They were related to his beliefs regarding the content of a presidential campaign.

The Conservative Candidacy: Case Study in the Focus of Attention

A cornerstone of Goldwater's philosophy was the principle that elections should offer the voters a clear choice. The need for a clear choice took on the attributes of a moral necessity; but Goldwater was also the most recent exponent of a belief associated with the candidacy of Senator Robert A. Taft during the 1940s: The Republican party would make a better electoral showing if it presented an unmistakable choice, rather than nominating a "me-too" candidate. Goldwater enunciated this belief when he appeared before the 1960 Convention to withdraw his own candidacy. He repeated it shortly after Richard Nixon's defeat.

We who are conservatives will stoutly maintain that 1960 was a repeat performance of 1944 and 1948, when we offered the voters insufficient choice with a me-too candidate.[16]

Goldwater's candidacy rested on the assumption that the majority of American voters hold conservative political attitudes and that a clear statement of conservative principles, if it did not win the White House, would at least cleanse the Republican Party of "me-tooism" and foreshadow the victory of a conservative Republican presidential nominee in a subsequent election. This assumption was consistent with Goldwater's speech to the 1960 Republican Convention, with his analysis of the reasons for Nixon's defeat, and with the thinking of Republicans who supported Robert Taft and deplored the nomination of Wendell Willkie and Thomas E. Dewey. It held that, when the Republican Party nominated a liberal presidential candidate who looked and sounded like the liberal Democratic candidate (except, perhaps, that he promised to administer the welfare state more efficiently and finance it without deficit spending) real Republicans were sufficiently offended not to vote at all. A "true" Republican candidate would bring these stay-at-home conservatives to the polls, and their sudden participation would insure victory.

This "woodwork myth of hidden conservatives" is easily tested using the techniques of political scientists, market analysts, and other practitioners of survey research. To validate the hypothesis, one would have only to prove that there were a substantial number—not hundreds, but hundreds of thousands—of potential Republican voters who sat on their hands rather than vote for a "moderate." In fact, however, every reputable examination of the question since at least 1944 has shown that it is Republicans who vote more frequently than Democrats and that the turnout of the most devoutly conservative Republicans reaches staggering proportions—96 or 98 percent—even when the Republican nominee is a liberal.[17]

Scholars at the Survey Research Center hypothesized that this misperception of American voting habits was based on familiarity with a particular aspect of public opinion which the conservative strategists mistakenly assumed was representative of the total. This particular "real world" of public opinion consists of expressions concerning public issues contained in letters addressed to public officials, including Republican Congressmen. The survey sample was analyzed to determine which of its members had ever written such a letter and how frequently they had done so. The analysis revealed that two thirds of such letters "are turned out by not more than three per cent of the population," and only 15 per cent of the sample had ever written to a public official.[18] Further analysis of the opinions of the letter writers demonstrated that those who write such letters are sensitive to the nuances of ideology, while the general population is not; letter writers fear the growing power of government, while the general population does not; and letter-writing Republicans preferred Barry Goldwater over all other contenders for the Republican nomination put together, while only one fifth of the non-letter-writing Republicans supported the Arizona Senator.[19] The authors conclude:

For ultra-conservatives who found a wide measure of social support and resonance for their views in the world of public opinion which they understood, it must indeed have been perplexing that uniquely at election time, and uniquely in vote totals, this vigorous support had a habit of evaporating. How could one interpret this gross discrepancy between what one heard and read about public sentiments and what happened at the polls? The easiest explanation was that strong conservatives in large numbers simply refused to go to the polls, however vigorously they would express themselves otherwise. And as soon as a useful reason was worked out as to why this willful non-voting should occur, a theory was born. It persisted in part because it was a handy tactical weapon; but it persisted in some part as well because the discrepant realities which helped to catalyze the theory also persisted . . . it is not a simple matter of fact *vs.* fantasy: both worlds are real, and have real effects on the political process . . . if the reality of one of these worlds was manifest on Election Day, 1964, then the reality of the other was equally apparent in the San Francisco convention.[20]

We have noted that the attempt to achieve Comprehensive decision-making may lead to misperceptions of reality when the decision-makers' focus of attention becomes narrowed. Because exhaustive effort has gone into the planning, data which challenges the assumptions of the plan may be ignored or discounted. This is particularly true when the environment does supply some cues which reinforce those assumptions.

Such cues were much in evidence as Goldwater rose to the leadership of the conservative movement. When a talk to a college political rally was received with nearly hysterical enthusiasm, it was easy to assume that the students present were representative of most of those on the campus. When many people wrote letters to urge the Senator's candidacy, it was easy to assume that many millions would react favorably enough to vote for him. When 42,000 cheering supporters welcomed Barry Goldwater to Los Angeles' Chavez Ravine in the late summer of 1963, it was similarly easy to assume that many of those who stayed home to watch the televised showdown battle between the Dodgers and the St. Louis Cardinals were also Goldwater fans. There were myriad reasons to ignore the systematic findings of the pollsters.

The Comprehensive model requires that the leaders of the organization agree on their goals. Barry Goldwater's goal was to present a conservative alternative. He naturally selected assistants and advisers who not only shared his attitudes on specific public policies but also agreed that a conservative candidacy would serve the best interests of the Republican party; indeed, that Goldwater had a good chance of winning.

This belief was not limited to Goldwater's inner circle. Thousands of Goldwater workers sustained their efforts in the belief that a "silent vote," so far undiscovered by the opinion analysts, would be delivered on election day. Our own interviews revealed this phenomenon, and so did survey research data.

A middle-level manager involved in planning the campaign tours told of the conviction that kept him going:

I guessed that the conservative voice would win. I made my pitch to the conservatives. From the acceptance speech to the end of the campaign, I believed this was the conservative year. That is, I did not necessarily make my pitch to Republicans as such but based it on those principles we [conservatives] had been enunciating for years.

Goldwater supporters found different cues in the environment to support the silent vote hypothesis. A Republican state chairman told us:

I felt that there was a social transformation [going on]. I have always seen youth as the bellwether. This time they failed me. I saw the idealism of youth [which in the thirties had been attached to liberalism] now becoming conservative and leading a whole new movement. I believed this, as did many other Republicans.

The search for cues which would support the basic premise of the Goldwater campaign was not limited to politicians in the field. A member of Goldwater's personal research staff, who was present at the presentations of private poll results by the Opinion Research Corporation told us:

I believed, along with many others, that there were a substantial number of voters who did not say that they supported Goldwater but nevertheless would vote for him. I took taxicab polls which were almost 100 per cent for Goldwater. [I believed in the silent vote] although we found no evidence of it in the polls.

The Opinion Research Corporation (ORC) was asked to make an inquiry into the "silent vote" during the campaign as part of a periodic survey. The Republican polling organization asked a sample if they knew of people who would probably vote for Senator Goldwater but would not admit it. Thirty per cent of the respondents replied in the affirmative. This datum was immediately broadcast in the *Victory Bulletin*, the newsletter sent by teletype from the Goldwater headquarters to the state organizations, in order to bolster sagging spirits. Not included were the reservations later published by Thomas Benham of ORC, who felt that the result was doubly skewed by Goldwaterite hopes that the "silent vote" would be influential and Democratic fears that it might. "Far fewer uncommitted people (16 percent) believed in these silent voters than did either Johnson supporters (33 percent) or Goldwater supporters (51 percent)."[21]

The belief in the electoral attractiveness of a conservative candidate was so central to Barry Goldwater's candidacy that it was not open to examination. The belief was held so strongly by his closest friends and advisers that it can only be described as an article of faith. Other possibilities were not admitted to the focus of attention.

We have seen the development of Barry Goldwater's affinity for the Comprehensive style of political organization and the origins of his belief in the efficacy of a conservative candidacy. These convictions developed at the same time and were no doubt related in Goldwater's mind. But neither was required by the other. A politician could be devoted both to Comprehensive organization and to liberal policies. The two tendencies would converge at that point in time when Goldwater would learn of a plan which used the tenets of Comprehensive organization to insure the presentation of a "true conservative" campaign.

Notes on Chapter 3

[1]The Ripon Society, *From Disaster to Distinction: A Republican Rebirth* (New York: Pocket Books, 1966), p. 18.

[2]Ripon Society, p. 22.

[3]Stephen Shadegg, *What Happened to Goldwater?* (New York: Holt, 1965), p. 267.

[4]Shadegg, p. 198.

[5]Shadegg, p. 77.

[6]Edwin McDowell, *Portrait of an Arizonan: Barry Goldwater* (Chicago: Henry Regnery, 1964), p. 66.

[7]McDowell, pp. 88-90.

[8]The quoted phrase is from Shadegg, *What Happened to Goldwater?*, p. 78.

[9]Theodore H. White, *The Making of the President 1964* (New York: Atheneum, 1965), p. 208.

[10]White, p. 208. The necessarily abbreviated account of Goldwater's background and experience offered here is based on both friendly and hostile accounts. See Shadegg, *What Happened to Goldwater?*, pp. 76-82; Richard H. Rovere, *The Goldwater Caper* (New York: Harcourt, 1965), pp. 21-38, 115-121, and McDowell, *Portrait of an Arizonan.*

[11]White, p. 89.

[12]The quotation is from Shadegg, *What Happened to Goldwater?*, p. 172.

[13]Harold Faber, ed., *The Road to the White House* (New York: McGraw-Hill, 1965), p. 72.

[14]For an analysis of events occurring in the 1960 Platform Committee, see Karl A. Lamb, "The 1960 Platform—Nixon Achieves Control" in Paul Tillett, ed., *Inside Politics: The National Conventions, 1960* (New York: Oceana, 1962), pp. 55-84.

[15]Theodore White makes this criticism in *The Making of the President 1960*, (New York: Atheneum, 1961), pp. 204, 315. Criticisms of Nixon from the opposite viewpoints of Goldwater and Rockefeller are offered in Robert D. Novak, *The Agony of the GOP 1964* (New York: Macmillan, 1965), pp. 9-24. The sketch given here of Richard Nixon as a political decision-maker draws upon these sources, conversations with members of Nixon's 1960 staff, and Mr. Nixon's own account in *Six Crises* (New York: Doubleday, 1962), pp. 293-426. Nixon's book accents decision-making in times of crisis, but its focus is more on personal psychology than on the development of systematic methods of decision.

[16]Faber, ed., *The Road to the White House*, p. 75.

[17]The evidence is summarized by Philip E. Converse, Aage R. Clausen, and Warren E. Miller, in "Electoral Myth and Reality: The 1964 Election," *The American Political Science Review*, 59 (June 1965), 323.

[18]Converse *et al.*, "Electoral Myth and Reality: the 1964 Election," p. 333.

[19]Converse *et al.*, p. 334.

[20]Converse *et al.*, pp. 335-336.

[21]Thomas W. Benham, "Polling for a Presidential Candidate: Some Observations on the 1964 Campaign," *Public Opinion Quarterly*, 29 (Summer 1965), 195-196.

4

The Comprehensive Plan

Raymond Moley's Memorandum

The Goldwater campaign was organized on the basis of a plan which promised to use Comprehensive organization to protect the purity of conservatism. On October 4, 1963, Raymond Moley addressed a memorandum to Senator Goldwater on the subject of political organization. Formerly a professor of economics and a speechwriter for Franklin D. Roosevelt during the 1932 campaign, Moley broke with the New Deal when it began to experiment with policies he considered unsound. In the years following, he became a conservative theoretician and adviser to Republican candidates in addition to writing a column of political and economic analysis for *Newsweek* magazine. Because Moley was a long-standing acquaintance of Goldwater, we may assume that the two men were in accord on fundamental questions—so much in accord that the basic premises underlying his memorandum did not require restatement.

These premises had been stated by Mr. Moley in his previously published writings, most notably in a book entitled *The Republican Opportunity*, first published in 1962 and issued in a revised edition in 1964. Mr. Moley postulated the existence of a conservative majority, awaiting mobilization by a truly conservative candidate.

The clamor of minorities is so vehement, their organized efforts so well directed, and their special interests so skillfully advocated that many political leaders discount or ignore the great majority who must bear the burdens of the superstate. . . . The claims of that majority are not dramatic . . . [but its members] are the potential fulcrum of political power. They are the Republican potential. [1]

Moley's second premise held that previous Republican candidates had failed to present a consistently conservative philosophy. Even if he began with the appropriate attitudes on some issues, each had been prey to the advice of the minor politicians who were forever pressing him to take a stand on this or that issue in order to appease the demands of this or that interest group. By responding to the wishes of minority groups, candidates imitated the Democratic strategy of building a coalition of minorities and permitted the appeal of conservative principle to be dissipated in compromise. Citing the late V.O. Key as his authority, Moley pointed out that "the politician seems to follow public opinion, while he actually leads it." And the moral politician—in contrast to the demagogue—will define the long-range public interest, rather than pander to the fleeting wishes of the electorate. Mr. Moley reserved particular disdain for systematic studies of public opinion.

Poll-taking has become a national obsession. In academic and business life this has assumed the fancy name of "opinion research." Those who pretend to leadership first determine what "the public" wants and then seek to give it, or, at least, promise to give it . . . but the measurement of public opinion is still a crude and fallible instrument. The perils such soundings face lie in sampling, in the large number of those interviewed who have no opinions at all . . . [in] the prevalence of prevarication, the changing of opinions from one day to another, and the shaping of questions which induce predetermined answers. [2]

The third noteworthy assumption behind Mr. Moley's memorandum was that Barry Goldwater would receive the Republican nomination—noteworthy because the Republican Convention was nine months in the future, and Goldwater had not reached a firm decision to seek the nomination.

The memorandum itself spelled out the organizational implications of what Moley considered to be the failings of past Republican campaigns. To remedy those ills, Moley prescribed a dual campaign staff. The candidate and his advisers, responsible for articulating conservative principles, would be shielded from the influence of the political technicians responsible for arranging campaign details.

The gathering of delegates before the nomination and the mobilization of the organization for the campaign later involve certain specific practical political talents. That activity should be headed by one or a group of individuals of experience and imagination. The person in charge of that side of the campaign should be directly responsible to the candidate.

On the other hand, the development of the issues and the gathering of materials for the candidate's speeches and statements require quite different capacities. A single individual should be responsible for this and in turn should be directly responsible to the candidate.

While it is essential that there be friendly relations between the two sides of the operation, they should not be mixed. In other words, the political operators should not interfere with or attempt to dictate the nature of what the candidate says. And on the other hand, the policy people should not dabble in the matters of practical political organization.[3]

Moley next suggested the composition of the group of experts constituting the policy side of the organization. And he sternly specified that "when speeches are formulated they should not be done by a committee ... Differences of opinion will suck the substance from what is said."[4]

Raymond Moley's memorandum provided nothing less than a blueprint for a Comprehensive organization. It promised the benefits of Comprehensive decision-making. Policy would be made by a compact group. Agreement within this group on the goal of presenting a conservative candidate would be complete and unquestioned: it was the single-minded purpose of the campaign. But the technical details, or means, of achieving that goal would be assigned to a separate group of practical politicians, and the concerns of the two groups would be rigidly compartmentalized. Although Moley specified that "friendly relations" should exist between the two groups, persons who later served in the Goldwater organization understood that liaison was to be effected by one or more individuals who, in essence, enjoyed membership in both groups. Thus the authoritative making and coordination of decisions. Thus the insulation of the speechwriters from the worries of the politicians in the field. Thus the guarantee that an unsullied conservative philosophy would be presented and the "Republican potential" would be mobilized.

Moley's plan left out of account the very factors which we have designated as the likely faults of the Comprehensive model. In providing a compact and semi-isolated policy group, he did not consider the risk that they might come to misperceive political reality, due to a narrowing of their collective focus of attention. In assuming that means and ends could be separated, with the means delegated to the "practical politicians," he did not consider the impact upon their morale of being excluded from influence on the design of the campaign's content. This presumed separation of ends and means ran the further risk of limiting the search for alternatives: By definition, the policy groups would not consider alternative means, and the logistical group would not consider alternative ends. Finally, Moley provided no method for explaining this bifurcation of the campaign organization to the lower echelons of the party or to the voting public. When John Grenier, Alabama Republican Chairman, was later assigned to an important post in the logistical segment of the campaign structure, journalists immediately charged that his appointment signaled Goldwater's acceptance of the policies and strategies of the Southern Republicans.

In common with most Comprehensive plans, Moley's scheme made scant provision for the costs of decision-making—particularly the costs in time and social agreement. (Campaign finance was not dealt with in the memorandum.) Time would be required to set up the policy group; the academic and other experts staffing it would have to obtain leaves of absence from their usual occupations. Additional time would be needed to establish smooth working relationships with the "practical" group.

Moley's easy assumption that the "pros" would readily abandon their claim to exert influence on the content of the campaign suggests that he gave little attention to the problem. The most serious problem of social agreement would arise when rank and file party workers who disagreed with the conservative purposes of the entire organization were nonetheless asked to labor in its ranks.

A final attribute of the Moley memorandum which was closely related to its underlying premises, but less closely tied to the predicted faults of Comprehensive decision-making, was its tendency to overestimate the impact of rational appeals to the electorate. It assumed that the formal campaign would have great power to sway voters.

> If I were the candidate, I would decide upon about six or at the most eight formal and definitive speeches, each on a specific subject, between January 1st and the convention. These should be done with great care and submitted to the country as a program. Then, after the nomination, the candidate should make about the same number of set speeches, perhaps even on the same subjects with some variations.
> As I look back on 1932, the success of Roosevelt in getting over to the country was due to the rather limited number of specific subjects that he spoke about . . . in each specific case, the people who knew the score . . . understood what he was talking about and knew that he had a program.[5]

This passage may be an example of the "congratulation-rationalization" effect at work on the memory of a veteran campaigner. Historians suggest that the central reason for Roosevelt's 1932 victory was the association of depression suffering with the name of Herbert Hoover. Alfred M. Landon's campaign manager wrote that "the Democrats could have tossed a cigar from the balcony of the Convention Hall at Chicago, nominated the man it hit, and won at a walk in November of 1932."[6]

The circle of close friends who served as Barry Goldwater's campaign advisers were largely amateurs in the realm of national politics. They were sensitive to the charge of amateurism, yet their instinct was to exclude the professionals of the Nixon and Eisenhower campaigns. The Moley memorandum resolved any lingering doubt. It gave the support of Moley's prestige and experience as a veteran campaigner to procedures which the Goldwater advisers already found attractive. Although the memorandum was not published until long after the election, its principles were freely quoted by Goldwater's campaign leaders. Three of our respondants described those principles before a fourth identified Raymond Moley as the author of the organizational plan.

Kitchel was his [Goldwater's] manager and acted as a bridge between the organization side and the policy-makers, or writers . . . My contributions were on the policy side.

Kitchel was *the* campaign manager with a foot in both camps—both the logistics organization and the policy organization. Otherwise these functions were kept separate. The reason for this kind of separate organization was based on the experience of F.D.R.

If there was any lack of interest in public opinion, it was because the general scheme was to base the campaign on what the candidate and his advisers believed to be the right policy rather than on the policies that people might want.

In his account of the campaign, speechwriter Karl Hess relates that "those concerned with issues and those concerned with nuts-and-bolts politics" were "separated as effectively as possible" on the advice of Raymond Moley. Hess then reports with dismay that the "pros" were unhappy with the arrangement.[7] Stephen Shadegg, the exponent of Comprehensive organization, describes the dual structure approvingly in a brief paragraph, labeling the organization "simple and direct."[8] But Shadegg later chronicles the tensions between the "think tank," or speech-preparation apparatus, and the political technicians, including Regional Directors (one of whom was Shadegg himself) and the Finance Committee. The politicians were particularly distressed because "Kitchel and Baroody had decreed that Goldwater would not lower himself by making a direct appeal for votes with speeches focused on local problems."[9] Both authors seem to accept the validity of Goldwater's version of a Comprehensive organization. When they later acknowledge the problem of social agreement, no suggestion is made that this problem was inherent in the organizational principles adopted for the Goldwater campaign.

A Non-Decision: Goldwater's Drift into Candidacy

The lateness of Goldwater's final decision to seek the nomination precluded the construction of an elaborate personal organization. Neither Goldwater nor his close advisers were prepared to solicit the contributions needed to support a complete staff before the commitment to candidacy was made. In September of 1963, Goldwater was asked about his apparent lack of a campaign staff or even a basic plan for converting his obvious support in the party into delegate commitments. He replied, "I'm doing all right just pooping around."[10]

Both the Comprehensive and Incremental models assume the activity of a strong and determined candidate. In different ways, each model assumes that the candidate is the master of his organization. He designs it to fulfill his purposes. In either model, the organizational machine is fueled by an ambitious candidate.

As we have suggested, however, much of Barry Goldwater's attraction for his followers was based on his apparent lack of conventional political ambition—the kind of ambition that leads political figures to adapt their political declarations to the prevailing winds of opinion. Goldwater did not behave as if he were determined to occupy the White House. Long after the press had tagged him as a possible candidate, Goldwater's references to the office were marked by a sincere humility. He once told an audience that no person without a college degree should ever be elected to the presidency.[11] A dedication to the conservative conscience left no room for the conventional kind of political ambition.

Formation of the Draft Goldwater Committee

Senator Goldwater clearly enjoyed his expanding public role after the 1960 election, but there were no signs that he was using his new popularity to build support for election to higher office. The organization of that popularity into a disciplined political force was carried on by a group of men and women who began operations without Goldwater's knowledge and worked for a year and a half without his blessing. The group, which came to call itself the National Draft Goldwater Committee, was eventually headed by Peter O'Donnell, Republican State Chairman of Texas. But its organizing genius was F. Clifton (Clif) White. The story of the activities of this group has been told often and well. In one account, Clif White stated disarmingly that "it was a significant victory as it represented the work of little people. It showed that the American political system is open, that individuals with some technical knowledge, faith and willingness to work, can elect a nominee for President."[12]

One of our respondents, an articulate aide of Clif White, described the successes of the White organization.

O'Donnell had to stay away from Goldwater–it was an honest draft, as Goldwater did not want [the nomination] . . . we went into counties and states on all levels such as the 10th District, any political entity that would elect delegates to the convention. In my state this meant cultivating the precinct delegates who elect the county delegates who elect the state delegates. [By working with the right precinct delegates, we went] all the way to the national convention. In [my state] this happened ten times in ten districts. We happened to get solid delegates starting from the bottom up and working for one and a half years before the Convention. This [cultivating the states where there would be no Primary election] was White's function throughout the [pre-convention] campaign . . . this was the smart thing to do as White knows the organization people in the states as no one else does in the Republican Party.

When the Draft Goldwater group was formed, Goldwater may have dismissed it as yet another collection of over-enthusiastic supporters. Clif White established an office in New York and continued to build the organization. He established solid lines of communication with both experienced Republican activists and those entering the Party specifically to support the Goldwater cause. The organization remained a tightly-knit structure, and many of its members developed great loyalty to White as their political commander. By the autumn of 1963, it was clear that Clif White's growing organization represented the active field forces of "the Goldwater movement."

Nevertheless, Goldwater continued to take little interest in the developing organizational effort. It became an external pressure over which he exerted little influence. A word from him could have ended its existence; instead, he chose neither to encourage nor to discourage the effort.

The Goldwater for Senator Committee

Goldwater's friends were concerned that, with the Republican Convention less than a year away, Goldwater would not be prepared to play the role history seemed to be preparing for him. Apparently they urged him to sanction the formation of a staff that would be ready to serve him if he should decide to seek the nomination. Goldwater finally yielded, and in the fall of 1963, Denison Kitchel opened an office in Washington, ostensibly to run a senatorial campaign. Kitchel was a 55-year old lawyer from Phoenix. Born in Bronxville, New York, he graduated from St. Paul's School, Yale, and Harvard Law School. Kitchel went to Arizona as a young man and developed both influence and affluence in the legal profession. Kitchel had little experience with the daily operation of political organizations. Like Goldwater, Kitchel had served as an Air Force officer and was accustomed to the ways of Comprehensive organizations.

Goldwater had not yet decided to run, and Kitchel felt he could not commit the Senator to such action. This meant that he was not prepared to begin assembling the logistical side of the dual campaign organization specified by the Moley memorandum. There was no reason for Goldwater to seek the aid of influential party members if he were determined not to become a candidate. However, since Goldwater had announced his intention of seeking reelection to his Senate seat, Kitchel felt that he could start assembling the policy segment of the campaign organization.

An electronic information storage system, the Recordak, was installed in the office. Operators began programming into it the remarkable record of Barry Goldwater's twelve years of public candor regarding political questions. This mechanical aid to Comprehensive decision-making reflected both a concern for chinks in the Senator's conservative armor and an exhaustive approach to their analysis. Kitchel next appointed Edward McCabe as Director of Research for Goldwater's "Senate" campaign. McCabe, a Washington lawyer, had known and worked with Goldwater since he came to the Senate. McCabe had been involved in four previous presidential campaigns and had served for five years as Associate Counsel and Administrative Assistant to President Eisenhower.

As Director of Research, McCabe established a network of conservatively oriented academicians at various universities in the United States. They would be ready to supply concepts and arguments to the issue-oriented substructure of the organization, where the ideas would be refined and finally produced in package form for the candidate's speeches.

Kitchel was drawn into contact with Goldwater's long-standing friends who would counsel him as the time approached for a decision regarding his candidacy. Richard Kleindienst, of Arizona, was one of these. Tony Smith, Goldwater's long-time press secretary, was another. The concern for issue positions brought the involvement of William Baroody, Sr. Baroody would eventually take a leave of absence from his post as President of the American Enterprise Institute for Public Policy Research (AEI). The Institute is a conservatively oriented foundation which performs research for members of both parties in Congress and publishes both long and short-range analyses of political issues. Although he held no official title in the Goldwater organization, Baroody would become the most influential member of its policy segment. Goldwater had used the services of AEI increasingly as his pronouncements were sought on a variety of public issues; he knew Baroody well and respected his intellectual powers and judgment. During the general election campaign, Baroody was recognized as Barry Goldwater's *alter ego* in matters of the intellect. Before long, Kitchel brought Dean Burch to Washington as his principal assistant. Burch, then thirty-five years old, was an Arizona attorney who had once served in Goldwater's Washington office.

A number of members of the House and Senate were enthusiastic supporters of Goldwater. Notable among them were Senators Norris Cotton of New Hampshire and John Tower of Texas. William Knowland, former Senator from California, was eager to begin constructing the framework of a Goldwater organization in that state. But Kitchel was not prepared to begin constructing the logistical side of a campaign organization. He kept a wary eye on the operations of the Draft Goldwater Committee, feeling that any close contact would provide more encouragement to the group than Goldwater wanted to give. Peter O'Donnell brought John Grenier to meet Kitchel at about this time. Grenier was Republican State Chairman of Alabama, and O'Donnell wanted to recommend him as an organizational leader for Goldwater. But Kitchel remained noncommittal. He felt that if he had either expressed like or dislike for Grenier, the Draft Goldwater Committee would have celebrated, feeling that "Goldwater is at last taking an interest in us!"

The operations of the Draft Goldwater Committee had gone "above ground" the previous April, when its formation had been announced, with Peter O'Donnell as Chairman. A strong disavowal from Goldwater would have killed the organization, leaving it without financial support. When he was tracked down by reporters, however, Goldwater merely announced that he would take no position on the draft movement, but that "they are going to have to get along without any help from me." Robert Novak records that "this was the kind of neutrality for which the Draft Goldwater movement had been praying."[13] It was also the kind of ambivalent decision that Goldwater made when internal principles offered no clear guide.

Goldwater's decision

The key decision of Goldwater to seek the nomination can hardly be labeled Comprehensive; neither can it be called Incremental. The first model would imply a careful examination of the alternative courses of action even-tuating in a decision that could be pinpointed in time. The second would have been evidenced by a series of marginal moves, following contacts with persons throughout the political arena, gradually "absorbing" uncertainty. But Goldwater remained ambivalent throughout the summer of 1963. Friends urged him to accept command of the forces recruited by Clif White. Goldwater yielded to the extent of permitting Kitchel to tend his political interests in Washington. But the Senator seemed determined to preserve his opportunity for saying "no." In itself, this determination could have been part of an Incremental pattern. But it was not coupled with positive efforts to ease his burdens of choice either through simplification or adjustment. His only "policy" seemed one of drift.

The reaction to Governor Rockefeller's remarriage made Goldwater's chances look better. An article defining Goldwater's foreign policy was pre-pared for publication in *Life* Magazine the third weekend in November. It would be the last step before the formal announcement of candidacy. But the assassination of President Kennedy came that weekend, and publication was canceled. In common with most Americans, Goldwater was thrown into an emotional tailspin by the events of that fantastic weekend, and thoughts of a possible candidacy were erased from his mind.

When the time for the political reassessment could no longer be put off, Goldwater found the prospect of campaigning against Lyndon Johnson ex-tremely distasteful. He had liked and admired John Kennedy and relished the prospect of engaging him in a political dialogue. Furthermore, he argued that much conservative sentiment had been aimed at Kennedy as a liberal target, and that some of this animus might not be transferred to Johnson. His friends replied that the conservative movement had grown up around Goldwater irrespective of John Kennedy. They held that Goldwater was the natural leader of the conservative movement; that he would remain so, regardless of Johnson's accession to the presidency; and that the momentum of the con-servative movement would be destroyed if he abandoned it by refusing to become a candidate.

Perhaps the appeal to duty as the conservative leader was the most influ-ential argument; perhaps it was not. Goldwater himself apparently is not sure exactly when the decision was made, or on what basis. Somehow, one Dec-ember day in 1963, Goldwater realized that he was going to make the race.[14]

A press conference was hastily arranged. On January 3, 1964, Goldwater appeared before the television cameras set up on the patio of his Phoenix home. Recuperating from a recent, painful operation on his heel, he appeared on crutches to speak of some of the principles of conservatism which would be the basis for presenting himself to the Republican Party. He would offer "a choice, not an echo." Then Goldwater boarded a plane for New Hampshire, where Nelson Rockefeller was already campaigning in the winter snows.

Testing the Comprehensive Plan

Up to the time of announcing his candidacy, Senator Goldwater had been swept along by external events and the decisions of others. He accepted his own position as a leader of the "conservative movement," but he had so far been more a captive than a leader. At last he was in a position to assume command of his personal political destiny, and the principles of the Moley memorandum seemed to provide the method. But there was no time to put them into effect.

The New Hampshire primary was a searing experience for Goldwater and his associates. For the first time, the gay spontaneity of Goldwater's style, which had won such enthusiastic support on the Republican banquet circuit, was placed before the full view of small groups of a skeptical electorate and the hostile analysis of the national mass media. Goldwater placed himself almost completely in the hands of his New Hampshire managers. He shook hands. He answered questions, often with little or no preparation. Plagued by the pain in his heel and the unaccustomed cold, he became exhausted. The unanimous verdict of both friends and critics was "overexposed."[15]

To Kitchel and Goldwater, the New Hampshire experience served chiefly to demonstrate the wisdom of the suggestions made the year before by Raymond Moley. An intimate associate of that time reported:

Goldwater's experience in New Hampshire strengthened our conviction that a dual organization was needed. We felt that his defensive responses to Rockefeller's charges in New Hampshire cost him much support there. That is, Goldwater listened too much to the New Hampshire politicians. Senator Cotton and others were always saying, "You must talk on Social Security," and so forth. This was a mistake, and by the time of the California primary, Goldwater decided not to react to the charges of the opposition. Upon entering California, Goldwater made a single statement at the airport on extremism and another single statement, later on, on Social Security. The rest of his time was devoted to presenting a straightforwardly conservative point of view.

The Moley memorandum had not specified ways to meet the crucial costs of campaigning (and decision-making): time, money, and social agreement. Time was in short supply when Goldwater opened his campaign in New Hampshire, but money was not. The Draft Goldwater Committee had raised $751,000 in support of the Senator's unannounced candidacy prior to January of 1964. When the poor New Hampshire showing led potential large contributors to have second thoughts, the practical politicians to whom such matters were delegated "made political financial history by applying market-research techniques to fund-raising." Direct mail solicitations were sent to the members of selected groups who "find the Federal government moving in on them"—physicians, small businessmen, dentists, and restaurant owners. Through this and other devices, Goldwater fund raisers were to collect $4.7 million before the Republican Convention, which was more than half again the total of $3 million collected during the period by national Republican party agencies.[16]

With financing in hand, the organizational effort expanded rapidly in order to make up for the loss of time. The headquarters supporting Goldwater's campaign soon came to employ one hundred persons. As early as February, it was possible to draw up the hallmark of Comprehensiveness, an organization chart.[17]

The National Goldwater for President Committee

The new organization was entitled the National Goldwater for President Committee. Its General Director was Denison Kitchel. The chart made clear that his supervision extended over both the policy-making and logistical elements of the staff. Kitchel used the best of the Draft Goldwater personnel, supplemented by some of Goldwater's long-standing political associates, to staff the logistical arm. The headquarters chief of this arm was Dean Burch, with the title of Assistant Director. The personnel of the policy group were those who had labored in the "Goldwater for Senator" office, including Tony Smith and Ed McCabe. As Research Director, McCabe was also officially subordinate to Burch. The most important addition to the group was Karl Hess, who had been working part time on the campaign but now left the American Enterprise Institute to devote full time to the preparation of Goldwater speeches. The New Hampshire experience confirmed the decision to limit Senator Goldwater's informal visits with both voters and the press and to rely more completely on television and on formal campaign addresses.

Under Burch's direction in the logistics wing were five principal sub-divisions: finance, public information, research, administration, and field operations. The last was the most extensive, as befitted an operation designed to court the convention delegations of 50 separate states. The nation was divided into eight different regions for the purpose of delegating the responsibility for the supervision of field operations. The Director of Field Operations was Richard G. Kleindienst, who would return to Arizona as a candidate for governor.

After an initial failure to find an appropriate role for Clif White, he was made cochairman of field operations with Kleindienst. Before long, White was put in charge of the 34 states where no primary campaigns would require the articulation of conservative principles. The gathering of delegates in these states was regarded as the task of a political technician, and White had demonstrated superb technical abilities. The Draft Goldwater Committee structures in those states continued to gather delegates with little information being passed up the chain of command to Kitchel or Goldwater. There is every reason to believe that Goldwater's close associates were not always aware of wounds opened in the state organizations by the operations of Clif White's associates. And White found the "Arizona Mafia" little interested in what he could tell them of the nuances of state party organizations.[18]

Although White's operations could gather nearly enough delegates to nom-inate Goldwater without the candidate proving his electoral attractiveness in primary elections, after the New Hampshire fiasco Goldwater and Kitchel felt that the only way to clinch the nomination would be to win a seriously contested primary. The next primary was in Oregon, where all candidates are by law placed on the ballot. The Goldwater campaign in Oregon was planned but never completely implemented. A series of appearances was canceled, for the multiplicity of candidates made a clear victory for Goldwater unlikely.

The California primary

Goldwater and his advisers decided to cut their losses in Oregon and con-centrate a major effort on California, which offered a rich harvest of 86 delegate votes. The speechwriters were established in the Los Altos Apart-ments on Los Angeles' Wilshire Boulevard. Command of Goldwater's army of volunteer workers was eased out of the hands of California leaders, including William Knowland, who were preoccupied with the bitter aftermath of pre-vious California campaigns. Eighteen days of hectic activity followed. But the basic enthusiasm already existed, as one of our respondents pointed out.

Goldwater decided during the California Primary that there would be no attacks upon Rocky. This worked well to an extent. Rocky lost California because he had no organization. He could win there only by offsetting [the Goldwater vote in] Southern California with a 3 to 1 Northern California vote. But in San Francisco, where 41 per cent of the voters were Goldwater supporters, we had 100 percent of the workers at the polls and in the precincts. Rockefeller did get a 2 to 1 vote but this was really a defeat. Rocky had a P.R. firm get the necessary 55,000 signatures [on nominating petitions] and they took up to the last minute. We got ours in a matter of hours, had planes waiting to carry them to their destination. The P.R. firm of Rockefeller's ended up paying as much as $1.50 per name.

The Goldwater workers in Southern California were amateurs. They were members of the Goldwater following, and they were attracted by his appeal to the old American virtues, a rock of certainty in socially mobile Southern California. Rockefeller had the mass media behind him, but Goldwater had the workers; and a suburban housewife who never receives callers may be favorably impressed by the cause that could bring a neighbor to her door. The Republican Chairman of Los Angeles County explained that "the Rockefeller group is class. The Goldwater group is the most messed-up, cluttered-up organization I've ever seen. But I think Mr. Goldwater is going to win at the doorstep."[19] Goldwater won the Republican primary in California by a margin of 59,000 out of more than 2,000,000 votes cast.

In terms of decision-making, the total impact of the primaries was to reinforce the predilection of Goldwater's most intimate advisers to follow the guidelines of the Moley memorandum. The New Hampshire experience demonstrated the need to implement Moley's recommendations; California seemed to prove their validity. Good organization was essential; an organization that succeeds is, by definition, a "good organization." The new organization chart of the Republican National Committee would be very similar to that of the Goldwater for President Committee. But was the headquarters organization responsible for Goldwater's winning the nomination? Or was it Clif White, who, drawing on his vast acquaintance with local Republican organizations, approached each state delegation as a unique problem in political persuasion—persuasion that did not take place at the public rostrum where Barry Goldwater was expounding the conservative faith?

Notes on Chapter 4

[1] Raymond Moley, *The Republican Opportunity in 1964* (New York: Duell, 1964), p. 89

[2] Moley, p. 141.

[3] The Moley memorandum, edited to remove references to personalities, was published as Appendix H of *The New Methodology: A Study of Political Strategy and Tactics* (Washington, D.C.: American Institute for Political Communication, 1967), pp. 191-193.

[4] *The New Methodology*, p. 192.

[5] *The New Methodology*, p. 193.

[6] John D. M. Hamilton in *Young Republican Magazine* (August 1938), p. 4. Hamilton's point was that the voters rejected Hoover in 1932 but responded positively to the New Deal in 1936.

[7] Karl Hess, *In a Cause that Will Triumph* (Garden City, N.Y.: Doubleday, 1967), pp. 31-32.

[8] Stephen Shadegg, *What Happened to Goldwater?* (New York: Holt, 1965), p. 194.

[9] Shadegg, p. 211.

[10] Robert C. Albright in *The Washington Post*, September 8, 1963. Quoted in Robert D. Novak, *The Agony of the GOP, 1964* (New York: Macmillan, 1965), p. 236.

[11] The Ripon Society, *From Disaster to Distinction: A Republican Rebirth* (New York: Pocket Books, 1966), p. 19.

[12] The quotation is from a paper delivered by F. Clifton White to the Western Political Science Association meeting on March 19, 1965, entitled "Selection of Delegates to the 1964 Republican Nominating Convention Related to the Thirteen Western States" (mimeographed), p. 12. White has since related the entire history of Goldwater's nomination in *Suite 3505* (New Rochelle, N.Y.: Arlington House, 1967). The best brief account of the Goldwater movement and its direction by Clif White and others is Theodore H. White's *The Making of the President 1964* (New York: Atheneum, 1965), pp. 88-97. The entire tragi-comedy of Republican events from 1960 to 1964 is related by Clif White's friend, Robert D. Novak, in *The Agony of the GOP, 1964, passim.* See also Shadegg, *What Happened to Goldwater?*, pp. 37-128.

[13] Novak, p. 131.

[14] This account of Goldwater's decision to run is based upon interviews with his close associates plus the reporting of Theodore White in *The Making of The President 1964*, pp. 94-97. The present authors did not interview the Senator, but White apparently questioned him closely regarding this crucial decision. See also Harold Faber, ed., *The Road to the White House* (New York: McGraw-Hill, 1965), pp. 14-15, and Clif White's *Suite 3505*, Chs. 12, 21, and 24.

[15] Stephen Shadegg blames the shortcomings of the New Hampshire campaign on the "lack of advance planning" *(What Happened to Goldwater?*, p. 98) but quotes Kitchel as saying, "In one way, New Hampshire was a good thing for we learned so much" (Shadegg, p. 100).

[16] The financial details are supplied in James W. Davis, *Presidential Primaries: Road to the White House* (New York: Crowell, 1967), pp. 215-216, 229. Quotations in this paragraph are from this source.

[17]The February organization chart is reproduced in *The New Methodology: A Study of Political Strategy and Tactics*, p. 154. The Goldwater primary campaign organization is described as yet further proof of the adoption of "The New Methodology" by American politicians. Insofar as The New Methodology represents a sensitivity to the most effective use of the mass media and a concern for "themes" and "images," the present authors would agree that it has substantially modified political campaigning in the last 15 years. If The New Methodology necessarily must include a Comprehensive style of decision-making, however, we suggest that the candidate will be courting trouble.

[18]*Suite 3505*, p. 267.

[19]Julius A. Leetham, quoted by Theodore White, *The Making of The President 1964*, p. 128. This brief chapter contains a compelling analysis of the impact of the primary campaigns on the voters. Primaries are also discussed in Novak, *The Agony of the GOP, 1964*, pp. 301-415, Shadegg, *What Happened to Goldwater?*, pp. 85-128, and Faber, ed., *Road to the White House*, pp. 19-44. The most complete account is Clif White's *Suite 3505*, which critics have labeled a "how-to-do-it manual" of presidential nominating politics.

5

Winning The Republican Nomination

The Pattern of Decisions in San Francisco

When Goldwater and his staff arrived in San Francisco, the majority of the delegates were his. Goldwater knew it; the press knew it; some of the public knew it. Yet elements of the Party persisted in opposing Goldwater through all the procedures of the Convention—the examination of credentials, the drafting of the platform, and the presentation of candidates. The treatment accorded his opponents by his supporters had wide-ranging consequences, yet Goldwater did not appear to sense trouble, and he eschewed the traditional gestures used by nominees to restore party harmony after the inevitable divisiveness of the Convention. Examples of such action include awarding the vice presidential nomination to the leader of an opposing faction, as John Kennedy did; making personal overtures to the defeated leader, as Eisenhower did to Taft; and stressing party unity in the acceptance speech.

Why was this grave political error committed? Why, throughout the campaign, did Barry Goldwater tell reporters that its least expected development was the failure of so many Republican leaders to support him? Why did Goldwater assume that the party rank-and-file would necessarily coalesce in his support, even if their leaders did not?

No single-factor explanation can supply a total answer to these questions, and we shall examine the circumstances of some crucial Convention decisions in detail. Each was in part determined by forces in the immediate environment. It is quite likely, for example, that Goldwater considered a Goldwater-Scranton ticket a real possibility until his sense of personal dignity was wounded by the famous letter prepared by Scranton's staff, signed on his behalf, and slipped under delegates' hotel room doors. The letter attacked Goldwater in vitriolic terms. But the general pattern of these crucial decisions becomes explicable when we suggest that possibly Goldwater and certainly many of his close advisers seriously misunderstood the nature of the Convention. Their attitude had the following stated or unstated components:

The Convention was "truly representative" of all Republican voters—and many independents—in the nation. This assumption, if logically analyzed, would have to include a belief that delegates were chosen in each state through an appropriate representative process. It would also have to ignore the fact that Goldwater's only primary election victory—and that by a slender margin—was in California.

The first ballot vote represented the true feelings of the Convention. This assumption would have to discount the probability that many delegates were bowing to the inevitable and supported Goldwater without enthusiasm to insure a place for their state on the bandwagon.

Throughout the campaign, Goldwater aides cited the magnitude of his first ballot vote as proof that he was the candidate preferred by the party rank-and-file, ignoring public opinion data which revealed that Goldwater was the choice of no more than a quarter of all registered Republicans. Interviewed after the election, "less than twenty percent of all Republicans recalled having preferred Goldwater at the time of the Convention."[1] The gathering of delegates from the non-primary states had been assigned to Clif White. As specified by the Moley memorandum, the policy group around Goldwater exercised no authority over the delegate-gathering, and the Clif Whites of the logistics organization were excluded from policy influence. The exchange of information was inhibited, further narrowing the scope of attention of the policy group. In terms of first-ballot votes, the results were impressive, so there seemed no reason to enquire further into the nature of the delegates themselves.

Many of the Goldwater delegates were newcomers. A comparison of Convention rosters reveals that 74.3 percent of the delegates had not been at either of the two preceding Conventions (in 1956 and 1960), although this was not an unusual turnover. Only 153 of the 1,308 delegates in 1964 had been delegates or alternates at the 1956 Convention.[2] As the late Paul Tillett surmised, the newness of the delegates was not so significant as the fact that they had come to the Convention bearing instructions from Clif White's delegate organization. They were not there to follow the cues of state political leaders. In effect, Tillett wrote, some state parties were infiltrated from below. In at least five states, for example, where pro-Goldwater slates had been defeated, dedicated pro-Goldwater delegates appeared in the presumably neutral or even anti-Goldwater delegations.[3]

Months after the election, a high official of the Goldwater campaign expressed amazement when told that three-fourths of the Convention were delegates who had not attended either of the previous Conventions. "When Barry got over 800 votes on the first ballot," he replied, "I just assumed that the Goldwater organization and the Republican organization were one and the same thing."

If such assumptions about the nature of the Convention had been valid, then the actions of Scranton, Rockefeller, Romney, and other opponents of Goldwater's candidacy could be viewed as the cacaphonous strivings of a small and impotent minority intent upon disrupting the harmony of the Convention when they found that its course could not be altered. The obvious treatment for such spoilers was to deny their demands, keep them from the public spotlight, and dignify their efforts with as little attention as possible.

Many apparently perceived the Convention in exactly these terms. A middle-range official of the Draft Goldwater Committee, who later worked in the public relations office of the Republican National Committee, habitually referred to Goldwater's Convention opponents as "those who would have denied the nomination to the Senator." Goldwater delegates revealed a particularly uncompromising attitude, as shown in a series of interviews supervised by Professor Aaron Wildavsky. Goldwater delegates told the interviewers that the prime quality of a presidential candidate should be moral integrity. They claimed that "principles are more important than winning." Wildavsky wrote:

One gets no sense whatsoever that Goldwater purists approached problems by inquiring how special circumstances might be taken into account in order to achieve desirable results. The pragmatic spirit was completely lacking. Indeed, the purists manifested amazingly little interest in specific issues . . . they are far more concerned about the need for substantial differences between the parties than they are about the differences themselves . . . political style thus becomes a substitute for politics itself.[4]

The Problem of Social Agreement

The Comprehensive model makes no provision for the cost of achieving social agreement; it may actually encourage decision-makers to ignore the problem altogether. But the American political party is not a Comprehensive organization. The support of state and local party units cannot be commanded. It can only be cajoled.

Barry Goldwater has never been accused of endorsing the attitudes of his most fervent admirers. He never claimed that the Republican nomination was his by some kind of divine right. Nevertheless, he seemed unaware of the damage to party harmony created by such an attitude on the part of many of his supporters. He did not perceive his own responsibility for acts of leadership which would help to promote social agreement. Important actions of the Convention did not find a place on his personal agenda for decision-making.

One of his close associates explained that the Senator approached the Convention as a constitutionalist. He felt that the various responsibilities of the Convention should be discharged by the officially designated organs of the party, just as the Constitution provides for the separation of powers.

The platform

Platform drafting was the business of the Platform Committee. Goldwater appeared before the Committee and stated, "I will not presume for a moment to tell you what should or should not go into this platform."[5] Speaking as "*this* Republican," he outlined conservative policy attitudes. He then departed, and he paid little attention to further proceedings of the Committee. Goldwater had confidence in the experience and outlook of Melvin Laird, the Wisconsin congressman who chaired the Committee.

In keeping with the belief of Congressman Laird and others that the Republican Party possesses a coherent and continuing attitude towards government, the national platform has been used by Republican Congressmen as a guide to legislative action more than have Democratic Congressmen used the Democratic platform. Laird's concern was to achieve a consensus on language within the Committee and then protect the resulting document from attacks from outside the Committee.[6] Laird rejected the various amendments to the platform proposed by the anti-Goldwater forces—Romney's on procedural grounds, others on the ground that they attacked the integrity of the Platform Committee. Thus Rockefeller, Scranton (represented by Senator Hugh Scott), and Romney made their public efforts to override the decisions of the Platform Committee through a vote of the entire Convention. Laird delayed the effort until long past prime television time by ruling that the entire document must first be read into the microphones to place it before the Convention. But the summary rejection of their amendments gave Goldwater's opponents public justification for abandoning the traditional practice of at least pretending to rally in support of the Party's nominee.

It is interesting to note the reactions of Goldwater intimates to the booing of Nelson Rockefeller by the Convention galleries. A member of the research staff based in Washington during the campaign told us;

> Being an astute politician, Rockefeller must have understood the Convention's [pro-Goldwater] attitude and therefore I must assume that he deliberately took the rostrum to provoke the incident that occurred. This type of approach would be consistent with some of the activities that he and his staff undertook during the California primary campaign.

One of Goldwater's conservative theoreticians suggested to us that those booing Rockefeller had been planted in the audience by the Rockefeller forces in order to discredit Goldwater. Clif White makes the same claim.[7] We reject it on the basis of personal observation.

One of the few persons who, at one time or another, could claim membership in both the policy and logistics segments of the campaign, offered a more complete account.

> Beginning in January, Rockefeller people told me often they were going to goad Barry into an open quarrel over extremism. I agree the basic issue wasn't frivolous if it were true but its use for many months was a tactic. The delegates, who weren't extremists and knew they weren't, were being told they were. They also knew that some proposals, such as the Romney amendments, would have been in the platform if Romney had offered them there as Laird asked him to. He didn't and the delegates felt he was more interested in prime TV time in the Midwest than in having his proposition adopted for its own sake. . . . Nelson wanted to provoke a fight and the Goldwater people among the hecklers were foolishly playing into his hands . . . granted Nelson overdid it. But he was fighting for the Presidency! That's never a kid-gloves affair, as witness the early LBJ-JFK rock-throwing.

In addition to containing the most charitable reference to Nelson Rockefeller of any of our interviews, this statement is notable for its sincere belief that Romney's battle to amend the platform was based on a search for publicity rather than a dedication to principle. Evidence indicates that the facts were more complex. On December 6, 1964, Barry Goldwater addressed a letter to George Romney in which he asked, in part, "Where were you, George, when the chips were down and the going was hard? . . . Many rank and file Republicans got a bad taste in their mouths when they saw leaders of their own party failing to support a national ticket." In his eleven-page reply, Romney detailed the presentation of his positions on extremism and other issues, on his own behalf and that of the Republican Governors' Association, to Chairman Laird before the Convention and to the full Platform Committee. Romney's specific amendment on "extremism" was introduced, he stated, by Richard Van Dusen, Michigan's member, during the final debate of the Platform Committee, but it was summarily rejected. Romney's letter continued:

You didn't read the platform adopted in San Francisco and you didn't know what amendments were being offered on the floor so you were obviously leaving many vital things almost entirely up to others, vital things about which you were not personally informed.[8]

The tangle of ambitions and motivations is difficult to sort out. George Romney no doubt hoped to build up his credentials as a party regular at the Convention, if he possibly could. But the decision-making structure of the Convention refused Romney (and his allies) any symbolic victory which could serve as demonstration to the Governor's constituents that his brand of Republicanism could at least gain a hearing in the national councils of the Party. Romney was then forced to seek a public confrontation. In his letter to Goldwater, Romney pointed out that opinion polls showed that Goldwater enjoyed the constant support of a scant third of the Michigan electorate. Romney's only chance to win reelection lay in disassociating his own candidacy from that of the Arizona Senator.

But this was the kind of evidence concerning political reality that was derided by Raymond Moley and systematically discounted by Goldwater's other advisers.

The one clear conclusion which emerges is that there were ample signals of dangerous disharmony in the Convention, but Goldwater did not heed them. Intent upon preparing the acceptance speech, Goldwater's policy group did not involve itself in the platform controversy. One respondent told us that the possibility of compromise at least on Romney's extremism amendment was discussed within the White delegate-watching group but was abandoned for fear that the Goldwater delegates—deeply offended by Governor Rockefeller's performance and in no mood for compromise—would not follow such instructions. Presumably, the idea was never suggested to Goldwater himself.

In summing up his attitudes towards the events of the Convention, a member of the policy group concluded:

There was considerable feeling in the Goldwater staff that any accommodations would have to come from the moderates. The platform was of the Party, not of Goldwater. Goldwater traditionally put little emphasis on platforms. Laird was the independent-minded man who ran the Platform Committee according to his own lights. In our mind we had by July more delegates than anyone else. Everyone had to accept this. I think we could have made this a little sweeter than we did. But it would have made little difference. The wounds were so powerful there was little room for better relations.

This comment no doubt reflects a reality: nothing that the Goldwater forces said or did at the Convention could have converted Nelson Rockefeller, for example, from being a bitter opponent to a happy state of enthusiastic support for the nominee. But the comment further suggests that little thought was given to the consequences of the display of disharmony at the Convention. The Moley memorandum had emphasized the power of the formal campaign to sway voters; it ignored the evidence which holds that many voters make their decisions during or just after the conventions. The atmosphere of the Convention, and the actions of the nominee within that atmosphere, together provide a better chance than any single event of the formal campaign to determine voting decisions.

This reality of modern political life seemed to make no impact on the decisions of Goldwater's policy group at any point during the Convention.

Selection of the vice presidential candidate

Goldwater's next chance to further party harmony came in his designation of a running mate. Some of the experienced politicians in the logistics group, including Clif White, hoped until late in the Convention that Goldwater would choose Scranton.

We have discovered no signs that the selection of William Miller was made as a result of a Comprehensive consideration of the alternatives and their possible outcomes or that it resulted from an Incremental process of bargaining and mutual adjustment. The decision itself cannot be pinpointed in time. A Goldwater confidant claimed it was made quite early.

Very early in 1964 everyone—including the Scranton forces—knew that Bill [Miller], whom Barry regarded and still regards as a personal friend, was a shoo-in for second place on a ticket Goldwater was sure to head barring a California [primary election] defeat.

It does seem clear that, if this were the case, the choice had not been effectively communicated to Miller.[9] Another friend gave a different account:

I talked to Goldwater about his plans. He stated he had not given it any thought, not even as to his Vice-President. So two days before the nomination, in the Mark Hopkins Hotel, he was still not clear as to who was to be his running mate; then, finally, he stated that it was to be Bill Miller. "Why Bill?" [I asked] "Well," [Goldwater replied] "Bill knows the organization, knows the party machinery, knows the members, and knows the language. But most of all he drives LBJ nuts."

Newsmen pointed out that Miller filled some of the traditional requirements that the ticket be balanced. He was from upper New York State, on the opposite side of the nation from Goldwater's home. He was a Catholic, which might help to win back some of the votes that had gone to John F. Kennedy. Goldwater pointed out that Miller, as a lawyer, would balance his own lack of formal legal training.

But the significant facts about William Miller were that he was a hard-hitting campaigner with a conservative voting record who was then totally unknown to most of the American public. The selection of Miller therefore brought no asset to the ticket in the conventional sense. His selection did nothing to woo the support of Democrats or moderates within the Republican Party. It did not add an illustrious name to the ticket to reassure voters concerning the quality of the man "a heartbeat away from the presidency." The selection only made sense as underscoring the determination of Barry Goldwater to offer a "choice, not an echo."

The acceptance speech

Finally, the closing public event of the Convention was the acceptance speech. The general impact of the speech cast it as the closing round in the battle for the nomination, rather than the opening salvo of a broadside directed at the opposition. Goldwater's advisers had intended the speech to be a reasoned and eloquent conservative statement, setting the stage for the political debate they hoped would follow. Instead, only a single statement survived, to be repeated throughout the campaign by pundits and opponents—the passing comment on extremism. ("Extremism in the defense of liberty is no vice. Moderation in the pursuit of justice is no virtue.")

These sentences were drafted by Harry Jaffa, a political theorist and student of Abraham Lincoln's career. They were prepared for a statement concerning the platform several days before the opening of the Convention, before Goldwater's opponents had decided to seek a public confrontation on the "extremism issue." Jaffa intended the statement to contain echoes of Lincoln's "house divided" speech as well as a reminder of Aristotle's conception of the Golden Mean as the pathway to true virtue.

Senator Goldwater's policy advisers liked the statement and decreed that it be saved for the acceptance speech. They believed that a single statement in response to the "extremism" charge would lay the issue to rest, for they assumed that the public would recognize the falsity of the charge. But the candidate was not particularly concerned with the possible consequences of the statement. To Goldwater, it was simply "something that needed saying," an aide recalled after the election, "and I'm sure Barry doesn't regret having said it."

After the Convention closed, campaign headquarters received a telegram praising the statement from a local chapter of the American Civil Liberties Union.

Two thousand words previously in Goldwater's speech, the "house divided" theme had been sounded when the nominee declared, "because of this Administration, we are a world divided—we are a nation becalmed." Just before the statement concerning extremism, Goldwater criticized "unthinking labels" to indicate his dismay at the pejorative use of the extremist tag by opponents who did not specify the real phenomena it presumably described. But the frenzied cheers of the audience prevented the perception of threads of logic running through the speech or the consideration of individual statements within their intended contexts.[10] To any but the most careful listener, it seemed that the Republican nominee was approving whatever tactics were labeled "extremist." In the context of the Convention—the conflict over a platform plank concerning extremism which received so little attention from Goldwater's policy group—this meant the tactics of the John Birch Society. To those who had fought for a plank denouncing the Birch society, it seemed a deliberate affront.

Thus was Barry Goldwater proclaimed the leader of a Republican Party more seriously divided than it had been at the opening of the Convention.

The Convention revealed the consequences of the particular form of decision-making adopted by Goldwater and his close advisers. They aspired to achieve a form closely akin to our Comprehensive model. Their actual style lacked the exhaustive search for information and the total consideration of possible consequences that the model calls for.

The predicted flaws of Comprehensive organization were now much in evidence. By excluding the professional politicians from policy influence, the policy group was cut off from information concerning the deep wounds in the Convention, just as it discounted information which contradicted its assumptions concerning the attitudes of the electorate. The focus of attention of the policy group was narrowed to the extent that Goldwater did not perceive any need to influence the operations of the Convention in order to enhance his own position in the eyes of the mass electorate. He therefore permitted a series of decisions which could serve his cause only if his opponents were in fact a small, noisy group with little influence in the Republican Party and even less within the nation at large.

... Delegates from the sixteen states with Republican governors gave Goldwater less than half their votes (214 for Goldwater to 238 for his opponents), while delegates from the thirty-four states with Democratic governors preferred Goldwater by an almost four-to-one margin (699 to 187). The vote of the states with Republican governors would have been even more markedly anti-Goldwater if there had been a chance of defeating him, but, in resigned despair, many Republican leaders bent to the Goldwater wind.[11]

Notes on Chapter 5

[1]Philip E. Converse, *et al.,* "Electoral Myth and Reality: the 1964 Election," *American Political Science Review,* 59 (June 1965), 325.

[2]Nelson W. Polsby, "Strategic Considerations," in Milton C. Cummings, Jr., ed., *The National Election of 1964* (Washington, D.C.: The Brookings Institution, 1966), p. 100. Polsby overstresses this factor, however, for an analysis of previous delegations would have revealed that the 1960-64 turnover was not surprising.

[3]Paul Tillett, "The National Conventions," in Cummings, ed., *The National Election of 1964,* p. 18. The states in which Goldwater delegates played prominent roles in presumably anti-Goldwater, or at least neutral, delegations, were Florida, Minnesota, New Jersey, New York, and South Dakota.

[4]Aaron Wildavsky, "The Goldwater Phenomenon: Purists, Politicians, and the Two-Party System," *The Review of Politics,* 27 (July 1965), 386 ff., p. 402. Clif White states that "Our delegates were a brand-new breed. Nothing could shake them." He further contends that Goldwater could have won the nomination on at least the second ballot even if Nelson Rockefeller had won the California primary. See *Suite 3505* (New Rochelle, N.Y.: Arlington House, 1967), p. 350.

[5]Goldwater's speech to the Platform Committee is reprinted as an appendix to his campaign book, *Where I Stand* (New York: McGraw-Hill, 1964).

[6]The continuity of policy positions, at least in the eyes of Republican Congressional leaders, through the 1960 Platform, the 1962 "Statement of Principles," and the 1964 Platform, is discussed by Karl Hess, who was involved in drafting all three documents. See *In a Cause that Will Triumph* (Garden City, N.Y.: Doubleday, 1967), pp. 60-76.

[7]*Suite 3505*, p. 398.

[8]Portions of the Goldwater letter and the full text of Romney's reply were released by Romney's office and printed in *The New York Times*, November 27, 1966. A significantly different account of the Romney amendment is offered by Karl Hess, *In a Cause that Will Triumph*, pp. 77-79. Hess trains his guns on Michigan National Committeeman John Martin, identified as Romney's "envoy." He does not mention Richard Van Dusen, Michigan's appointed member of the Platform Committee.

[9]A perceptive account of William Miller's political career is found in Harold Faber, ed., *The Road to the White House* (New York: McGraw-Hill, 1965), Ch. 9. Faber effectively attacks the claim that Miller "rigged" the National Committee and the Convention in favor of Goldwater, and he describes how Miller learned of Goldwater's decision regarding the vice presidency.

[10]The context has been ignored since the speech was delivered. In the 1966 revision of his *Nominating the President: The Politics of Convention Choice* (New York: Norton, 1966), p. 267, Gerald Pomper casually refers to "the Republican party's nomination of a defender of 'extremism.' " For the acceptance speech, see Goldwater's *Where I Stand*, Ch. 1.

[11]John H. Fenton, *People and Parties in Politics* (Glenview, Ill.: Scott, Foresman, 1966), p. 111.

6

The Hazards of Comprehensive Organization

Barry Goldwater's acceptance speech was finished, the 1964 Republican National Convention adjourned, and the delegates swarmed into busses and cars for their trip from the Cow Palace to the swank hotels on San Francisco's Nob Hill. The parties lasted far into the night, and Theodore White finally fell asleep to the mingled strains of "Dixie" and "The Battle Hymn of the Republic"—North and South at last agreed on Goldwater's nomination.[1] Could a similar harmony be created within the electorate?

Voter opinions are formed by the impact of events and impressions which either reinforce or challenge established loyalties toward a particular partisan label. Many impressions are received in advance of the formal opening of the campaigns. If impressions reinforce each other to become a firm decision, the voter may "tune out" the oratory of the campaign itself. Whatever else it accomplished, the Republican National Convention supplied strong images. Its conflicts made headlines and filled the columns of political interpretation; the raw drama of the raucous rejection of all "moderate" proposals paraded across the television screens of all who had the patience to watch.

Barry Goldwater did not violate any of the formal rules of the Convention. The disaffection of the Rockefellers and the Romneys could not be blamed on any positive act of the nominee. His disavowal of leadership—or his determination to let the Convention proceed according to its own rules—was complete. However, spectators naturally associated Goldwater with the events of the Convention. The inclination to judge the candidate by the behavior of his supporters was not discouraged by most of those who reported the Convention in the mass media.

The result was that Senator Goldwater would have difficulty convincing the electorate that he spoke for his party, rather than for the uncompromising faction that had dominated the Convention. This difficulty was exploited by the Democratic campaigners. Hubert Humphrey gleefully referred to Goldwater as "the temporary spokesman of the Republican Party," and Democratic television commercials criticized Goldwater against a background of scenes from the Republican Convention showing the feet of delegates trampling the discarded campaign portraits of Scranton, Rockefeller, and Romney.

There was even a divisive factor in the Goldwater camp itself. For nearly two years, a small group had worked for the nomination of Barry Goldwater under the direction of F. Clifton White. Riding in an elevator on the final morning of the Convention, White learned by accident that Dean Burch was to be appointed Chairman of the Republican National Committee. White had openly sought the position; he and his group had every reason to expect some tangible reward for their considerable labors. But all of them were excluded from the inner circle surrounding their victorious candidate. Stephen Shadegg describes the group's stunned reaction at such treatment by "the candidate they had created."[2] (One imagines the emotional state of poor Gepetto when Pinocchio suddenly kicks him in the shins.) At their own post-Convention party, one of the group suggested there was still time to "dump Goldwater and go with a candidate of their own. White killed the insane idea."[3]

Clif White boarded a plane to Hawaii two days later without leaving word of his destination. His loyal associates were still prepared to work for Goldwater, but they felt no particular compulsion to respect the nominee's judgment. Their new mood was to work for Goldwater, but on their own terms.

There was no sign that Goldwater and his policy group were any more aware of this potential disruptive force in their own organization than they were of the growing division within the rank and file of the Republican party. If they were aware of such problems, other realities claimed their attention as they faced the. thousands of decisions necessary for mounting a national campaign.

Decisions at the Top

A supreme irony of the Goldwater campaign was that, although its structure was based on criticisms of the organization of previous campaigns, no
member of the staff had been free before the 1964 Republican Convention to
make careful plans for the conduct of the general election. The Comprehensive model requires careful preparation, so that goals may be defined, alternative means considered, and probable consequences studied. But such preparations were not made, and we conclude without surprise that the affinity of
Goldwater and his close advisers for the Comprehensive style of decision-
making was more an aspect of their total approach to political questions than
it was a conscious choice between explicitly defined methods of approaching
political decisions. One of Goldwater's inner circle told us:

> I now think that we should have established a separate unit to work on the assumption
> that the nomination was in hand and make plans for the general election campaign. But
> this is hindsight, and it did not occur to us at the time. The only separate planning took
> place in the four-day period just after the close of the Republican Convention. Meetings
> were held in Washington while Senator Goldwater was yachting off Southern California
> and Congressman Miller was resting at his home in New York State . . . All through the
> campaign, I felt that we should have a week or ten days with nothing else to do when we
> could just think things through. But of course there was no such chance.

The Comprehensive model requires that many decisions be reached, long
before the campaign opens, on the basis of the best information available,
after careful consideration of possible consequences. The organization may
then be designed specifically to implement those decisions. The Moley
memorandum provided just such a design for the candidate's personal campaign staff. It assumed that a conservative campaign could win, and it guar-
anteed the purity of that conservatism. The Moley design did not include
specifications for the entire Republican party, and Goldwater had not
attempted to rethink his criticisms of the Nixon campaign. Confronted with
the need to make immediate organizational decisions, Goldwater returned to
his previously established convictions. He announced his intention of
imposing a Comprehensive-style structure upon the Republican party. One of
our respondents described the initial meeting.

> Goldwater called us 50 state chairmen into his suite at the Mark Hopkins in San Fran-
> cisco and said to us that Burch was to be his man and that if we had any questions to
> channel them through the Republican National Committee. He said this campaign was
> going to be different, that he was going to run his own campaign. "If you want to stay
> with me, you can. If you want out, do it now." He did not want to talk to six different
> people when he was in a state. He wanted to be able to call the chairman and settle all
> questions.

The nominee's announcement was received with considerable enthusiasm. A common criticism of the Nixon campaign had been that it was hampered by the confusion of competing organizations. National campaigns, said the critics, should be directed from a single headquarters. This organizational judgment was made by several elements of the party; it was independent of ideology. On February 5, 1964, Republican National Committee Chairman William Miller had reported to his colleagues in the House Republican Conference that all "the serious presidential candidates" had agreed to accept arrangements for conducting the national campaign "under one roof" at the National Committee's* headquarters in Washington's Cafritz Building.[4]

Following this announcement of a unified command for the campaign structure, Goldwater departed for Newport Beach, California, and his version of the traditional candidate's post-Convention rest. Key advisers then flew to Washington for meetings which would consider the details.

The four days of planning sessions held by their principal staff assistants while Goldwater and Miller were resting from the labors of the Convention were remarkable both for the persons excluded from attendance and the topics excluded from the agenda. Basic principles were a matter of mutual agreement and were not opened for discussion. All decisions were concerned with the details of presenting the campaign.

The list of persons involved in this initial discussion included Denison Kitchel as Campaign Director; Tony Smith, Goldwater's veteran Press Secretary; Warren Nutter, principal speechwriter; Lou Guylay, the incoming Director of Public Relations for the Republican National Committee; Dean Burch, the newly appointed Republican National Chairman; John Grenier, Burch's choice for Executive Director of the RNC; Peter O'Donnell, the official head of the former Draft Goldwater Committee; and, finally, William Miller's representatives, William Warner and Robert Smalley, Campaign Manager and Public Relations Director, respectively, for Miller's campaign. The most conspicuous absentee was F. Clifton White, the single person most responsible for Goldwater's triumph in San Francisco.[5]

An important item of discussion centered on the best times and places for the presentation of the most important points of Goldwater's conservatism. The result was a scheme calling for seven major campaign speeches in seven

*Unless otherwise specified, the term "National Committee" will be used throughout this volume to refer to the headquarters and staff of either the Republican (RNC) or Democratic (DNC) National Committees. In its official sense, the term refers to the organization of National Committeemen and Committeewomen (one of each sex from each state) appointed by the quadrennial National Convention of each Party to handle its affairs until the next Convention.

major cities. (The Moley memorandum had specified "about six or at the most eight.") This plan had to be abandoned. It had been hoped that the first opinion polls performed by the Opinion Research Corporation after the opening of the general election campaign would provide clues as to the aspects of conservatism which would find the most enthusiastic response in the electorate. But the polls showed that negative responses dominated public awareness of Barry Goldwater's positions on issues. Specifically, respondents expressed fear that he might initiate a nuclear war and abolish the social security system. Any hope that the Democrats would participate in a "reasonable" debate on the issues vanished with the showing of the famous "daisy girl" television spot* in early September. The Democratic advertising agency was as aware as ORC of the impact of the "nuclear issue" upon public thinking.

It was soon clear that no campaign dialogue would materialize; Goldwater could not even expect to define the campaign issues. Much of the early phase of the campaign was devoted to defending the candidate against the effects of this fearful public image. When we asked him about surprise decisions in the campaign, a close friend of Goldwater's cited this decision as proof that, no matter how much Goldwater's people wanted it otherwise, they were forced to modify their original plans.

Theodore White reports the agony suffered by Denison Kitchel as he went to bed each night, vainly seeking a way to free his candidate from the burden of the "nuclear thing."[6] Goldwater's campaign was intended to present a conservative philosophy, by definition an appeal to reason. But fear and other strong emotions are hard to modify through rational appeals. Voters seemed unable to give their full attention to Goldwater's words. Strong emotions stimulate selective perception, and voters heard either what they wanted to hear or what they expected to hear.

Content of the Republican Campaign

The actual content of the campaign was not startlingly different from previous Republican campaigns. Most of Goldwater's positions and rhetoric had a familiar ring. One of his close associates commented on this phenomenon:

His opponents painted Goldwater as a guy advocating positions very different from other Republicans. Close analysis will show that the speeches in this campaign were essentially

*See below, pp. 194-201, for an account of Democratic television advertising.

the same basic Republican gospel preached by Nixon in 1960, Eisenhower in '56 and '52 and Dewey before that. . . . In 1964 I noted on several occasions the shocked reaction of some Goldwater fan in an audience when he heard the Senator endorse the Eisenhower-Dulles foreign policy or advocate a stronger NATO alliance. This came as news to such people even though his public utterances for more than a decade had been on precisely that line. The same can be said for his over-all record in the Senate. His color, personality and phrase-coining somehow lent credence to the impression he was different from the others when in reality their basic standards were all cut from the same mold.

In general, Goldwater proposed a reduced role for the federal government in the domestic society and economy, while he favored a hard line in foreign policy. After reviewing the campaign's content, Professor Stanley Kelley, Jr., found that the vaunted "true conservatism" of the Goldwater campaign did not differ dramatically from the content of previous Republican campaigns, "although it differed considerably in tone." Kelley writes:

It was Senator Goldwater's stand on domestic issues that made his campaign differ in a fundamental way from the Eisenhower and Nixon campaigns. The difference was not primarily ideological. Goldwater's attack on "the regimented society," "handouts,". . . and on "centralized power" paralleled attacks by President Eisenhower on "big government," "paternalistic direction by Washington bureaucrats," and socialized medicine . . . but General Eisenhower took pains in 1952 to assure voters that a vote for him was *not* a vote to repeal the New Deal. In 1964 Senator Goldwater gave no such assurances.[7]

If Goldwater's campaign had not been haunted by a few stark phrases he had coined on the banquet circuit before becoming a candidate, and if the electorate had been willing to judge his attitudes only by the polished phrases of his formal campaign speeches, there would be some reason to endorse the judgment of speechwriter Karl Hess that Goldwater's positions in the campaign represented the ideological center of the "regular" Republican party.[8]

The Goldwater statements concerning social security which Democratic television commercials exploited with such devastation had been made before the campaign began. The same was true of other Goldwater statements, including his suggestion that the Eastern seaboard states be "sawed off," and proposals concerning national defense which were articulated in the idiom of relaxed generals conversing over a cocktail rather than in the prose used by presidential candidates.

Goldwater's advisers knew of the existence of such statements; their information storage system kept track of them. Yet their initial planning assumed that there would be a campaign dialogue based on issues raised by Senator Goldwater's formal campaign speeches. Goldwater's planners did not appreciate how deeply held were the attitudes toward him already formed by the electorate. They did not realize how easy it would be for the Democratic Party to campaign against the incautious Goldwater of the New Hampshire primaries, paying little heed to the Republican nominee.

When the Democratic attack probed these chinks in his conservative armor, Senator Goldwater doggedly restated his positions, wearily defending himself in an effort to communicate the fullness of his attitudes on national defense and the social security system. He was placed in the curious position, for the candidate challenging the incumbent, of having to defend his record—not the record of what he had done, but the record of what he had said. This defensive posture kept the issues alive and reinforced the voting decisions of those who had selected President Johnson.

Goldwater's campaign did eventually have an impact on those who held their voting decisions in abeyance. Professor John H. Kessel has analyzed a series of opinion surveys roughly matching important stages in the campaign. He found that the Republican campaign did have an impact on the electorate: "Independents and Democrats who postponed their decisions until the campaign were more likely to vote for Goldwater than those who decided early."[9] Support for Johnson remained relatively stable, but support for Goldwater did grow measurably over the level recorded at the time of the National Conventions.

Thus there was a segment of the electorate which behaved in the manner anticipated by Goldwater and his policy group. The error was in assuming that this particular part of the real world represented its totality.

Although the responsibility for formulating the content of Goldwater's campaign was determined by the Moley memorandum, nagging questions remained as to the best method of presenting that philosophy through the mass media. The Republican National Committee had retained the Leo Burnett agency, which laid some potentially important foundations for the Republican presidential campaign even before the Convention—including the scheduling of a segment of Republican television time at the conclusion of the Democratic National Convention. The Draft Goldwater Committee had also retained an agency. But the expertise of Madison Avenue was not represented on Goldwater's personal staff, and his organization functioned throughout the primary election period without a Director of Public Relations. Filling this position had been one of Denison Kitchel's earliest preoccupations, but he could not find a person with the necessary qualifications who would accept the appointment. Finally, after the Convention, he obtained the services of Lou Guylay, a veteran of the Republican National Committee, who had performed the same role for the Eisenhower and Nixon campaigns. Since Guylay was already affiliated with a firm, it became the official advertising agency. The "Goldwater account" passed into the hands of yet a third agency.

If the standards of the Moley memorandum were applicable, the tasks of the advertising agency might be regarded as part of the supporting technical staff of the campaign, quite apart from the group assigned the task of articulating the conservative philosophy. But it is not easy to separate content from the techniques of presentation. This does not mean that political campaigning should be tailored to the practices developed for merchandising soap; it does mean that the public relations expert can advise campaign managers on the best means of capturing voter attention. At the very least, he will have knowledge of the expected attention span of the average voter and may suggest concentrating messages to fit within that span.

In describing the initial planning session, one of our respondents explained:

> One of the items discussed was the use of television. The ad agency people wanted to use spot announcements. I felt that Goldwater's personality and ideas required a longer exposure on television to come through. Our thinking eventually shifted to the 30-minute program rather than the one-minute spot.

This decision seems to have been based upon the determination to present the conservative philosophy rather than a willingness to consider the advice of persons experienced in the use of mass media. Goldwater's managers felt that the candidate himself was the most effective spokesman for his cause. But there are inherent restraints upon a candidate required to plead his own case which are not present when another person presents a message on his behalf. The decision to concentrate on presentations of the candidate limited the dramatization of issues and themes.

Could the Goldwater half-hour programs reach the audience they had to reach if voting decisions were to be influenced? The answer was supplied after the event by Dean Burch, Chairman of the Republican National Committee:

> After days of painstaking preparation—with time stolen mostly from sleep, because you don't dare disappoint the party faithful who've gathered at rallies and prop-stops—you finally make your pitch to your largest TV audience. But it turns out that you capture your maximum number of voters—seven-plus million for a sober discussion of foreign policy—while at the same time, on a rival network, 28 million eyes are glued to screens tuned to the perils of Peyton Place.[10]

The lengthy Goldwater performances thus reached an audience that needed no further convincing. The audience's devotion was tested, for trailers filmed by Hollywood actor Raymond Massey appealed for funds at the conclusion of each show. The response was unprecedented. It constituted the largest number of small contributions ever received by a political campaign and supplied further real evidence which contradicted the gloomy forecasts of the opinion surveys. It seemed that Raymond Moley's "Republican potential" was clearly being mobilized.

Eventually, Goldwater's staff recognized the necessity of coordination between the functions of articulating the conservative position and the presentation of that position through the mass media. Charles Lichenstein, Deputy Research Director of the Republican National Committee, became the chief liaison agent between the campaign staff and the technical unit which prepared Goldwater's television shows. Lichenstein had performed a similar function during the California primary campaign, and his experience in previous campaigns had made him familiar with political usages of the mass media. The assignment was made on an emergency basis. The Moley memorandum had not provided for such coordination. After the election, several members of the campaign organization complained that they got very little help from the experts of the advertising world. Said one respondent, "they bought air time and newspaper space. But we had to supply all the ideas."

Despite their ritualistic consultation of public opinion data and the considerable sum they paid a private polling organization, the conception of how voting decisions are made held by Goldwater's closest advisers was more closely akin to that of John Stuart Mill than it was to the knowledge of contemporary political science. They regarded the electorate as made up of atomistic individuals, open to persuasion by reason and with a predisposition in favor of conservative policies. Rather than question this basic assumption concerning the nature of the voter, the initial planning conference was devoted to such questions as the selection of speech topics and the kind of television presentation to be emphasized. From its inception, the attack on Republican "me-too" candidates had called for the rejection of a politics of coalition-building in order to provide the voter with an intellectual choice. Yet, in a compounding of ironies, a legacy left this intellectual candidate by one of his departing advertising agencies was a campaign slogan with anti-intellectual implications: "In your heart, you know he's right."

"Go hunting where the ducks are"—The Campaign Strategy

The "grand strategy" of the Goldwater campaign had in fact been stated by the Senator years before. It was related to the basic premise of the "hidden conservative vote" and to "the Republican potential" of Raymond Moley's writings. Its first premise was that Goldwater could count on the states which Richard Nixon carried in 1960, because Nixon's defeat resulted from the disaffection of conservatives who could not stomach his presumed concessions to liberal attitudes. The number of conservative defectors had not been large enough in those states to tip the balance against him; there would be no defectors if Goldwater were the candidate. Goldwater's route to victory would then be through those states where the defection of conservatives had defeated Nixon, the areas which Nixon had not carried but which contained many voters who would find a conservative philosophy attractive.

The men around Goldwater did not consider "strategy" in the sense of tailoring appeals to the expressed wishes of various groups within the electorate. One of Goldwater's close advisers told us:

The general plan for the campaign was established fairly early. It was a regional strategy based on the notion that little campaigning would be needed to win votes in the South, no amount of campaigning could win electoral votes in New England and on the East Coast, but that votes could be won in the Midwest and on the West Coast. As the Senator said, "Go hunting where the ducks are."

The respondent went on to say that the feeling behind this strategy was simply that the conservative philosophy would find the most adherents in the South, the Midwest, and on the West Coast. Thus it was not a regional strategy in the conventional sense of designing a program which offered the satisfaction of diverse political demands to stimulate support in enough states to constitute a majority in the electoral college. No promises would be made to identifiable regions or groups. Even when he was forced into a defensive posture by the Democratic attack, Senator Goldwater did not abandon this principle of his campaign. To the amazement of observers, the Republican nominee stressed exactly those aspects of his position which were least likely to please a particular audience. On September 16, in Knoxville, Tennessee, he referred to his conviction that parts of the TVA complex should be sold to private enterprise. Two days later, in Appalachia, he attacked President Johnson's "phony" poverty bill. On October 26th, at Madison Square Garden, Goldwater declared, "if I had to cater to every special interest in the country to get elected, I wouldn't want the job."

But the highly Incremental process of "catering to special interests" has long been considered a major function of American political parties. The party is one of the leading agencies capable of effecting a compromise between the competing demands of regions and interest groups. Over the span of American history, divisive conflicts have been resolved within each of the major parties and have thus been prevented from becoming issues between the parties which could divide the nation.

So ingrained in American political habit is the partisan practice of seeking out regional and group demands which can be incorporated into the party program that many commentators could not accept at face value Goldwater's attempt to demonstrate the integrity of his conservatism. They assumed that, through some perverse staff miscalculation, Goldwater was unaware of the beliefs of his audiences. What was communicated to the electorate was the notion that Barry Goldwater did not offer responses to the political needs or desires of specific groups; Lyndon Johnson did. The effect of Goldwater's disclaimer of interest in such groups was reinforced by Johnson's expressions of concern for them. The positive identification of Johnson with expected group benefits, and the negative identification of Goldwater, with which the campaign began, were both increased by the campaign.[11] Those who disagreed with the proposition that "Washington is getting too powerful for the good of the country and the individual person" voted almost unanimously for Lyndon B. Johnson.[12]

Although seven key speeches were assigned to seven major cities at the initial planning conference, there had been no time to fill in the details of the regional plan. No further allocation of campaign time to key areas was made, and the problems of the Tour Committee—where should the candidate speak next week?—later consumed much valuable time for the highest echelons of the Goldwater organization.

Persons who were excluded from campaign policy-making because of working in the logistical side of the organization criticized the allocation of campaign time to areas. One respondent complained that Goldwater made several unproductive trips to solidly Democratic urban Chicago, when he could have influenced votes by appearing in the suburbs. Another respondent complained that Goldwater kept revisiting Texas, long after opinion polls demonstrated he had no hope of carrying that state. Yet another complained bitterly of Goldwater's failure to appear in Virginia.

But the net result of decisions allocating the campaign effort to localities was to make the Goldwater campaign little different in its regional emphases from the Nixon campaign of 1960. Professor Stanley Kelley, Jr., found that "the Republican Presidential campaigns in 1964 and 1960 . . . differed only marginally in the states selected as the foci of the most intensive campaigning."[13] Indeed, Professor Kelley found that the allocation of campaign effort by the Goldwater planners made mathematical sense. He constructed an index of the expected value of campaigning by assigning a value to a combination of the electoral votes of individual states with the closeness of the race in each state as revealed in final election returns. He then compared the differences in campaign time spent in the states with the index of campaign value and found that the Goldwater allocation of campaign effort correlated with variations in the state index to a value of .84. This was slightly higher than the "efficiency" of the Johnson campaign. Of course, this measure of efficiency is not an indication of the ability of the campaign to influence voters.

We now have before us the broad outlines of the Goldwater strategy of presenting conservatism without compromise. In its oratorical trimmings, in many of its issue positions, and in its regional emphases, the formal presentation of this conservatism differed little from the campaigns of previous Republican candidates. By definition, however, this conservatism was not tailored to fit the demands of particular regions and groups. As Raymond Moley specified, the conservative impact would not be dissipated by heeding the anxieties of local politicians.

Goldwater and Civil Rights

But where does Goldwater's treatment of the civil rights issue fit into his strategic conceptions? How can this picture of the goals of Goldwater's campaign be reconciled with the outcome of the election? For the Republican candidate carried only Arizona and the five states of the deep South which had voted for segregation and the Dixiecrats in 1948.

Some of the harshest criticisms leveled at Goldwater's campaign have centered upon his attitudes toward the revolutionary social advance of the American Negro in general and federal civil rights legislation in particular. Most of these criticisms begin with the assumption, either stated or implicit, that Goldwater's approach to the issue was copied from Machiavelli and that its most important component was an attempt to cultivate a substantial "white backlash" vote.[14] If the assumption can be proven correct, then the picture of Goldwater as a Comprehensive decision-maker must be modified. At least on the civil rights issue, Goldwater's behavior would exhibit some of the attributes of the Incremental model.

Support for such an assumption can be found in the sequence of Goldwater's statements and actions regarding the issue. At one time he had been a member of the National Association for the Advancement of Colored People, and campaign biographies gave him credit for integrating the Arizona Air National Guard. He voted for the Civil Rights Acts of 1957 and 1960, but he was warmly received in the South during and after the 1960 campaign. In 1961 he announced that the Republican party had no hope of winning the Negro vote "as a bloc" for years to come. The rioting and bloodshed associated with civil rights activity in Northern cities in 1963 was followed by the candidacy of Governor George Wallace of Alabama. Goldwater's vote against the 1964 Civil Rights Act and his victory in San Francisco became the signal for Wallace to withdraw. Goldwater then courted Wallace's following by opposing "violence in the streets."

The picture is of Goldwater deliberately moving from a moderate or even liberal stance on racial problems toward a position tinged with racism. The evolution of Lyndon Johnson's position seems to have been just the opposite, reflecting the shift from the limited constituency of Texas to the search for a national consensus. But an equally plausible explanation of Goldwater's attitude could be that his view of the governmental actions permitted by the Constitution remained static, while national policy changed dramatically.

Roy Wilkins, Executive Secretary of the NAACP, was sitting in a corner of the galleries when the Republican platform was endlessly read into the television microphones at the Republican National Convention. Mr. Wilkins was asked if he thought American Negroes would be impressed by Senator Goldwater's past expressions of sympathy for Negroes and their cause. He replied that Negroes are not so concerned with motivation as they are with results. The important question was what actions Goldwater's feelings for Negroes led him to take. His vote on the 1964 Civil Rights Act supplied the answer.

All the evidence given us by Goldwater's associates indicates that Goldwater's attitude on this issue reflected a personal searching of his conscience rather than a calculation of political effects. One of Goldwater's legal advisers told us that he counseled Goldwater to vote against the 1964 Act because two sections of it violated the U.S. Constitution, although he was certain that the Supreme Court would find the Act constitutional. Thus Goldwater was encouraged to reject the concept of positive law enunciated in its modern form by Chief Justice Charles Evans Hughes when he said that "we live under a Constitution, but the Constitution is what the judges say it is."[15] A pragmatic or politically Incremental view of American legal processes would certainly be based on deferring to the authority of the U.S. Supreme Court. But Goldwater declared that he had sworn an oath to uphold the Constitution of the United States and therefore could consult only his own interpretation of its meaning.[16]

One of Goldwater's staunch admirers and close assistants told us:

On this civil rights thing, Goldwater was told by the practical politicians that the vote here was crucial. Goldwater refused to compromise. His philosophy denied the possibility of compromise. Of course the politicians disapproved. Goldwater did change his mind, however, when it was apparent that he was wrong. At first he was opposed to the use of Federal troops enforcing integrated schools. Then he studied this question for weeks and decided that what the situation needed was a good constitutional order and that meant Federal troops enforcing it if necessary. He said this all through the South. . . . There was never any question of his changing his positions in order to win.

Because of the importance of the so-called "Southern Strategy" in the eyes of the Draft Goldwater Committee, we asked several Goldwater intimates about the role this concept played in making early decisions for the general election campaign. A highly placed executive in the logistics segment of the campaign organization told us:

You don't have to campaign on race to win votes in the South. Of course when the Senator talked about "State's Rights" in the South, it may not have meant the same thing to his audiences as it meant to him.

A member of the policy group made essentially the same point: "A Southern strategy as such did not exist. You don't need a strategy when people are crying for you."

An outside observer has compared Goldwater's treatment of the racial issue with John F. Kennedy's treatment of the religious issue in 1960, stating that Kennedy never explicitly asked for the Catholic vote but designed his campaign appearances in a way that would assure the maximum stimulation of concern on the part of Catholic voters. Similarly, Goldwater did not have to ask for a racist vote, for he was certain to receive whatever votes were motivated by bigotry.[17] Another informant told us that Goldwater actually felt little confidence about winning Southern votes, feeling that Southern voters would perceive Lyndon Johnson as "one of their own," regardless of Johnson's statements and actions on behalf of the Negro since entering the White House.

We are told that Goldwater once considered abandoning his candidacy for fear that it would stimulate racial violence, and we know that Goldwater called upon President Johnson and "volunteered to eliminate entirely any appeal to passion of race in the fall campaign, to which the President agreed in private compact."[18]

A member of the policy group told us of Goldwater's request for a speech on segregation that would not be racist in tone. The assignment proved more difficult than anticipated, and this particular speech was labored over for several weeks. The eventual outcome was Goldwater's speech on October 16th in Chicago which pointed out that the right not to associate must not be jeopardized in the process of assuring the freedom of association.[19] We know that Goldwater rejected the film *Choice* because he found it racist. But we also know that Goldwater's effort to make a major campaign issue of street violence and the deterioration of respect for law and order was interpreted as referring to the tactics of the Negro social revolution in the flimsiest of disguises. Presumably, Goldwater's concern was with the decay of the quality of American life as evidenced by rising crime rates, juvenile delinquency, and an apparent lowering of the standards of ethical conduct expected of public officials.

Few observers have questioned the sincerity of Goldwater's expressions of sympathy for the Negro cause. The conservative conscience no doubt placed a value on the dignity and worth of individual human beings, but it also forbade granting the government additional powers to intervene in the ordering of relationships between individual citizens. The constitutional principle ranked higher in his order of values than did the humane impulse, and Goldwater's personal position, in our judgment, at least remained consistent. He proposed no solutions for the most pressing social problem of the era.

If the political technicians had followed the candidate's lead concerning racial issues throughout the campaign, and if local Republican organizations had in fact been subordinate units in a strict chain of command, Comprehensive organization could have served the candidate well in this controversial area. Neither of these requirements of the Comprehensive model was achieved.

The initial approach to the question of seeking the Negro vote by Goldwater's managers at the Republican National Committee was consistent with the candidate's position. In fact, it was more consistent with his desire to avoid racial issues than it was with the principles of Comprehensive organization. The Minorities Division of the Republican National Committee had functioned for nearly two decades to maintain contact between the national Republican Party and local Negro leaders and organizations. Before the Convention, the Minorities Division had made careful plans for a campaign attacking Lyndon Johnson's early civil rights record. But they were plans suited to the campaign of nearly any candidate except Goldwater. The freshness of

Goldwater's vote against the Civil Rights Act made Lyndon Johnson's attitudes as a Texas Senator irrelevant.

The Director of the Minorities Division was Clay Claiborne, a remarkable Negro politician from New Jersey. Although his Division was abolished, Claiborne was appointed a Special Assistant to the Director of Campaign Organization, with a press release stating that the appointment marked the determination of the Goldwater campaign not to abandon any group of voters to the opposition by default. But Claiborne was assigned an isolated office several floors removed from the center of National Committee operations. When he prepared materials aimed at attracting Negro votes in the District of Columbia, their distribution was hastily interrupted by one of the former Draft Goldwater Committee personnel, presumably out of fear that Democrats would distribute them among Southern whites.

In a Comprehensive organization, very specific duties are assigned to each position. There is no room for workers without tasks. Clay Claiborne was initially retained as a public relations gesture. His children needed money to continue in college, and he stayed on, although it was clear that no plans would be developed to make use of his skills and contacts. In the final days of the campaign, a party tactician conceived the notion of wooing Negro support away from Johnson and Humphrey in key states by stimulating a write-in vote for Martin Luther King. Like many ideas born late in a losing campaign, this one was never referred to Goldwater or Kitchel. Claiborne was ordered to have the handbills printed which would urge this course of action on the Negro voter. Claiborne reluctantly complied, placing the printing order with a New Jersey firm.

Because the organization sponsoring them was not designated on the handbills, Democrats properly complained that they violated the New Jersey election laws. Claiborne was indicted on this charge. The case was finally brought to trial in the spring of 1966, after several delays. The prosecution could not establish willful duplicity on Claiborne's part, and he was acquitted.

The incident constituted a travesty of the announced intention of the Goldwater campaign to win electoral allegiance on the basis of a conservative philosophy alone. This misguided effort to stimulate racially motivated voting had no parallel in the actions of the nominee. Carefully avoiding racial issues, Goldwater ignored the supposed "white backlash." Negro leaders managed to dampen the growing fervor of their urban followers. The summer of 1964 saw little of the mob violence which would have provided inescapable linkage between racial attitudes and the Republican candidate's discussion of disorder in the streets. The "white backlash" did not develop.

On the other hand, election returns suggest that Barry Goldwater's devotion to constitutional principle was perceived in the South as support for racial segregation. Goldwater's strongest showing was in the deep South, and particularly in the "black belt" counties, where white voters are intent upon maintaining the old racial order.[20]

We must conclude that the treatment of civil rights issues in the Goldwater campaign revealed two flaws in his pattern of decision-making. First, the organization did not respond to the example set by the candidate's moral perceptions of the issue. Complete social agreement on such a personal matter can hardly be expected. The main error lay in assuming that the lower echelons of the organization could be controlled. The second flaw was built into the assumptions concerning the rationality of the electorate upon which the Goldwater campaign was founded. Goldwater had to assume that Southern voters could hear conservative doctrine and disassociate it from the racial overtones that have been traditionally attached to it in the South. No doubt a few voters did this, particularly editorial writers, but their number was tiny.

Response to the Unexpected

If Goldwater maintained a delicate balance on the tightrope of his conscience concerning civil rights, there were other times when unexpected circumstances required adaptations of his Comprehensive plan. Because one of the dangers of Comprehensive decision-making is inflexibility, it is important to consider some of these incidents.

The problem of party unity, which caused little concern among Goldwater's policy group at the Convention, was forcibly brought to their attention by its aftermath. Party leaders reported a barrage of requests that they disassociate themselves from the Goldwater candidacy. One governor of a New England state reported that his mail ran five to one against Goldwater, and voters he greeted at public functions warned him against supporting the Arizona Senator. General Eisenhower, who had held himself aloof from the scramble for the nomination, permitted reports of his dismay at the spectacle of the Convention.

The Hershey meeting

The first response to these pressures was an attempt to explain and justify the statement on extremism through the medium of a public exchange of letters between Barry Goldwater and Richard Nixon. At the urging of Edward McCabe, Mr. Eisenhower agreed to sponsor a conference between Senator Goldwater and the state and congressional leaders of the Republican party. The meeting was held on August 12th in Hershey, Pennsylvania. A respondent who was present described it to us.

As I recall, the Hershey meeting . . . was a milestone of sorts at the time. It served to underscore that the positions advocated by Goldwater and Miller were, in fact, the same basic gospel preached by practically all leaders of the party for twenty years. In this, Hershey may have been a major communications breakthrough at the time as well as a major party unity move.

In a normal year, it would seem incredible that, a month after the National Convention, the nominee should require "a communications breakthrough" in his relations with Republican governors, congressmen, and the former President of the United States. Barry Goldwater was asked to justify his campaign positions to this distinguished audience as a price for their support.

After greetings by Governor Scranton, statements by Richard Nixon and Dwight D. Eisenhower, and introductions by Goldwater of his campaign assistants, the Republican candidate read his prepared statement. Although the statement consisted of "very quiet language," it had been pieced together by Edward McCabe from previous Goldwater speeches. It was "in no way a softening of the Goldwater position,"[21] but its effects were mollifying. Goldwater next called upon Chairman Dean Burch of the Republican National Committee to comment upon organizational plans, and the meeting was then opened up for questions.

A transcript of this meeting has since been published. It is dreary reading. It reveals considerable extemporaneous skill and knowledge on Goldwater's part as he responded to questions on specific issues, but his responses were essentially negative in tone. Various state leaders raised the questions they felt were most important to their own constituents and suggested approaches they hoped the national campaign would adopt. Although he responded courteously, Goldwater gave no indication that their counsel would be heeded. Questioners returned again and again to farm policy. In regard to this issue, Goldwater stated, "we are having—pardon the expression—a hell of a time getting Republicans to agree on what the platform means." But, he announced, a group of eminent agricultural economists were laboring with farm state congressmen to define a satisfactory position. As each party leader worried about Goldwater's position, or his image, on various issues, Goldwater explained—with growing exasperation—that his position had been stated on the issue; all he could do would be to repeat it. When Governor Romney raised the question of civil rights, Goldwater replied, "George, I don't know how I can say it any stronger or any oftener than I have said it."

Governor Rockefeller returned again and again to the question of extremism, and Charles Percy of Illinois worried about both "backlash" and "lashback"—the propensity of Republicans to vote for President Johnson. The meandering and repetitive nature of the discussion indicates that Goldwater could not satisfy his questioners either on specific issues or on general strategy. Goldwater brought no new vision, no grand program or principle, which could unite the men of power in the Republican party and send them forth to do political battle with renewed faith in the outcome. The closest attempt—and that a sorry one—was made by William Miller, who identified "two main premises" of the coming campaign on which "Republican leaders must be in accord": a firm foreign policy and fiscal responsibility at home.

Goldwater yielded to conventional political pressures in agreeing to attend the meeting. No Republican presidential campaign conducted with the open hostility, or even the total silence, of Dwight D. Eisenhower, would make sense; Eisenhower had enjoyed the largest and most enthusiastic following of any Republican leader in more than a generation. But there is no sign that Goldwater and his close advisers had any patience with the idea of a gathering in which Goldwater was required to explain his policies to other Republican leaders. Nor did they feel that the participants in this Republican Summit should combine to offer a common policy. They believed the 1964 Republican National Convention had been a representative assembly of the Republican Party. The nominee was the legitimate spokesman of that Party, regardless of what policy attitudes might be held by past leaders whose lease on legitimate authority had expired. And they were convinced that the conservative campaign should not be compromised by concessions to practicing politicians.

This perception was not lost on the Rockefellers and Romneys who faced electorates in volatile, two-party states. They were well aware of the public reaction in their areas to the Goldwater candidacy. At that late point, nothing said at the conference could have caused them to offer their names and organizations to Barry Goldwater. Those who came hoping to find reasons to discount the image of vindictiveness created by events in San Francisco, as magnified by Goldwater's critics and opponents, were reassured. The breach between the Republican nominee and several party leaders was partially healed. But the harmony effort was an isolated incident that did not extend to the lower echelons of the party. Such an extension was incompatible with Comprehensive decision-making.

The determination to perfect a Comprehensive organization managed through the Republican National Committee was specified in Goldwater's formal statement at the Hershey conference and elaborated by RNC Chairman Burch, who stated, "we have two words that we are trying to use as a keynote of this campaign. The first is *organization* and the second is *coordination*."

The Citizens' Committee for Goldwater-Miller

Moments earlier, however, Senator Goldwater had confirmed the appointment of General James W. Doolittle and Mrs. Clare Booth Luce as co-chairmen of the newly created National Citizens' Committee for Goldwater-Miller. This organization represented a major modification of Goldwater's original Comprehensive plan. It was the organizational result of the belated realization that a unified party effort in behalf of the Goldwater candidacy could not be expected.

Such extra-party organizations are usually established to provide a home for independents and even members of the opposition party who support the candidate but cannot bring themselves to support his party, and they have been important adjuncts to Republican presidential campaigns since the development of the Willkie Clubs in 1940. The device holds out a promise to the Republicans of attracting a temporary majority to the banner of a popular candidate, by creating an organizational home for those who are dissatisfied with the Democratic administration but cannot identify themselves as Republicans. With victory achieved, careful political leadership would bend other party office-holders in a liberal direction in order to consolidate the personal victory of the candidate on the basis of stable party strength. Citizens' organizations played important roles in both of the Eisenhower campaigns, but President Eisenhower did not supply the leadership needed to expand the base of partisanship. Goldwater criticized the independent efforts on behalf of Eisenhower and Nixon for draining away funds and energy which should have been devoted to rebuilding the regular Republican Party.

None of our respondents explained the rationale for establishing the Citizens' Committee in 1964. The facts seem to yield but one interpretation. The single person most responsible for winning the nomination for Barry Goldwater was F. Clifton White. In the process, White established working relationships with Goldwater enthusiasts in most of the states. Although

White attempted to recruit members of the regular Republican hierarchy to staff the state Draft Goldwater organizations, he found in many cases that he could work only with the members of minority factions within the party or with individuals who were attracted to party work for the first time by the possibility of a Goldwater candidacy.

White therefore commanded forces loyal to Goldwater in those very states where the regular party organization demonstrated little enthusiasm for the national ticket. It was a campaign resource too powerful to be neglected, but Goldwater's initial dedication to the regular organization, as expressed in his Comprehensive criticisms of the Nixon campaign, substantially delayed providing for the inclusion of White's forces, although they offered the most powerful weapon for reshaping the party in Goldwater's image.

When Clif White returned from his Hawaiian trip, he was asked to contact Goldwater, who asked him to head the Citizens' Committee. White objected that such efforts are intended to organize the labors of those who are unable or unwilling to identify themselves with the party. White argued that he would not feel comfortable as the leader of an extra-party organization. It was finally agreed that White would function as executive director of the Citizens' group, while its figurehead leaders would be Mrs. Luce and General Doolittle.[22]

Thus the Goldwater campaign adapted belatedly to the divisive effects of the Republican National Convention. The Hershey conference represented a recognition that a public gesture was required in behalf of party unity; establishing the Citizens' Committee was an admission that party unity could not be reestablished, and that other arrangements would be needed in key states. Some Goldwater partisans no doubt viewed the establishment of the volunteer organization as a vehicle for cleansing the party of its more liberal elements.

True to his promise that the campaign would be conducted through the state party headquarters, Goldwater attempted to bring White's network under the control of the regular party. State chairmen were given veto power over the appointment of the Citizens' for Goldwater-Miller chairmen in their respective states. The official channels of communication and command were designated as running from RNC headquarters to the state headquarters and only thereafter to the Citizens' groups in each state. Furthermore, the Citizens' group was conceived as an adjunct to the logistics arm of the campaign structure. Clif White was regarded as a political technician, excluded from influence on policy-making.

The Jenkins case

A third example of adaptation to an unexpected event was provided by the arrest of Walter Jenkins, close aide to President Johnson, on a morals charge. The fact of Jenkins' arrest was not published until a week after the event, and the RNC staff played a significant role in bringing about that publication.

Theodore White recounts how Abe Fortas and Clark Clifford, intimates of President Johnson, made the rounds of Washington newspaper offices pleading with editors to keep the story private. The story had been received earlier by the Chicago *Tribune* and the Cincinnati *Inquirer* (both Goldwater papers) but they chose not to publish it. Staff members of the Republican National Committee had learned of the incident within 48 hours of Jenkins' arrest.[23]

Dean Burch, aided by Lou Guylay, the Public Relations Director of the National Committee, contacted friendly newspapers in the Midwest and announced he would hold a press conference regarding a suppressed story. Editors of these papers in turn put pressure on their news services in Washington to release the story. Finally, the story moved out over the press service wires, and the press conference was not necessary.

One of our respondents considered this action on the part of the Goldwater staff an important public service:

Dean Burch deserves much of the credit for getting the Jenkins situation out to the public. If he had not had the courage to "call the hand" the Administration and the press probably would have succeeded in killing the story. Incidentally, the Jenkins case and the Austin television monopoly were not exploited by the candidate. [Goldwater] did not believe in doing this. As thanks he gets blamed for running "the dirtiest campaign" in history.

The campaign organization had reacted Incrementally, without seeking advance approval. Senator Goldwater was not informed of Burch's plan.[24] When the scandal became public, it seemed to offer proof of Goldwater's charges of "moral decay." Some of the young Goldwater supporters at National headquarters were elated, but the candidate did not enlarge on the incident. He responded to his own conscience. Theodore White has written:

Here, if ever, was demonstration of his charge of "moral decay," of sickness of soul, of bestiality in Babylon. Yet the Goldwater painted as a killer by the Democrats could not bring himself to hurt an individual; urged by his young men to hammer the issue, to make the most of it as if a gift had been given him—he simply refused. He referred to the episode in the weeks following only rarely—and with conspicuous lack of relish.[25]

The uninvited supporters

With its casual assumption that the campaign could be controlled from a single headquarters, Goldwater's policy group discounted the fact that campaigns involve much more than the actions of the candidates. Diverse groups, both invited and uninvited, either support the campaign effort or attempt to profit from its atmosphere. The behavior and attitudes of the uninvited can hardly be controlled from on high, yet their actions, associated with the candidate in the mind of the public, may seriously damage his image. One such phenomenon was the spate of "hate books" attacking either Lyndon Johnson or the so-called Eastern Establishment of the Republican party. Published as commercial ventures, these books had no connection with the Goldwater campaign, and they were explicitly repudiated by Dean Burch on behalf of the Republican National Committee. Nevertheless, critics continued to attack Goldwater by attacking the books.[26]

But invited groups could also damage the image, as the raucous Goldwater fans had done in booing Governor Rockefeller in San Francisco. In the closing weeks of the campaign, Goldwater visited Austin, Texas, the home city of President Johnson. His motorcade passed through deserted streets, but he entered an auditorium packed with screaming enthusiasts. When Goldwater mentioned the President's name in his speech, it was greeted with a deafening chorus of boos. Taken aback, Goldwater took a moment to remind his audience of the dignity of the presidential office. Its incumbent, he suggested, should never be the subject of such rudeness.[27] At this late point in the campaign, Goldwater was acting as if he realized that he must reach beyond those already dedicated to his cause—and that the larger audience could be repelled by the actions of those immediately present. But this was a reaction to the naked emotions of a campaign rally. It did not signal a change in the pattern of decision-making.

Notes on Chapter 6

[1]Theodore H. White, *The Making of the President 1964* (New York: Atheneum, 1965), p. 220.

[2]Stephen Shadegg, *What Happened to Goldwater?* (New York: Holt, 1965), p. 168.

[3]*The Making of the President 1964*, p. 206.

[4]"Report of Republican National Chairman, William E. Miller, before the Republican Conference, House of Representatives, Washington, D.C., February 5, 1964" (mimeographed), p. 10.

[5]The inclusion of Peter O'Donnell in this initial group seems to have been an act of courtesy rather than a sign of eagerness to incorporate the experience of the Draft Goldwater Committee into the general election campaign. Stephen Shadegg (*What Happened to Goldwater?*, p. 176) states that Grenier backed O'Donnell for Director of Political Organization, but "O'Donnell was unacceptable to the Goldwater high command." O'Donnell had no assignment in the national campaign, and Wayne Hood was eventually made the Director of Political Organization.

[6]White, *The Making of the President 1964*, p. 330.

[7]Stanley Kelley, Jr., "The Presidential Campaign," in Milton C. Cummings, Jr., ed., *The National Election of 1964* (Washington, D.C.: The Brookings Institution, 1966), p. 65 text and n. 68. Apparently Kelley does not consider Goldwater's repeated efforts to clarify his position on social security as attempts to "assure" the voters.

[8]Karl Hess, *In a Cause that Will Triumph* (Garden City, N.Y.: Doubleday, 1967), p. 53.

[9]John H. Kessel, "The Impact of Strategy: The 1964 Presidential Campaign," paper prepared for delivery at the 1966 Annual Meeting of the American Political Science Association, p. 6.

[10]Dean Burch, Speech to the Law School Forum of Yale University, March 16, 1965. Press release of the Republican National Committee, March 17, 1965, p. 3.

[11]John H. Kessel, "The Impact of Strategy," p. 10.

[12]Kessel, p. 14 and Table 10. "Almost unanimously" means that 90.2 per cent of those who felt the national government has not grown too strong voted for Johnson; 69.9 per cent of those who felt that it has grown too strong voted for Goldwater.

[13]Kelley, "The Presidential Campaign," p. 75. Kelley lists the ten states to which Nixon, Kennedy, and Goldwater gave the largest amount of their scheduled campaign time (p. 75, n. 94), and comments that seven of the Nixon states appear on the Goldwater list. Goldwater replaced Michigan, Iowa, and Missouri of the Nixon list, with Texas, Arizona, and Indiana.

[14]The most vigorous analyses of this kind are found in The Ripon Society, *From Disaster to Distinction,* (New York: Pocket Books, 1966), pp. 27-32, and in George Gilder and Bruce K. Chapman, *The Party that Lost Its Head* (New York: Knopf, 1966), pp. 207-209. For a more puzzled account of one of Goldwater's Southern campaign trips, see Richard H. Rovere, *The Goldwater Caper* (New York: Harcourt, 1965), pp. 133-150.

[15]The issues posed by the Supreme Court's practice of judicial review may be studied in any constitutional law text. A useful discussion is Howard E. Dean, *Judicial Review and Democracy* (New York: Random House, 1966). Chief Justice Hughes' famous statement is analyzed by Professor Dean, pp. 154 ff.

[16]Goldwater's Senate speech opposing the Civil Rights Act because he found Sections II (public accommodations) and VII (fair employment) unconstitutional is reprinted in his campaign book, *Where I Stand* (New York: McGraw-Hill, 1964), pp. 94-97.

[17]Jerry Landauer, writing in *The Wall Street Journal*, July 17, 1964. Quoted in Milton C. Cummings, ed., *The National Election of 1964*, p. 52.

[18]White, *The Making of the President 1964*, p. 236.

[19]The speech is quoted extensively in White, *The Making of the President 1964*, pp. 331-332. White calls it the best speech of the campaign, "a genuine intellectual effort."

[20]The analysis of election returns is performed by Bernard Cosman in *Five States for Goldwater* (University, Alabama: University of Alabama Press, 1966). See also Philip E. Converse, *et al.,* "Electoral Myth and Reality: the 1964 Election," *American Political Science Review*, 59 (June 1965), p. 330.

[21]Hess, *In a Cause that Will Triumph,* p. 166. The transcript of the Hershey conference, rescued from a RNC wastebasket, is published as an appendix to Hess' volume, pp. 166-231. Quotations from the transcript in this chapter and the next are from this source.

[22]The account of the conversation between Goldwater and Clif White is in Shadegg, *What Happened to Goldwater?*, pp. 185-186.

[23]White, *The Making of the President 1964*, p. 367.

[24]Hess, *In a Cause that Will Triumph,* p. 142.

[25]*The Making of the President 1964*, p. 369.

[26]There were similar efforts aimed at the Republicans, including a phony "psychoanalysis" of Barry Goldwater. The Democrats seemed to receive less blame for their existence. The "battle of the books" is described by Charles A. H. Thompson, "Mass Media Performance," in Milton C. Cummings, Jr., ed., *The National Election of 1964*, pp. 138-142.

[27]One of the authors was present at the Austin rally. Theodore White was in the press section; his description of the Texas campaign tour is found in *The Making of the President 1964*, pp. 337-339.

7

The Republican Organization in Action

In spite of the embarrassment it could cause, the grass roots enthusiasm for Barry Goldwater was his most impressive political asset; indeed, it was the most striking political phenomenon of 1964. The reality of this enthusiasm provided constant evidence to contradict the predictions of the opinion analysts concerning the outcome of the election.

The problem of converting this enthusiasm into politically productive labor was approached according to the tenets of Comprehensive decision-making. The first step required by the model is the definitive establishment of organizational goals.

With the help of volunteers from the National Federation of Republican Women, Dean Burch and John Grenier set in motion at Republican National Committee headquarters one of the largest scale exercises in the setting of goals ever undertaken by a political party. It was the expansion to a national basis of an effort previously successful in individual congressional districts. Ray Humphries came to the National Committee from the Congressional Campaign Committee to direct the operation. It consisted in specifying "vote quotas" for every state and every county that could be broken down even into precinct quotas. National headquarters thus could advise the precinct captain how many votes he should deliver as his fair contribution to national victory. But the delivery of those votes was viewed as a problem of local political organization. There was no mechanism by which local campaign needs could be considered by those planning the national campaign. The "vote quota" scheme is a classic example of Comprehensive decision-making. And it revealed the classic faults of Comprehensiveness. Because the quotas were assigned from on high, they could not mobilize the knowledge and energies of the very persons who would have to give them life.

The Field Organization

In his talk to the 50 state chairmen at the close of the Convention, Barry Goldwater insisted upon establishing a single organizational structure with direct lines of command and communication. This was in the best tradition of Comprehensive organization. An Incrementalist would study the situation in each state and work with those persons most capable of producing results, even if it were necessary to establish multiple points of contact. The initial formation of the Citizens for Goldwater-Miller organization seemed to be guided by just such a purpose. When questioned by Governor Romney at the Hershey conference concerning the mode of operation of the Citizens' groups, Dean Burch replied:

> Governor, we are going to have to resolve this on a more or less State-by-State basis. In certain States we feel that by working within the existing structure of the Republican Party . . . we will be organized down to each precinct, and in that case the Citizens would become more or less a fund-raising and psychological group. In certain States, if the organization within the State is not down to the precinct level, then we will have to supplement that either by building up the State organization or with the Citizens' groups.*

In spite of the Incremental sound of Burch's statement, alternate channels of communications were not established, and the Citizens' organizations remained officially subordinate to the regular State parties. The position of the Citizens' groups was harshly criticized in our interviews after the election. The criticisms were based on experience rather than on theory. Some respondents felt that this aspect of the organizational plan was implemented entirely too well.

We talked to one lady who held a secretarial position in the head-quarters of the California Citizens for Goldwater Committee. It was late

---

*See above, pp. 102-105, for an account of the Hershey meeting.

in the campaign, and she felt that Goldwater would lose. She blamed this not on any shortcomings of her candidate but rather on the fact that information and directions were going from the Republican National Committee to the headquarters of the California State Central Committee. This was a disaster, she felt, because the staff at the regular party headquarters in general had supported Rockefeller in the presidential primary. "It's all going down the drain," she said. "To think that it took ten or fifteen years of people having meetings in their living rooms to get this organized. And now it's all going down the drain."

On the other hand, we were told that the decision to use the regulars had not been carried out. A professional Republican manager put it this way:

To sum it up, there were too many knuckleheads running the organization–nice guys with no political experience. They did not know the organizations and the people who traditionally run the state presidential organizations. Goldwater said that he was going to run his campaign through the state organizations and then he did the very opposite. He did what he criticized Nixon for. In fact he outdid Nixon. He had promised to run the campaign through the regulars and regular channels and instead brought in his Arizona Mafia who were political amateurs. For example, in Virginia we exceeded our quota by 20,000 and still lost by 80,000. In California we turned the organization over to the amateurs, Reagan and Brennan, who went around and worked outside the state organization. We lost there by 1,000,000 while [Senator-elect] Murphy won by 800,000.

The most strongly stated point of view was offered by an assistant to Clif White who had labored with the Draft Goldwater Committee for the six months preceding the Republican National Convention:

Now here [let me describe to you] the biggest blunder of the campaign. It can only be attributed to Goldwater and his attempt to unify the party after the nomination. [He said] it would be run by the Republican National Committee and the state committees which is the policy that should normally be followed. However, this was not a normal year. We [the Draft Goldwater Committee] had organizations of people in every state. Some of the people heading state organizations were moderate and liberal Republicans. But the [Draft Goldwater] committeemen and women were conservatives.

There were three groups during the campaign. First, the regulars; second, the [Republican National] Committeemen and women, who were made powerless; third, state and county chairmen who go back to the Draft Goldwater days. Who did Goldwater turn the organization over to? The unfavorable group, that is, the regulars. But this was an exceptional year because of the change in the philosophy of the Republican Party as well as in the party organization. For example, California was highly organized with Goldwater committees. We had two brilliant people, a committeeman and a committeewoman, who were pro-Goldwater then. They were not kooks. After the nomination they were relegated [to positions of no importance] and did not take part in the general election. This was an awful loss which later showed up in the election. We handed back the organization to the wrong people in states like California. This caused disarray and did not endear Goldwater to the people who had voted for him in San Francisco. [The Draft Goldwater group] were not authorized to run until about four weeks after the nomination. We lost steam and never really recovered the momentum we had built up to the nomination. The Citizens' Committee did not even meet until the second or third week in August.

This mention of a "change in the philosophy of the Republican party" and the suggestion that specifying a subordinate role for the Citizens' organizations was a misguided move aimed at party unity are in stark contrast to the picture of the political world held by Goldwater's policy-making group. They claimed until long after the Convention that the Arizona Senator spoke for the conservative majority of Republicans and that any organization should exhibit clear lines of authority. In this view, the liberal candidates (with their disruptive volunteer organizations) were the interlopers.

Several of our respondents complained that the scheme for working with the regular organizations broke down because Goldwater's Regional Directors were persons who had worked in the Draft Goldwater Committee. The Regional Directors turned to the people they knew and used those contacts, often bypassing the established party leaders. The time pressures of the campaign supplied an excuse for such actions, but the motive was widely regarded as an effort to remake the party in a Goldwater pattern. Heading the list of those shunted aside were the Republican National Committeemen and Committeewomen, who are the official liaison agents between the national party and the state parties. This was regularly cited as an important reason why Dean Burch was later voted out as Chairman of the National Committee. Interviewed during the fight over the Chairmanship, a National Committee veteran stated:

Last week Burch and maybe Kitchel and Grenier began to call some of the state leaders in order to butter them up—to cover up for the miffs that they had committed during the campaign. Their purpose was to continue control of the party. However, their actions of August and September ruined these chances.

Interviewer: Isn't it true that Goldwater met with his state chairmen in the Mark Hopkins Hotel in San Francisco and stated that the campaign would be run through the regular organization?

Respondent: Yes. But this plan was never carried out because the people in charge only dealt with Goldwater people. The whole campaign was based on mistrust of some [established party leaders]. They only trusted Goldwater supporters. This was true in every state. Take my own state of — — — — — . The Draft Goldwater leaders were not popular. Before the Convention, Goldwater delegates were chosen by the worst possible means. But our State Chairman thought he had a commitment from Goldwater as to how many Goldwater delegates should be in the delegation. He fell for this line from the Goldwater people, and after the Convention, only Goldwater people were allowed to do any work.

When executives of the RNC were reproached for appointing only Goldwaterites as Regional Directors, they cited the exception of Fred Scribner, legal counsel of the Republican National Committee. Scribner did indeed direct Region 3 (New England), and he was no Goldwaterite. But New England had already been written off as too solid a liberal stronghold.

Senator Goldwater's field organization compiled a list of impressive accomplishments. It produced the largest army of precinct workers yet seen in American politics. According to the estimates of survey researchers, the Republican workers made several million more contacts than did the Democrats. At least in this campaign, personal contact was particularly effective.[1] Barry Goldwater's defeat would have been of even greater magnitude without the campaigners at the doorstep. The precinct workers were furnished with adequate supplies to support their mission. Door-to-door canvass kits were finally produced in abundance; there were plenty of instruction books, literature, and campaign stickers. It seems unlikely that these workers labored with increased dedication because a "vote quota" had been sent down from national headquarters; for the Goldwater movement had enjoyed a substantial mass base from its inception. The army of workers would have been in the field regardless of what type of organization was established to coordinate their efforts. They were caught up in the excitement of a presidential campaign involving the hopes, ambitions, and energies of thousands of people. To channel those energies, yet prevent diverse ambitions from causing serious conflicts, is the major challenge of campaign planning.

The effort to impose a Comprehensive style of organization on the field forces hampered their effective use. If Goldwater had, in fact, been nominated by a Convention which was truly representative of the party rank and file—and uniformly so in every state—the initial prohibition against volunteer organizations would have been completely appropriate. In some states, the Draft Goldwater personnel were friendly toward, if not almost identical with, the regular party structure. In others, they were dissident elements that had been fighting the regular leadership for years. The effort to bring the volunteer group under the wing of the regular organization simply added to the inevitable clash of ambitions and ideologies. Rather than regarding the Citizens' Committees as temporary groups formed for campaign purposes alone, the effort to include them within the regular chain of command made their activities seem aimed beyond the election toward control of the local parties.

In spite of his belated efforts at the Hershey conference, Barry Goldwater gave the impression of campaigning just as he had won the nomination—as the champion of a faction, not the leader of a united party. This outcome was exactly the opposite of Goldwater's intention; its cause, at least in part, lay in the attempt to implement the principles of Comprehensive organization.

The Reorganization of National Headquarters

According to long-standing custom, the presidential nominee appoints a new Chairman of the Republican National Committee. When the candidate's personal campaign staff is a separate organization, as was Richard Nixon's, the coming of a new National Chairman may make little difference to the party civil servants who run the national headquarters between presidential elections. But the logic of Goldwater's decision to run his campaign through the National Committee—widely praised at the time—required much more than simply a change in top management. Dean Burch and John Grenier came to the National Committee with a mandate to remake it in the Comprehensive image.

As State Chairman in Alabama, John Grenier found that modest organizational work yielded impressive Republican results. Politics in the Alabama Democratic party has long been a matter of personal factionalism, so the Democrats have developed little more than rudimentary organization. By both training and experience, Grenier was a devotee of the Comprehensive style. Young, crisp, and decisive, he was characterized as "an ex-Marine drill instructor." In midcampaign, a reporter described him as establishing "a clear line of authority not unlike a military table of organization."[2] Theodore White saw both Grenier and Dean Burch as "handsome, neat, and efficient as the most attractive junior executives of American Tel & Tel or General Motors."[3] They seemed determined to apply the principles of sound business organization to an enterprise that had become run down and rather seedy.

As an executive of the logistics arm of the campaign organization, Grenier fulfilled a technical, rather than a policy-making function, at least in the eyes of the Moley memorandum. But reporters and Republican workers did not necessarily separate policy from technique (ends from means). Grenier's appointment was widely regarded as proof that Goldwater had adopted the racially tinged "Southern Strategy" of pre-Convention enthusiasts.

Burch and Grenier came to the headquarters of the Republican National Committee in Washington's Cafritz Building to find offices that had been occupied continually since the Eisenhower victory of 1952 without major remodeling. They found a staff which had been directly involved in the campaign of 1956 but had played only a peripheral role in 1960. Furthermore, it was a staff that had received the attention of only part-time directors in recent years, because of the practice of naming members of Congress to the National Chairmanship. Contrary to public report, it was not a staff that had been purged of all but Goldwaterites by William Miller. Even if this had been Miller's intention, his duties as a congressman did not permit that kind of attention to the operations of the National Committee.

The approach of the new Republican managers was to redesign the new organization from the top, rather than to inquire what persons were already on the job and what they were doing. Immediate decisions were made to remodel the offices and to modernize the telephone service. Even before the new organization was completed, the offices were swarming with carpenters, painters, telephone men, and the inevitable furniture movers.

The first step in rebuilding the organization was to draw up a budget, allocating money as yet uncollected among the various activities that the organization should perform. The next step was to design an organization chart on the basis of the functions specified in the budget. No chart of the existing organization was available. A pre-Goldwater National Committee executive told us, "We've never bothered with an organization chart. We found it only makes people worry about how big their square is." But Burch and Grenier found the chart essential to their style of operation. As new positions were created and staffed, the chart was revised. At least three printed versions of it were distributed to the RNC staff during the fourteen weeks of the Goldwater campaign. The time and attention this matter received was in marked contrast to the indifference toward it exhibited by the Democratic leadership.

With slots established by the organization chart, the next step was to recruit the personnel to fill them, or else reassign persons already on the payroll. Equipment and furniture would then be installed in the newly partitioned offices to serve the needs of that specialized office. The final step would be to communicate the nature and design of the headquarters organization to the rest of the party, so that requests for help could be handled, contacts made, and a thousand details of logistical support organized for the campaign.

Dean Burch, John Grenier, and their principal assistants labored around the clock to establish the new organization. By August 16, the bulk of the decisions had been made and were ready for communication. Five weeks after the Convention, the state chairmen were called to the National Committee headquarters to learn how the campaign organization would function. Each was provided with a *Republican State Chairman's Handbook* providing a potpourri of information, ranging from an organization chart of the Republican National Committee to helpful hints on planning a state party headquarters.

The new staff structure was a classic example of the Comprehensive approach to the making of decisions. The organization charts, the chains of command, and the definitions of authority were all included. John Grenier had practiced his organizational presentation at a series of regional campaign schools for key workers. In these presentations, Grenier described the implementation of the principles of the Moley memorandum in terms of good organization. He began by describing the National Party Headquarters as the "nerve center" of the campaign, where decisions would be made with authority and communicated to lower echelons in the states. There would be a wealth of volunteer help, he stated, which the state organizations would have to direct, while it would be the task of national headquarters to ensure that the campaign in all fifty states would be operating on the same track at the same time. He announced that this would be a close election in which organization would make the difference.

Explaining the changes made at national headquarters, Grenier stated that the ultimate decision-makers were Goldwater, Miller, and Denison Kitchel. These three men had been assigned offices on the third floor of the Cafritz Building. Also on the third floor was the home of the policy group described in the Moley memorandum: the research specialists, the academicians, and the speechwriters. Their office was just down the hall from the suites set aside for the candidates and for Kitchel. Grenier described this group as the personal staff of the candidates and of the Campaign Director for the purposes of policy formulation. Policy would be implemented, Grenier said, through Dean Burch with the advice of the Steering Committee which would be meeting every weekend. Thus the dual structure of the campaign organization was made explicit. But its implication—that policy formation was to be strictly separated from its implementation by technicians—was not pointed out.[4]

One of our respondents who was present at the State Chairmen's meeting told us of his certainty, upon seeing the organization charts, that Goldwater would win. The prestige of the Comprehensive form of decision-making and coordination could cloud the perception of reality. Five weeks had elapsed since adjournment of the Republican National Convention—five weeks in which voting decisions could have been influenced. Instead, Goldwater's chief lieutenants were busy remodeling the National Committee offices, redesigning the campaign organization, and preparing for a formal campaign to open on September 1. The time costs of Comprehensive decision-making have nowhere been better exemplified.

A more important cost unaccounted for in Goldwater's Comprehensive plan was that of achieving social agreement. To redesign an established human organization is always painful to those persons whose working relationships are disturbed. Many Republican National Committee staff members had misgivings about the Goldwater candidacy. Efforts viewed by Burch and Grenier as attempts to create a more efficient organization were viewed by the incumbent staff members as an attempt to purge all those who were not dedicated Goldwater adherents. There was a good deal of jockeying for personal influence and the trappings of power as the newcomers arrived.

One of the first directives issued in the name of John Grenier was that all materials going to the mimeograph room would have to be approved by a particular Administrative Assistant. This person was a militant Goldwater supporter, a newcomer to the Cafritz Building, and particularly aggressive in gathering the square footage of floor space she felt her operations required. Persons who had been at the National Committee for years were required to write memoranda explaining the work of their offices and the need for the materials usually duplicated by the mimeograph room. John Grenier explained afterwards that this requirement was only made so that a measure of cost control could be instituted. At the time, established Committee staff members felt that this requirement was intended to harass them and to "purify" the propaganda output of the Committee. Later in the campaign, the same Administrative Assistant took it upon herself systematically to destroy historical files of the National Committee stretching back nearly fifty years. She felt that the Goldwater Republican Party needed that space. She preserved only a Calvin Coolidge campaign button.

Press accounts at the time stressed just such conflicts as these to support the thesis that Goldwater's goal was control of the National Committee. The insistence upon strict lines of authority did lead to the resignation of several experienced persons—particularly those who saw themselves as demoted. Goldwater made a gesture toward unity between the newcomers and the career employees when he invited all staff workers in the Washington area to breakfast with him at a Washington hotel on two different Monday mornings. Relaxed and beaming, Goldwater recounted his recent experiences on the campaign trail and told the most successful of his campaign jokes. Professional staff members were astonished that the candidate would devote the time and resources (more than a thousand persons attended the breakfasts) to the entertainment of workers already laboring in his behalf.

The most serious questions of social agreement arose within the ranks of the Goldwaterites themselves, when the authority of the policy group was challenged by the veterans of the Draft Goldwater Committee effort who found themselves relegated to the role of political technicians.

The policy group itself was not definitively formed until the beginning of the Convention, for the various experts making it up had to obtain leave from their normal occupations. Although Edward McCabe retained the title of Director of Research, he was used increasingly to maintain liaison with the highest echelons of the party—first with General Eisenhower, then with William Miller. The operating chief of research activities, as Deputy Director of Research, was Charles Lichenstein, a former political science teacher at Yale and Notre Dame who had worked on the staffs of United States senators, the 1960 Nixon campaign, and the Republican research organization founded by Dr. Milton Eisenhower. As a professional political staff member, he brought a wealth of experience to the policy group, but his emergency assignment to the function of television coordination removed that experience from some of the decisions of the policy group. The principal speechwriter in residence at Washington headquarters was Dr. Warren Nutter, University of Virginia economist, as Karl Hess was assigned to travel with the campaign plane. Coordinator of contributions from the conservative academic community was Dr. W. Glenn Campbell, on leave as Director of the Hoover Institution on War, Revolution, and Peace, of Stanford University. (Nutter's hand-lettered sign near their adjoining offices read "Political Issues from Soup to Nuts.") A principal assistant was Richard A. Ware, on leave as Secretary of the Relm Foundation of Ann Arbor, Michigan. Liaison between the policy group and the candidates was looked after by Tony Smith, Goldwater's loyal press secretary now partially sidelined by illness. And the acknowledged leader of the policy group was William Baroody, Sr., who held no official title.

These six men—Baroody, Lichenstein, Nutter, Campbell, Ware, and Smith—formed the core of what Stephen Shadegg referred to as "Goldwater's think tank."[5] And the group functioned effectively to control the output of the campaign—the speeches, television scripts, pamphlets concerning issues, and responses to letters demanding, "What does Senator Goldwater think about . . . ?" One of the strict policies of the group was that no promises would be made in response to the specific demands by pressure groups for changes in governmental policy.*

Another policy was the blockading of the campaign portals against the entry of the lunatic fringe attempting to ride Goldwater's conservative coattails. When one celebrity delivered a television broadcast supporting Goldwater which was received with such enthusiasm that the RNC switchboard was flooded with demands for a rerun, a member of the policy group exclaimed, "My God! Maybe we should have let the kooks surface before this!"

The scholarly bent of the members of the policy group meant that factual data included in Goldwater's speeches received more careful checking for accuracy than the usual campaign speech. But this strict authority over campaign content was resented by members of the logistics wing of the organization—particularly by those who had labored for Goldwater long before the members of the policy group were enlisted or Goldwater even agreed to become a candidate. The question of coordination between the two sides of the campaign organization had been handled in the Moley memorandum through the suggestion of "friendly relations," but Kitchel was aware that more formal organizational devices would be needed.

The basic campaign schedule was planned so that the candidates would be on the road from Tuesday through Saturday and would spend Sunday resting while subordinates prepared questions requiring decisions. On Monday they would record television programs before attending a major strategy conference. One of the participants explained the schedule to us:

*One afternoon when Tony Smith was absent and could not exercise his usual surveillance, a policy group subordinate sent a mildly favorable response to a Florida association of grapefruit growers. One of William Miller's staff sent a letter to a numismatical hobby magazine over the Congressman's signature promising to effect a change in certain practices of the U.S. Mint. A theory of the grand Goldwater coalition was formulated on the spot: amateur radio operators, coin collectors, and grapefruit growers.

The weekly schedule for the campaign was laid out so that there would be strategy meetings on Sunday involving a rather large number of persons while the candidates were resting. On Monday, after doing whatever was needed for television, Goldwater would be able to meet to discuss strategy with his most intimate circle of advisers. Goldwater and Miller were both to have been present. These meetings came off only about three times during the campaign. It seemed that the television people always needed the candidates longer than we had planned. On one occasion Bill Miller was absent because he was sick or just plain exhausted. At the Sunday meetings, there was a constant undercurrent of frustration on the part of the political activists because Goldwater's policy advisers did not respond to their suggestions regarding the substance of the campaign, that is, the nature of statements that Goldwater should make on specific issues.

Apparently the Sunday meetings were intended to bring together technical experts to seek their advice on technical matters and insure that all were working together in the implementation of policy. But any hard decisions on "strategy," in the traditional sense, were reserved for the Monday meetings between the candidates and their close policy advisers. In practice, these meetings were secondary to "whatever was needed for television." To call the Sunday group a "strategy committee" was an error soon discovered by its members.

This viewpoint was confirmed by one of Goldwater's closest advisers:

The Sunday meetings were not meetings of the "inner circle." Such meetings were intended for Mondays, but few of them took place due to the burden of preparing television broadcasts. The result was that all campaign decisions were on an *ad hoc* basis, in spite of our desire to make them on other bases.

This was one of a number of comments we heard indicating that the original Comprehensive plan of the campaign proved inapplicable because of the pressure of events and infinite details involved in a national campaign. In fact, the response of yet another close adviser suggests that there was not complete agreement within the top levels of the organization concerning the nature and purpose of the alleged strategy meetings.

They were really two different groups. The alleged strategic committee was composed of Goldwater, [Leonard] Hall, [Ray] Bliss, [Dean] Burch, [John] Grenier, Wayne Hood, Lou Guylay, Bill Knowland, Ralph Cordiner, Bill Miller, Bill Warner, and Clif White.* This group was to meet every Sunday and Monday in Washington. But this never quite came off. The real strategy group was Baroody, Miller, Goldwater, and Kitchel.

*Leonard Hall was formerly Republican National Chairman; Ray Bliss, the State Chairman from Ohio, would succeed Dean Burch as Chairman of the Republican National Committee; Wayne Hood was Director of Campaign Operations, serving directly under Grenier; Lou Guylay was Director of Public Relations; William Knowland was the former Republican Senator from California; and William Warner was the vice presidential campaign manager.

The procedures adopted for coordinating the work of the policy group and the practical politicians did not function to broaden the focus of attention of the policy group. A contributing factor was the absence of Denison Kitchel from headquarters. When illness struck Tony Smith, Kitchel joined the campaign plane to serve as the principal buffer between Goldwater and the annoyances of the campaign trail, which ranged from hostile reporters to confused schedules. As General Manager of the campaign, Kitchel officially supervised both wings of the campaign structure. But he was seldom available to provide the communication between them.

The result of organizational bifurcation was to alienate the experienced politicians (such men as Leonard Hall, William Knowland, and Ray Bliss) who felt qualified to offer advice regarding both the substance and techniques of the campaign and probably did not accept the propriety of a distinction between the two. These men did not break any previous commitments, but they were not inspired to seek new resources or energy that could be devoted to the Goldwater campaign.

Frustration and alienation soon permeated the middle echelons of the logistics segment. Stephen Shadegg records its culmination in a frontal assault upon the authority of the "think tank" by certain of the Regional Directors with the aid of members of the office of the Finance Director.[6] But when Goldwater himself was finally reached, he proved unwilling to modify the structure of the organization.

Problems with Financial Management

Dissent had apparently been building up for some time among the campaign's financial managers. Goldwater had announced his intention not to bankrupt the party; he found in Ralph Cordiner, Chairman of the Board of General Electric, a Finance Chairman as opposed to deficits in the party as he was to increasing the debt of the federal government. Cordiner was assisted by Jeremiah Milbank, Jr., William Middendorf, and J. Stetson Coleman, the chief fund raisers of the Draft Goldwater operation. The Moley memorandum had not dealt with campaign finance, but its logic required that financial managers be regarded as but a special type of practical politician performing technical duties in the campaign structure.

The unforeseen consequence of establishing a powerful financial directorate was that a potential veto power over the decisions of the policy group was also established. Because campaign contributions usually come in late, finance managers normally borrow money against the credit of the party. Their power to refuse any particular request on the basis that no funds are available is most important in the field of advertising, for the mass media do not do business on credit. Political advertising must be paid for in advance. Before it was replaced as the RNC advertising agency, the Leo Brunett Agency had tentatively reserved some prime television time slots. One of these would have come at the conclusion of the Democratic National Convention. When the time came to pay for this reservation, the campaign coffers were empty, and Goldwater's newly installed financial officers directed that the time be canceled.

Some of our respondents claimed that as the campaign progressed, the men in charge of finance made suggestions ranging from the appropriate newspaper to be used for a particular advertisement to the request that Goldwater take a specific stand on Proposition 14, the state constitutional amendment on the California ballot which repealed fair housing legislation.

Since those who control the money have the potential power to influence campaign policies, candidates ordinarily choose persons for this role whose policy judgment they trust. However, Moley's principle of separating policy-making from logistical functions made it difficult for Goldwater to recognize the problem. Prestige in the financial community would seem to have been a reason for selecting Cordiner for the National Committee position. Cordiner's principal assistants had performed valiantly for the Draft Goldwater operation, and it seemed appropriate to retain them. But this, like many Goldwater decisions, was made under the pressure of time, without full opportunity for the Comprehensive analysis of possible alternatives and their consequences.[7] The resultant conflicts meant loss of time and waste of energy.

Because federal law provides that no political organization may spend more than $3,000,000, national campaigns can only be financed by setting up a multitude of organizations to raise funds. Adherence to the letter of this law requires that they be managed by separate directorates, and there is no legal requirement that any of them cooperate with the central campaign manager. In 1964, the Goldwater campaign finished in the black because of the large number of small contributions received at the last minute in response to television appeals. Most of these appeals were made by the National TV for Goldwater-Miller Committee, with headquarters in Los Angeles. This committee had been formed in Los Angeles because many wealthy contributors were located on the West Coast. Instead, small contributions poured in, and the managers of this committee proved more interested in conservatism than they were in the Republican Party. The excess funds were kept in California. They were not returned to Washington to help the National Committee dig its way out of the morass of the Goldwater defeat. The proudly announced surplus of the campaign was a mirage. Months later, the Los Angeles committee contributed funds to the campaign of a conservative candidate for high office in the Young Republican National Federation.

Notes on Chapter 7

[1] John H. Kessel, "The Impact of Strategy: The 1964 Presidential Campaign," paper prepared for delivery at the 1966 Annual Meeting of the American Political Science Association, pp. 7-8.

[2] Jerald Ter Horst, "The Grenier Plan for the G.O.P.," *The Reporter* (October 8, 1964), p. 25.

[3] Theodore H. White, *The Making of the President 1964* (New York: Atheneum, 1965), p. 317.

[4] The source of this paraphrase of Grenier's talk to party workers is a tape recording of his speech to the Regional Campaign School held in Dallas, Texas, in the files of the Republican National Committee.

[5] Stephen Shadegg, *What Happened to Goldwater?* (New York: Holt, 1965), p. 211 and p. 233.

[6] Shadegg, pp. 232-237, 240-241.

[7] Goldwater had paid inadequate attention to financial requirements from the beginning. He announced his candidacy on January third without knowing who would arrange for financial support. As a professional campaign manager, Stephen Shadegg was shocked at this oversight. See *What Happened to Goldwater?*, p. 90.

8

The Failures of Comprehensive Organization

The attempt to achieve a Comprehensive coordination of decisions created more difficulties than it solved. Assuming the validity of a central set of decisions about campaign ends and means, Dean Burch and John Grenier further assumed that these decisions would impose productive order upon the many operating decisions which carried out the campaign. Unhappily, no allowance was made for the cost of failing to achieve social agreement. Many members of the campaign organization, including some with important responsibilities, did not agree with the campaign goals perceived by Goldwater's policy advisers. They felt that insistence on pure conservatism was a path to political suicide, yet they clung to their positions as career employees of the RNC. Many National Committee employees had developed special contacts over the years in various states. Their goal came to be the preservation of those contacts in spite of the Goldwater candidacy. In some cases, they implored their friends to work for the local ticket, even if they did not care to support the national candidates. The Moley memorandum ignored the loose federalism of the American party system and the fact that local labors supporting the national ticket are performed voluntarily. They cannot be commanded.

The Fate of RNC Subdivisions

The party civil servants were well aware that the national headquarters of an American political party, particularly in the period between presidential campaigns, is little more than a holding operation. Regardless of their personal opinions, it was not the role of the RNC staff to advance one faction, ideology, or strategic design within the party over another. Insofar as the RNC activities before 1964 were guided by a common strategy, it was one of coalition-building.

National headquarters had for many years carried on at least token efforts to organize support for the Republican Party among identifiable groupings within the national electorate. It included a Minorities Division, concerned with wooing the Negro vote; it had a Nationalities Division to solicit the support of Americans of foreign parentage; it had a Labor Division which tried to win what allegiance it could away from the Democrats within the ranks of organized labor; it had a Farm Division with a similar mandate; and it had specialists dealing with veterans' organizations and with Senior Citizens. The National Committee even supported an Arts and Sciences Division, which had the awesome task of organizing support among professors for local and national Republican candidates. Each of these offices attempted to maintain national contact with its constituent interest groups. The only specific regional effort was the Southern Division, commonly known as Operation Dixie.

All of these offices, in turn, were part of the Campaign Division, which was headed by the Executive Director of the Republican National Committee, Mr. A. B. ("Ab") Hermann. A one-time professional baseball player, Hermann entered politics as the organizer of an aggressively liberal Young Republican group (for the Coolidge era) in New Jersey in 1924. After serving as New Jersey state chairman, he came to Washington to work both at the National Committee and the Congressional Campaign Committee. He became Executive Director at the Cafritz Building headquarters early in the Eisenhower Administration, and he supplied permanent leadership as a party civil servant under a succession of Republican National Chairmen. Hermann was one of those men who, because of his vast political acquaintance and powers of persuasion, aided by long-distance telephone calls, tied the local elements of the Republican Party into the semblance of a national political organization through the Incremental process of mutual adjustment.

When John Grenier replaced Ab Hermann as Executive Director, Hermann was named Special Assistant to Dean Burch. In this role, his acquaintance with the leaders of the Republican Party was put to use in answering correspondence, screening visitors asking to see the Chairman, and responding as well as he could to the questions and demands of those leaders who called him to complain about aspects of the Goldwater campaign.

The Campaign Division was disbanded. Some of its constituent elements were kept under the direction of the Republican National Committee, but most of its functions were transferred to the Citizens for Goldwater-Miller organization. Others disappeared. The labor and farm organizations—little more than one-man offices—were in effect disbanded, as their directors resigned. The only functions to be kept within the Cafritz Building and the Republican National Committee were the Nationalities Division and the Arts and Sciences Division.

The Nationalities Division was headed by Congressman Edward J. Derwinski of Illinois. For several years it had sought the votes of those of recent foreign descent, particularly from Eastern Europe. The Nationalities Division argued that the hard-line foreign policy of the Republican Party would be most likely to roll back the Iron Curtain and win their homelands back for the free world. The Nationalities Division had a well-developed program of local affiliates, public events, and publicity. It was a going organization based on attitudes compatible with Goldwater's campaign positions. The Goldwater managers supported the Nationalities Division with an increased budget and intervened little in its work.

The Arts and Sciences Division, on the other hand, was taken out of the category of campaign organization and was placed under the Research Division. The theory supporting this decision was that intellectuals and academicians would be available to feed ideas and concepts into the mill where they might find their way into Goldwater's speeches. However, of 10,000 Republican academicians identified over the years by the Arts and Sciences Division, only 300 responded affirmatively to a mailing requesting their help for the national ticket.

The Southern Division disappeared, for the Goldwater campaign was intended to mark the coming of age of the New Republican South. The South simply became Region VI, one of seven regional divisions of the campaign effort. The highly respected director of the Southern Division was Lee Potter, Republican National Committeeman from Virginia. Potter was assigned to the Tour Committee and spent the campaign arranging the travels of former President Eisenhower and Richard Nixon. A Tennessee legislator, Sam V. Claiborne, became the Southern Regional Director, but John Grenier was considered the effective director of the Southern campaign. With Grenier (who had served the Draft Goldwater Committee) available, Potter was not needed, regardless of his contacts and abilities.

Of course, many of Potter's friends assumed that his displacement signified more than was apparently intended. They assumed that it marked the assault of the Goldwater managers upon the established Republican organization, as well as the abandonment of Potter's essentially moderate approach to Southern voters in favor of more radical tactics. Once again, insistence upon the Comprehensive principle of clear lines of authority created problems not anticipated by the Moley memorandum.

Conflicts with the Citizens' Committee

Comprehensive organization was not achieved at the national campaign headquarters. The most notable consequence of attempting to achieve it—or assuming that it would automatically establish itself—was shown not by conflict between Goldwater newcomers and career professionals but by disagreements between the candidate himself and Clif White's Citizens' Committee. Significantly, the Citizens' operation was run, not from the Cafritz Building, but from the Duryea Building on Connecticut Avenue, originally leased by the Draft Goldwater Committee.

Although Goldwater announced his determination to avoid building a coalition of minorities, the task of arranging the support of organized interest groups was assigned to the Citizens' organization, and some career employees were transferred there from the RNC. As an extra-party organization, the Citizens' group could not pretend to bind the Republican Party to specific promises. Any serious wooing of, for example, organized labor implies willingness to promise some concrete advantage in return for help in contacting the membership of the organization. But staff members at the Citizens' Committee could not promise a *quid pro quo*. An official of the Citizens' organization who had labored in the Nixon campaign pointed out this deficiency. He had developed a promising contact with a union group in the Midwest, but he was unable to take even preliminary steps toward exploiting it.

In addition to organizing activities in several states, the Citizens' headquarters made substantial contributions to the national campaign. Characteristically, Goldwater began with little campaign literature ready for distribution. Funds were short, and the National Committee finance managers were not eager to support the production of a flood of expensive brochures. According to Lou Guylay, law prohibited the National Committee from selling campaign literature, but the Citizens' group could distribute it in return for contributions. The result was that these small but traditional items supporting the campaign were designed, produced, and distributed to local organizations by the Citizens' headquarters.[1]

Separated physically from the National Committee headquarters, the personnel of the Citizens' Committee were not so closely bound to the control of the Cafritz Building's third floor "think tank." This may have facilitated the production of minor campaign literature, but it eventually developed into one of the major internal crises of the Goldwater campaign.

The Citizens' Committee headquarters was largely staffed by persons who worked closely with Clif White during the Draft Goldwater Committee days. Many developed strong personal loyalties to White. Coupled with their feeling that White's abilities were not adequately recognized was their resentment of the circle of advisers surrounding Goldwater, who seemed to be relative late-comers to the cause.

Crisis Over "Choice"

As the campaign wore on without seeming to gain the offensive, the tendency to reject the judgment of those planning its content was redoubled. It seemed to the Citizens' Committee staff that the basic themes were moral decay, bribery, violence in the streets, and the image of President Johnson as a political wheeler-dealer. To dramatize this issue, a television film, *Choice*, was planned. According to Clif White, Senator Goldwater himself approved the idea for the film.[2] But none of the Senator's policy advisers was involved in its development. The film was produced under the direction of Rus Walton, publicity director of the Citizens' organization. As former Executive Director of the conservative United Republicans of California organization, Walton had contacts in the film and television industry. The film was made up of clips previously shown on television but extracted from their original context. Scenes of street rioting, frenzied dances, and other less attractive aspects of modern American society were displayed. A speeding automobile, similar to one driven by President Johnson, was intended to link his Admini- stration with the theme of national moral decay. One brief sequence of a girl in a topless bathing suit made the newspaper headlines when the film achieved premature publicity. But the most striking aspect of the film was the fact that pictures of street rioting showed whites battling Negroes. Without seeking permission from Goldwater's policy group at the Republican National Committee, the Citizens' organization arranged sponsorship for the film. It was scheduled for nationwide television showing on October 22. A member of Goldwater's inner circle later explained:

I realize now that we did not know enough about what the Citizens' organization was doing. We had confidence in Clif White as a technician; and he was present at the Sunday conferences. We simply assumed that no checkup was needed.

This crisis is an excellent illustration of the fact noted above—that the Comprehensive style makes no provision for the cost of achieving social agreement; it does not even recognize the problem. Goldwater's principal associates assumed that the mere communication of campaign goals (ends and important means together) at the Sunday meetings would suffice to win the adherence of all elements of the organization to those goals. No provision was made for the divergence in experience, styles, and convictions among the persons joined together in the campaign.

When Denison Kitchel saw *Choice* he was outraged. But plans for showing the film were so far advanced that only the candidate himself could halt their implementation. A showing was arranged for Goldwater. One of our respondents was present at that showing.

Politicians as soon as they saw [the film] saw three things—nudes, pornography, and immorality—which are dangerous to any politician. This movie was never cleared with the top—and all of a sudden we were confronted with a factor which we did not know how to handle. . . . Goldwater looked at it without saying a word. He turned to my son who watched it with me and asked him what he thought of the film. My son said he liked it. Goldwater said it was a racist film and he would not use it. This film shows you how an election is run—the sudden and unanticipated decisions meeting you at every step.

At this point, a two-day suspension in campaigning was necessitated by the death of former President Herbert Hoover. Both Goldwater and Johnson attended the services in New York. After the funeral, the Goldwater campaign staff flew to Los Angeles the night before a whistle-stop campaign trip through the Goldwater heartland of Orange County. Before the train's departure, Goldwater held a press conference in his Los Angeles hotel. It was conducted according to the usual rules permitting no direct quotation. The *Los Angeles Times* that morning reported that a Young Republican leader in the area had resigned his position in order more effectively to promote the showing of *Choice*.

A reporter asked Goldwater for his reaction to the film. "It is not salacious," the candidate snapped, "it is racist." Goldwater explained that he had ordered the cancellation of all plans for showing the film and that he repudiated the film completely. He then granted permission for this remark to be directly quoted.

Thus the assumptions of the Moley memorandum failed their most severe test. Not all persons in the campaign structure could be assumed to agree that the presentation of the candidates should be left to the policy-making segment of the organization. Clif White was regarded as a "technician" and was relegated to a relatively isolated, subsidiary position, when many persons felt that he should have been appointed Chairman of the Republican National Committee. Surrounded by friends from the Draft Goldwater Committee, White and his associates developed their own concept of how the campaign should be waged. This concept was very nearly implemented, although the candidate and his close advisers found it despicable. Technique and content, means and ends, could not be so easily separated.

The Case Against Comprehensive Decision-Making

After describing two models of decision-making and coordination, we predicted:

The campaign leader who strives for Comprehensiveness will either find his decisions difficult to reach or will be led to narrow his focus of attention to exclude data which his original plan did not encompass. In any case, his decisions will be hard to enforce . . . The mistakes he makes will be large and noticeable, and his campaign will be marked by severe problems of discipline, sharp internal conflict, and missed opportunities. (See p. 37.)

But we also suggested that no model can encompass all the decisions which go to make up a presidential campaign and that the behavior of human beings is rarely uncomplicated enough to fit within the boundaries of abstract models. With an outline of decision-making in the Goldwater campaign now before us, we are faced with two questions: (1) Did the events described actually constitute a test of the Comprehensive pattern of decision-making, or did they only test the assumptions made by Senator Goldwater and his associates concerning the nature of the American electorate? (2) If Comprehensive decision-making was tried and failed, was the magnitude of Goldwater's defeat caused, at least in part, by that failure?

To answer the first question, we must determine whether the attitudes and behavior of Senator Goldwater and his associates approximated the specifications of the Comprehensive model closely enough to support our claim that they made a determined effort to put its principles into operation. As we have indicated, a major requirement of the Comprehensive pattern was missing. Goldwater and his policy-makers did not conduct an exhaustive search for information, nor did they carefully consider alternatives and their consequences before specifying the goals of the campaign and selecting the chief means of achieving them. Instead, the goal of presenting conservatism without compromise grew from the political observations and experiences of Goldwater and his close associates. No exhaustive consideration of alternatives was perceived as necessary, and most decisions were reached with neither difficulty nor delay.

But Barry Goldwater and his close advisers, devoted to presumptions of clear authority and delegated responsibility, limited their foci of attention to exclude much crucial information. As Admiral Yamamoto, speeding toward Midway Island, ignored the possibility that his code had been cracked, Barry Goldwater's policy group ignored or discounted the opinion polls. The isolation of the policy group from other elements of the organization caused its members to remain ignorant of the early stages of discontent in their own organization and to disregard the potential harm of well developed dissent in the party at large.

But the exhaustive consideration of alternatives is impossible in the world of politics, for it is a world of imperfect knowledge. Evidence is selected from the real world which confirms the assumptions of the Comprehensive plan, and other data is systematically excluded from the decision-maker's focus of attention. The requirement of an exhaustive consideration of alternatives will not be met by any actor in a political situation, for the lack of perfect knowledge would make decisions impossible to reach. We therefore conclude that the Comprehensive style of coordinating decision-making received as complete a test in the Goldwater campaign as is likely in any campaign.

The belief in the power of conservatism to attract votes was intricately connected with the attractions of Comprehensive decision-making in the minds of Senator Goldwater and his policy advisers. The Incremental adjustments of the Nixon campaign seemed to them an abandonment of principle. The Moley memorandum promised that Nixon's "mistakes" would not be repeated and that Goldwater's policy advisers would not need to adjust their plans or compromise their viewpoints in response to signals from the lower echelons.

Moley's plan was based on the same misperceptions of voting behavior that were shared by the Republican candidate and his decision-makers. Principles of Comprehensive organization were so completely associated with assumptions concerning the nature of the electorate that their consequences are difficult to separate. They were tested simultaneously, for the Comprehensive organizational structure prevented campaign leaders from receiving, or at least taking seriously, signals which contradicted their assumptions about the voters.

To establish our contention that the attempt to coordinate decisions Comprehensively affected the magnitude of Goldwater's defeat, we must attempt to separate these two kinds of consequences. The separation begins by pointing out that the flaws predicted in analyzing the model were very much in evidence throughout Goldwater's campaign organization. Social agreement was not achieved; all elements of the organization did not uniformly accept the goal of presenting a dignified and relatively intellectual conservative ideology which carefully skirted any involvement with racial bigotry. The attempted separation of policy-makers from political technicians eventually caused intense internal conflict. It served to limit the focus of attention of the top decision-makers, insulating them from real knowledge concerning the electorate, the party, and the headquarters staff. In short, Comprehensive organization was not achieved, but the effort to establish the Comprehensive coordination of decisions burdened the Goldwater campaign with significant costs in social conflict coupled with the waste of time, money, and human energy.

At what point did these costs have an impact on the magnitude of the electoral outcome? The dual campaign structure of the Moley memorandum seemed to work well during the period before the Convention. Clif White operated to help political conservatives gain control of the Republican party at the precinct level, thus assuring conservative delegates to the Convention. In the California primary campaign, Goldwater's appeal was most effective, directed at an electorate of registered Republicans, large numbers of whom were already militant conservatives. Goldwater and his planners were led to believe that both the assumptions and details of the Comprehensive plan were correct.

The costs of Comprehensiveness mounted steadily thereafter. The clearest consequence of the Comprehensive pattern occurred at the Republican National Convention. The focus of attention of the policy-makers did not include the operations of the Platform Committee, and they overestimated the intellectuality of the audience for the acceptance speech. The opportunity to improve party harmony vanished. A series of events ensued which effectively portrayed Barry Goldwater as the candidate of a strident faction, rather than a united party. This impression was not lost on the minds of voters. In November, Goldwater received the support of very few Democrats outside the deep South and only a scant three quarters of the Republicans. The "hidden conservative" vote did not materialize.

Paradoxically, however, the effects of Comprehensiveness which acted to increase the magnitude of Goldwater's national defeat may have served to increase his margin of victory in the deep South. The attempt to separate policy-makers from technicians was not appreciated by either the press or the public. The inclusion of Southern leaders in the logistical wing of the organization may have seemed a signal that the "Southern strategy," with its overtones of bigotry, was being adopted. Conservative slogans such as "states' rights" have long carried racial overtones in the deep South; the segment of the public which could separate conservative doctrine from its unintended segregationist connotation was very small. But the isolated policy group discounted the kind of evidence which establishes this fact.

His vote in the deep South can hardly be cited as a success of Goldwater's Comprehensive plan. For the *goal* of that plan was to win votes on the basis of a conservative philosophy as unsullied by racism as it was uncompromised by concessions to local politicians. Comprehensive decision-making and assumptions concerning electoral behavior again combined to defeat Goldwater's purpose.

We conclude that Comprehensive decision-making was tested in 1964 and found inappropriate for American politics. But the Senator and his friends did not approach the campaign in an experimental mood. The edifice of the Goldwater campaign may be compared to the philosophy of a medieval theologian who orchestrates the theme of the Christian faith to the tune of Greek rationalism. The first principle is a matter of faith. If the first principle is accepted, however, the details seem logically necessary and the totality convincing. Belief in a hidden conservative vote was the article of faith; Raymond Moley's plan for Comprehensive decision-making supplied the details; and the general prestige of "good organization" reinforced the logic of combining the two.

When election night brought crushing defeat, the basic article of faith was not called into question. Although the magnitude of his defeat had been clear when the polls began to close, Barry Goldwater delayed his concession statement until more votes were counted, so that he could announce that more than 25,000,000 Americans had chosen the conservative philosophy.

The members of the Republican National Committee met in Chicago on

January 21st and 22nd, 1965, to ratify the agreement by which Ray Bliss of Ohio succeeded Dean Burch of Arizona as Chairman of the Committee.

Barry Goldwater delivered a speech which, like so many before, combined personal humility with an aggressive defense of the conservative cause. He begged his fellow partisans to cease blaming each other. Nobody could be blamed but himself, for the ultimate responsibility for all decisions of the campaign rested with the candidate. The conservative vote was yet to be mobilized. Conservatism remained the natural philosophy of the Republican party, and the managers of the party should seek better methods of "merchandising" it.

The faith endured.

Notes on Chapter 8

[1]For a more complete account of the early crisis in the production of campaign literature, see Stephen Shadegg, *What Happened to Goldwater?* (New York: Atheneum, 1965), pp. 187-188.

[2]F. Clifton White, *Suite 3505* (New Rochelle, N.Y.: Arlington House, 1967), p. 414.

Part 3

President Johnson
and the Use of Incrementalism

9

The Kennedy Team and Lyndon Johnson

Those who make it their business to describe presidential campaigns have been all but unanimous in depicting the 1964 Democratic campaign as a masterpiece of centrally directed, unified, and successful decision-making. In the words of their leading craftsman, Theodore H. White, Lyndon B. Johnson led "as masterful a campaign as the Democrats have ever conducted."[1] The extent of Johnson's victory was unprecedented. He received 61 percent of all the popular votes cast, surpassing Roosevelt's 60.8 percent in 1936 and Harding's 60.4 percent in 1920. Equally important was the wide distribution of Johnson's electoral strength. His vote fell below 60 per cent of the total in only 24 states and below 55 per cent in only nine.[2] Here was an electoral outcome of a degree and range that might be expected from ideal procedures of campaign decision-making.

Decisive victories have a way of looking well planned. They invite the retrospective impression that strategies were fully reviewed and clearly chosen, and that the various tactical moves and projects were carefully devised to implement these strategies. In the aftermath of the overwhelming Democratic victory, many campaign leaders with whom we talked exulted over the political management they had seen: "This was a near perfect campaign"—"It couldn't have been better"—"It was extremely well coordinated"—"It went beautifully"—"Just like clockwork." A few were more cautious, their assessment captured by one who remarked, "I don't know; success clouds our judgment." All agreed that 1964 was better organized than 1960. For many of those on the "inside," the latter, while tremendously exciting, was not the unblemished organizational triumph depicted by some reporters. "You can't run a campaign from an airplane" and "There were four or five men who tried to do everything and it won't work," were typical criticisms.[3] These personal observations bear eloquent testimony to the fact that presidential election campaigns are such complex social transactions that it is virtually impossible for individual participants to comprehend all their manifold events. Participant assessments tend to rest upon direct, sometimes idiosyncratic personal experiences, and to be organized around standards of evaluation that are unconscious and unarticulated.

Using the criteria set forth in Chapter 2, we propose that Incrementalism far overshadowed Comprehensiveness in the Democratic campaign. Exhaustive analysis, coherent planning, and unified direction were indeed attempted, but they have been substantially overstated as characterizing the processes of Democratic decision-making in 1964. A commitment to "rational" decisions and organization was widely shared by Johnson's campaign leaders. As events unfolded, however, there was no slavish devotion to this ideal, and Comprehensive aims melted smoothly into Incremental practices. This finding might seem to contradict the conventional wisdom about a president's control over his reelection effort, the dominating political resources of the White House, and Lyndon Johnson's own determination to exercise close personal control over all facets of his campaign. Such factors were important, but we shall see that they took effect in ways which emerged in the end as an Incremental approach to making decisions.

The Opening Decisions: Kennedy Prepares for Reelection

The initial plans for the Democratic presidential campaign were made long before the spring of 1964. Some grew slowly from indeterminate origins, yet a number of major decisions were made before John Kennedy's death in 1963. On November 12th of that year what might be called the Kennedy campaign team of 1960, augmented by Richard M. Scammon (Director of the Census), met with the President to take up concrete questions of strategy and organization for 1964. These veteran politicians—Lawrence O'Brien, Kenneth O'Donnell, Ralph Dungan, Richard Maguire, John Bailey, Theodore Sorensen, Robert Kennedy, Stephen Smith—foresaw with keen anticipation a well-managed, centrally organized effort. They considered many ideas, but none which departed radically from their experience or their established operations. Indeed, the Incremental cast of the discussion is illustrated by the acceptance of "the Bailey-Scammon strategy" in dealing with the South in the national party organization (to *gradually* reduce its strength, starting with an adjustment of delegate seats at the National Convention).[4] It was a session of high esprit, seen by its participants as the opening of campaign planning.

Yet it was also a continuation. Beginning as early as 1961, the time, place, and allocation of delegates to the Democratic National Convention had been actively considered, while target states and areas for a massive registration drive had been identified. Certain programs such as operations focusing on women, minority groups, and voter registration had been initiated, to be carried out from the National Committee. In the case of one or two it can be argued that the program was intended primarily to promote legislative goals of the Kennedy administration, but most of these efforts were aimed directly at the 1964 election.

The immediate forces behind such early decisions are worth noting. For the most part they originated in the Democratic National Committee. The fact that National Committee staff members serve at the discretion of the president tends to obscure the real physical, social, and functional distances separating party headquarters from the White House.[5] It is true that Committee leaders hold their jobs at the President's "pleasure"; but the busy chief executive may not know just what his pleasure is, or care on a day-to-day basis what is being done about it at party headquarters. Furthermore, the assumption that the National Committee of the party in power is populated exclusively by the "President's Men"—faithful extensions of his perception and will—ignores the subtle and variegated political forces playing upon the Committee and the diverse backgrounds of its personnel.[6] These forces were very much in evidence during the period of our study.

Although pictured as a unified community of Kennedy appointees, the Democratic Committee was more like a multiple satrapy. In the words of one of its leaders, "Kennedy could say Yes or No, but [these were] Kennedy people, O'Donnell people, Bailey people, Bobby people, and all were sort of fighting each other." Despite their differences, Committee leaders recognized that their performance would be judged primarily by the development of party organization and popular support for the Kennedy administration. The 1964 campaign would be the payoff. Thus, there were strong motivations for DNC operatives to invent and develop programs which would give them control over political resources and enhance their positions on the "Kennedy team." It was a situation dominated by projects—often in competition with each other for resources and attention—being urged on the White House by Committee leaders through varying channels of access.

The programs for voter registration, minority groups, and women's activities—headed, respectively, by Matthew Reese, Louis Martin, and Margaret Price—were good illustrations of this point. Each of these National Committee operations enjoyed knowledgeable and vigorous leadership between 1960 and 1964. Each constituted an "interest" which had to bargain with other interests for money, personnel, and attention. Treasurer Richard Maguire thus occupied a focal point as a matter of course, and he used his position to participate in every area of this early campaign management. The resulting processes of decision were similar in character but diverse in outcome, as reflected in the following comments:

We got off the ground in '61, soon after the election. The National Committee took the initiative, not the White House. Of course, everybody was involved in the practical aspects. Everybody had ideas, so no one could be called the single originator. In 1961 we made a decision about minorities: that we would register the unregistered Negroes. We held a series of meetings at the Mayflower [Hotel in Washington] with the leaders of various minority—especially Negro—groups . . . All these discussions were about the problem, not how to proceed. The Negro vote was good if we could cultivate it. [But] how do you get enough money?

About March [1964] it was agreed with Matt Reese to do a volunteer Voter Registration drive. This involved budget and personnel, and it was integrated with the National Voters Registration Program. All this was the result of thinking in June 1963. I did some of the initiating, but I don't think any one person makes a decision . . . In that same meeting I presented the idea to get money to put the President on TV. I wanted some project, other than registration, where women could be out doing something for the President . . . [and] we would have gotten $100,000 if we wouldn't have run into competition from Maguire. The decision was made with the Chairman [John Bailey] and Maguire in '63 that we could do this—and then we had to wait, and relook. The main finance drive was going and we were stopped—and we didn't start again until after the convention.

Thus between 1961 and 1963, various programs with promising applications to the 1964 campaign emerged within the National Committee, pushed by leaders trying to strengthen their own areas of specialization and responsibility. The resulting operations reflected a complex process of integration with other programs, and of bargaining among leaders with different interests and bases of power in the White House-National Committee-state party-interest group system. Negro groups, for example, influenced state leaders (such as governors and mayors), the White House, and congressmen to support National Committee programs (e.g., registration) of concern to them. At the same time, they worked directly to organize and finance these programs with the Committee leaders responsible for them. The leaders could use this "clientele" support to press for Committee backing amidst intense competition for scarce resources. It is quite clear that the pattern of decision-making during this period was anything but Comprehensive. Rather than centralized initiative from the White House, pressures for action often arose from below, from a diverse array of interests and proponents, and decisions were reached as the result of many different interchanges in many different places.

Kennedy's November 12th (1963) meeting in the Cabinet Room revealed the fact that important questions had already been resolved, and many courses of action had already been taken, even if in a small way. The distribution of delegate seats at the National Convention, a strong registration effort, and the use of the National Committee as campaign headquarters—all had already begun.[7] New decisions tended to modify existing programs and to choose among a few alternatives.

The Coming of Lyndon B. Johnson

No less than for the nation as a whole, the death of President Kennedy came as a traumatic shock for the evolving campaign staff. There was every reason to anticipate demoralizing and, in the end, seriously disruptive effects. Yet two factors operated to minimize both. One was the new President's determined moves to achieve continuity. Within hours of the assassination, and continuing through the days that followed, Johnson moved decisively to keep the "Kennedy team" intact and to make it his own.[8] At neither the White House nor the National Committee were there major replacements or even notable changes in personnel. Although addressed to Congress and the nation, Johnson's words, "Let us continue," applied equally to the world of Democratic politics. Stephen Smith (John Kennedy's brother-in-law), who had come to the National Committee in September and was to be its Executive Director, soon left, and Clifton Carter (a long-time associate of and campaigner for the new President) later replaced him; but otherwise the staff remained substantially as it had been.

The second factor was more subtle and is expressed in the following remarks by a Committee leader:

.. Steve [Smith] came, and then there was a problem between Smith and X, and Smith and Y. Y and I had problems. After the assassination, we buried the hatchet. We saw that a lot of this was pretty trivial. Power lessened. Your sense of security was less. But people began getting down to the real job [of preparing for the campaign] .

Thus the fragmentation, which could have been expected to increase, actually declined. Lyndon Johnson did not follow Kennedy's practice of selecting a number of close political associates—Robert Kennedy, Kenneth O'Donnell Lawrence O'Brien, for example—who could speak for him and serve as divergent sources of power in the National Committee and elsewhere. Instead, "he gave the impression that the President was involved in the details fairly intimately, much more than Kennedy."

At the same time it should not be inferred that the President began at once to intervene at the party headquarters. Despite the definite uncertainties and emotional shock, a common remark by the political leaders preparing for the campaign was, "I found things a little easier under Johnson"—a feeling that was, of course, not universally shared by all members of the White House staff and the National Committee. Each of these persons had his own situation, his own understanding of what was involved in the transfer of presidential power, and his own image of the incoming President. But each knew that the nature of this President would affect every aspect of his work.

If the character of Barry Goldwater was a pervasive element in Republican decison-making, it is even more apparent that the style and personality of Lyndon B. Johnson had a direct bearing upon Democratic practices. Goldwater's effect upon the process of decision-making began long before 1964. I took many forms and molded the very context within which decisions had to be made. The impact of Lyndon Johnson, on the other hand, was at once more direct, more dominant, and more restricted.

As political types, the two candidates were a study in contrasts. These contrasts are particularly relevant because they are cues to the different way the men guided campaign decision-making. They also help to explain the personal relationship between the two and their feelings toward each other

The first contrast involved power. Barry Goldwater was uncomfortable in the presence of power. We have seen that he neither sought it for himself, nor admired it as an instrument of social policy, nor developed complex skills in its exercise. Lyndon Johnson's desire for power and his facility in its use have become a legend in his own time. Within the arena of congressional politics he was a master of interpersonal influence. He used power; he enjoyed power and he aspired to power. From the very start of his public career, he had been its warm and devoted student.

No man in American history became President with a greater relish for power or with more experience in its exercise than did Lyndon B. Johnson . . . .

. . . Through all of [the many Johnsons] runs a common theme: the theme of power, unifying all his disparate sides. Whether exhibitionistic or unpretentious, whether considerate or insensitive, the single thrust of his long career has been the acquisition and the use of power. Johnson was born with the instinct of power, and long before he reached the White House he knew exactly where it rested, how to obtain it, and most important, how to exercise it—sometimes with restraint, sometimes without.[9]

The new President's orientation to power was not simple, either in its dimensions or in its explanations. The extent of his ambitions, and the intensity of his concentration and frustration, mark Johnson as an inviting subject of future psychological analysis.[10] For us, however, too little is known about his childhood and early adolescence to make speculations worthwhile. It is as a practicing politician from the hill country of Texas that we have the story of Lyndon Johnson, stretching back to 1931.[11] Late in November of that year, Richard M. Kleberg, a manager of the King ranch, won a special election to Congress from the 14th district. He took Lyndon Johnson, then 23 years old, along to Washington as his secretary. Johnson had done manual labor, worked his way through Southwest Texas State Teachers College, taught a grade-school class (mostly of poor Mexican-American children), and, following his graduation, had also taught public speaking for more than a year in a Houston high school. Reinforced by the influence of his mother, an elocution teacher herself, this short career in education left lasting impressions upon Johnson. It helped shape his sympathy for better schools, especially for underprivileged children. But teaching was not enough. His ambitions were greater. The evidence we have indicates that throughout these early years Lyndon Johnson struggled to distinguish himself, to do better than others, and to expand his career.

He did not start from the bottom, though the bottom was clearly visible from where he lived and worked as a youth. His father, Sam E. Johnson, had been a successful businessman and the Johnsons were part of what others have called the "gentry of Blanco county." They held this status despite the serious losses Sam Johnson suffered in the 1921 depression which plagued the family during the entire decade. For young Johnson, times were hard and life was hard. He was no stranger to extreme poverty and deprivation. But the life of his father and of his grandfather before him gave Lyndon concrete standards of individual initiative and accomplishment, and sufficient status to ease his initial steps.

Johnson's grandfather had served in the Texas legislature as a Populist, and his father, also a member of the legislature, was deeply involved in the political life of the state. As a boy, Johnson was thus intimately exposed to the language and concerns of politics. Our knowledge of political socialization, of the influence of the family on later political thinking and activity, makes it clear that this political interest, experience, and encouragement of his family was an important factor in Lyndon's background. (When he was born, his grandfather is said to have exclaimed, "A United States Senator was born tonight!")[12] It is true that while a student he served as secretary to the college president; but the youthful teacher might never have come to the attention of Representative-elect Kleberg had his father been unknown in the political community.

If the sketchy outlines of these early Texas years do not reveal the source of Lyndon Johnson's intense drive for power, they do suggest the initial lessons he learned about the techniques—how power was to be achieved and exercised. Political results were not gained by verbalizing lofty principles or sending written memos from remote positions of constitutional authority. They were achieved instead by direct, personal influence over the men whose support was needed to get something done. Such men knew what they wanted; they had to be persuaded through argument, intimidation, and pay-offs that their own interests would best be served by going along. In this process there was no substitute for personal contact and understanding. The most forceful application of personality and reasoning, tailored to fit the individual needs and weaknesses of fellow leaders, was required for the exercise of power. It was no task for the faint-hearted or the amateur.

As he served his Washington apprenticeship with Kleberg, returning to Texas in 1935 as state director of the National Youth Administration, and then, in 1937, in running for and winning a congressional seat of his own, Johnson learned and perfected these techniques of personal influence. He served through six consecutive terms of Congress (with time out for a seven-month leave as a Naval Reserve officer following Pearl Harbor), lost a special election to the Senate in 1941, and then came back (by an 87-vote margin) to enter the Senate in 1948. There he became Minority Leader in 1953 and Majority Leader in 1955. Known as "The Treatment," Johnson's techniques of influence became a legend. Here is how they are described by Evans and Novak:

The Treatment could last 10 minutes or four hours. It came, enveloping its target, at the LBJ Ranch swimming pool, in one of LBJ's offices, in the Senate cloakroom, on the floor of the Senate itself—wherever Johnson might find a fellow Senator within his reach. Its tone could be supplication, accusation, cajolery, exuberance, scorn, tears, complaint, the hint of threat . . . Its velocity was breathtaking, and it was all in one direction. Interjections from the target were rare. Johnson anticipated them before they could be spoken. He moved in close, his face a scant millimeter from his target, his eyes widening and narrowing, his eyebrows rising and falling. From his pockets poured clippings, memos, statistics. Mimicry, humor, and a genius for analogy made The Treatment an almost hypnotic experience and rendered the target stunned and helpless.

One Texas politician who was talked into changing his mind on a key issue by Johnson explained that he really had no choice. "Lyndon got me by the lapels," he said, "and put his face on top of mine and talked and talked and talked. I figured it was either getting drowned or joining."[13]

The political philosophy of The Treatment eschewed a commitment to ideology for a commitment to effective legislation. Ralph K. Huitt stresses this point in his analysis of Johnson's leadership in the Senate. He quotes Johnson himself:

"The thing you must understand is that no man comes to the Senate on a platform of doing what is wrong. They will come determined to do what is right. The difficulty is finding an area of agreement. . . ." To do that, "first you must have a purpose and an objective and the vision to try to outline what the national interest requires, what the national need is. Then you lay that on the table, and are as reasonably patient and as effective as you can be, from a persuasive standpoint."

This is the way to "do the possible" and pass bills—the pragmatist's test of legislative achievement. . . .

What emerged from Johnson's own statements and from examples of his work was the view that good legislation is not the product of oratory and debate but of negotiation and discussion, designed not to make issues but to find common ground that equal, independent and dissimilar men could occupy.[14]

But for Lyndon Johnson these methods were more than just mechanisms of policy achievement. He enjoyed them. They, and the elaborate patterns of social goals and activities that he wove around them, were a fascination and satisfaction in themselves. They were Johnson's politics, and his interest in politics was consuming, unrelenting, and unrelieved. The enormous energy and force of personality reflected in The Treatment were not unleashed only on weekdays or between the day-time hours of 9:00 and 5:00. For Johnson, politics was a full-time, all-encompassing vocation. There was no room for the type of diversion Barry Goldwater found in shortwave radio or desert photographs.

. . . the fact is that Johnson's job is politics, his hobby is politics. He does some hunting, cattle-counting and fence-checking when he is in Texas but his chief activity with friends is talking. And the only subject he stays on for any length of time is politics and politicians.[15]

This single-minded concentration on the affairs of political life has often been attributed to deep-seated needs for personal achievement and the admiration of others. In any case, many commentators have remarked about Johnson's combination of immense, restless energy, a complete devotion to politics, and personal vanity. Theodore White describes him:

> This was not a vanity of person so much as an obsession with self; and an obsession with self and self-performance so deep as to recall all the insecurities and awkwardness he had first brought with him to Washington from the hardship and reaching of his past. As a young Congressman back in the Roosevelt days, he was remembered as one of the best, most vigorous and earthiest conversationalists of the younger thinkers who were then remaking America. But he could go to a dinner party, talk like a man possessed of enormous force, then, when the conversation passed to someone else, droop his head, doze off in weariness as others talked, then come awake and seize the conversation by main force and carry it back to himself.[16]

Propelled by these inner forces, Johnson had driven himself unmercifully. The heart attack he suffered in 1955 interrupted, but did not permanently alter, the intensity of his drives and activities or his sensitivity to criticism.

Johnson's political abilities received less exercise after 1960. His frustrations over the lack of power and the slender opportunities to use his energy and skill, as Vice President, were well known to close associates. He understood the limitations of his position, and kept his feelings in check. As President, however, there were no such limitations, and Johnson plunged into the role with all his resources and all the techniques he had developed in the House and Senate. Long after the first blush of novelty and excitement had passed, the personal characteristics that distinguished the "Speaker" of the "little Congress,"* the Texas politician, and the Majority Leader of the Senate, were seen in the presidency. Professional observers found this a source of comment and concern:

> The restless pace of [Lyndon Johnson's] life and his unrelieved concentration on his work are such a source of wonder to his aides that they are constantly afraid he will go beyond the point of human endurance. . . .
> . . . the Johnson system of government is enough to fell a brewery horse. He is still trying to run the Presidency as if it were merely a continuation of his one-man show in the Senate. He has to be in on everything. He is uneasy with institutions [and] finds it difficult to delegate responsibility. . . .
> From this savage routine he has no escape, unless it is the ranch, and even there he works with much the same ferocious energy. His only game is politics, his only relief, good news.[17]

---

*This was an unofficial gathering of congressional secretaries. Johnson won the distinction while he worked for Kleberg. It was an early sign of his political abilities. White, *The Making of the President 1964*, p. 38.

This was the Democratic candidate in 1964. He was a man who strove for power, who loved politics, who hungered for personal recognition and public approval. His political style was vigorous, intense, personal, verbal, and tough. His experience in American politics and government was vast. He assumed the office of president as a strong professional politician, confident of his knowledge and skills. His power was now bolstered by the preeminent authority of his office. In personal confrontations he exhausted associates and intimidated opponents. "He dominated any room by walking into it and any conference by taking his seat."[18] One of the campaign leaders who worked closely with the President remarked that when the two candidates met in the White House to discuss ground rules of the campaign, "Goldwater was scared to death of Johnson, in every way . . . He [Goldwater] didn't say much." Even if we discount the partisan tone of this comment, it is clear that most men found a competitive encounter with Lyndon Johnson to be a trying experience.

It is now also apparent that more than power marked the personal characteristics that separated the decision-making patterns of the two leaders. Their attitudes toward politics, their commitment to ideology, their styles of personal influence and expression, and their political experience, were others. Each characteristic had a discernible effect upon the way they made decisions and the way they related to other decision-makers. Barry Goldwater's background and personality had a manifold impact upon the Republican campaign. The more immediate influence of the Democratic President's approach to decision-making can be seen in the initial "Johnson take-over." The message went out to every Democratic leader that the new President wanted to know and approve of all campaign plans. Meetings were arranged between the President and a large proportion of these men. A smaller but still substantial number made frequent visits to the White House. A few were in almost daily contact with the President.

Leaders of the formal party apparatus were, however, only a segment of the whole group with whom Lyndon Johnson discussed party politics and the forthcoming campaign. There were many others, and altogether they reflected the President's quarter century of political life. Some were "bright young men" of Roosevelt's New Deal, others were old friends from Texas, others were trusted members of his Senatorial staff, and still others, of course, were inherited directly from John F. Kennedy. Within this group was a diversity of political styles and views, and much experience. There were many strong personalities, and there were powerful political figures in their own right. All members of this extended group were not equally close to Johnson, but he talked and listened to an impressive number of them before making his decisions.

As a decision-maker, the President was not impulsive, and he certainly was not "pushable." He dominated his staff and had a tendency to make demands that were excessive and arbitrary. Precisely how he finally reached decisions was usually shrouded in mystery.

But it is . . . known that the President's decision-making is an arcane process; he absorbs the opinion all around him, lets it percolate inside him in some mysterious, instinctual way and then issues a decision "when it is ready." This makes it difficult for any one person to be sure what part he played in the President's decisions.[19]

There was no mystery about his unwillingness to rush ahead.

In order "to be able to move right or left or backwards or forwards," the President refuses to make up his mind until the last minute—and even then, after the last minute, he is likely to change it. . . .

"He's as cautious as an old coyote," a Texas friend has said. "He'll lift his muzzle to the wind and sniff, then he'll trot on a few feet and smell the spoor, and lift his muzzle to the wind again."[20]

With his caution against final commitments, his determination not to be "boxed in" by decisions of others, his desire for many and divergent opinions before making a choice, his sensitivity to criticism, his eagerness to deal personally with other leaders, and his tendency to make last-minute changes, Lyndon Johnson combined motivations and techniques which would open the way for Incrementalism. His impulse "not to let go," to control even minor decisions of those around him, made him by no means the perfect Incrementalist. But his keen judgment of what was politically effective following a martyred predecessor led him to choose campaign leaders of exceptional experience and competence. The effect of these men, as they operated within the "natural" circumstances of a presidential campaign, was to counterbalance Johnson's wish to be in on everything and to reinforce other aspects of his personal style which fostered Incremental decision-making.

Notes on Chapter 9

[1]Theodore H. White, *The Making of the President 1964* (New York: Atheneum, 1965), p. 294. Rowland Evans and Robert Novak take a sharply different view, however. They remark: "His campaign organization–disorganization was the better word–defied schematic description." *Lyndon B. Johnson: The Exercise of Power* (New York: The New American Library, 1966), p. 466.

[2]Good presentations and analyses of 1964 voting data can be found in *Election '64: A Ripon Society Report* (Cambridge: Ripon Society, 1965); Harold Faber, ed., *The Road to the White House* (New York: McGraw-Hill, 1965), pp. 270 ff.; White, *The Making of the President 1964*, Ch. 13; and Richard M. Scammon, ed., *America at the Polls* (Pittsburgh, Pa.: Public Affairs Press, 1965).

[3]In general, Robert Kennedy came off poorly and Kenneth O'Donnell very well in the assessments made to us four years later. For example, "Bobby Kennedy was an amateur. Kenny O'Donnell did his thinking for him."

[4]White, *The Making of the President 1964*, p. 28.

[5]The location of the DNC has been relatively stabilized in recent years at 1730 K Street. While this is only a few blocks from the White House, it is not across the street or down the hall. We shall have more to say later about the effects of physical distance on political relationships and decision-making.

[6]The authoritative statement on the National Committees does not emphasize this point, but contains material supporting it. See Cornelius P. Cotter and Bernard C. Hennessy, *Politics Without Power* (New York: Atherton, 1964), Chs. 4 and 5, in particular.

[7]White, *The Making of the President 1964*, p. 28, gives a faithful account for the meeting but places too little emphasis on the decisions which preceded it. See Faber, ed., *The Road to the White House*, pp. 152-153.

[8]Evans and Novak, *Lyndon B. Johnson*, pp. 338-344 ff.

[9]Evans and Novak, pp. 1, 4.

[10]For notable instances of such analysis, see Alexander L. George and Juliette L. George, *Woodrow Wilson and Colonel House* (New York: Dover Publications, 1964); and Sigmund Freud and William C. Bullitt, *Thomas Woodrow Wilson: Twenty-Eighth President of the United States: A Psychological Study* (Boston: Houghton-Mifflin, 1967).

[11]The descriptions of Lyndon Johnson's youth and early career tend to be quite repetitive in their details. The best are Evans and Novak, *Lyndon B. Johnson*, Ch. 2; Faber, ed., *The Road to the White House*, Ch. 12; White, *The Making of the President 1964*, esp. Ch. 2; and William S. White, *The Professional: Lyndon B. Johnson* (Boston: Houghton-Mifflin, 1964), Chs. 6-9.

[12]Faber, ed., *The Road to the White House*, p. 127.

[13]Faber, ed., pp. 104, 229. Also see Ralph K. Huitt, "Democratic Party Leadership in the Senate," *American Political Science Review*, 55 (June 1961), pp. 333-334, esp. p. 338.

[14]Huitt, pp. 337, 341.

[15]Ben H. Bagdikian, "The 'Inner Inner Circle' Around Johnson," *New York Times Magazine*, Feb. 28, 1965, p. 78.

[16]White, *The Making of the President 1964*, pp. 53-54.

[17]James Reston, *The New York Times,* Nov. 4, 1966. The same point is emphasized in Faber, ed., *The Road to the White House,* pp. 134-135.

[18]Tom Wicker, "Lyndon Johnson is 10 Feet Tall," *The New York Times Magazine,* May 23, 1965, p. 23.

[19]Bagdikian, "The 'Inner Inner Circle' Around Johnson," p. 84.

[20]Stewart Alsop, "The Face of the President 1966," *Saturday Evening Post* (Sept. 24, 1966), p. 24.

10

"Let Us Continue"—The Opening Pattern of Democratic Decision-Making

In the early months of the election year indications persisted that the President intended to build upon, not supplant, the campaign plans and personnel already in place and operation. By February the National Committee had been significantly enlarged with Johnson appointees, yet with very few exceptions, they did not replace resident staff members. Decisions also had been reached about additional facilities and certain basic organizational features for the campaign. The process of this decision-making had several characteristics which were to be found throughout the rest of the year.

Basic Decisions in the Pre-Campaign Period

First, the President was boss. He did not delegate campaign authority. But the change from Kennedy's practice was subtle, reflected mainly in the conviction that Johnson himself wanted to be fully informed about what was going on and would say so if he did not like what he heard. In actual practice, Committee and other campaign leaders were careful to send reports about their plans and operations to the White House, but only a few—Clifton Carter (DNC Executive Director), Kenneth O'Donnell (Executive Director of the Campaign), Richard Maguire (DNC Treasurer), and to a lesser extent John Bailey (DNC

Chairman)—were in direct contact with the President. At this early stage of campaign preparations, Lyndon Johnson was indeed the boss, but great fragmentation persisted in the processes of decision. It was caused by functional specialization, the shortage of time and money, and the lack of direct communications between many operating heads and the White House.

Second, there was no overarching strategy giving explicit cues about substance and timing to the various decision-makers. Rather, the obvious fact of an approaching election, experience in and understanding of what a campaign involved, and the diverse realizations by party leaders that they had better "come up with something," generated a situation in which decisions and pressures for decisions were coming from numerous individuals and groups in the party structure. The universal belief that the White House could veto, or ignore, or be displeased with any proposal also led to considerable restraint in carrying plans forward independently. But this belief did not lead to strategy. The fragmentation can be seen in the following statements by some of the top leaders about early strategy-making.

We had the thing laid out, from the organization standpoint, early in February. That is, we decided to have state coordinators and to run the campaign through the National Committee. Strategy is something you devise day by day. Our basic strategy all the way through was to show that the President had a firm hand on the switch. That he was responsible, experienced, and generally a man to have confidence in.

In the first place, our overall plan was revised three times.... The reason for an early strategy plan was to give us a frame of reference.... That early, of course, there was no clear feeling about who [the Republican candidate] would be. [But] strategy is not too much dictated by the opposition nominee. We worked out priority areas ... a 12-state priority.

I came in January [1964]. There was very little long-term planning, but discussions and decisions about the campaign were made from the very beginning.

It is quite clear that certain strategic-type decisions were reached or reaffirmed quite early. Target states and areas were selected, as were images that the President and his campaign would try to project. Money-raising schemes were developed to produce the needed revenue. But few of these plans had the scope to be called a strategy, and those that did were exceedingly vague. The exception was the designation of target states in the Voter Identification Program, yet this rather sophisticated registration plan, based on the assumption of a relatively close election, seemed less relevant as the expansion of Johnson's victory became an alluring possibility.[1] It tended to be watered down during the summer and fall.

Third, almost all of the decisions made by early February were continuations of decisions that had been reached earlier. Some had been implemented and could be seen in on-going programs. These included the decision to run the campaign through the National Committee, the selection of techniques and target areas for the registration program, and the definition of the basic image to be presented of President Johnson (a firm, responsible man, in full and sober control). Some of these early choices had been rather formal and institutionalized (e.g., at the National Committee meeting in November 1963), while others were the result of diverse patterns of individual action, especially at the Committee level. Still others, such as the use of state coordinators and the organization of citizens groups, were dominated by the traditions of campaign politics. The spirit of overall coherence was at this point limited to those in direct contact with the President—men like O'Donnell, Carter, Maguire, Walter Jenkins, and Bill D. Moyers. For them, campaign planning was simple and sensible, as yet unsullied by complications of many competing projects and leaders, and eased by the strong position of an incumbent President.

Lyndon Johnson was moving deliberately to gain control over the existing party organization and to give unified direction to the development of a campaign design and apparatus. He expanded or modified existing plans and staff, thus minimizing bitterness over lost jobs and programs and the confusion of new leadership. His task was significantly reduced by the common belief among party and White House leaders that the President *is* the boss; that every element of the political situation is his business; and that the campaign of an incumbent president *is,* ultimately, run from the White House. One campaign leader, and close friend of the President, expressed it this way:

The President was the man. . . . You've got to remember that the Democratic Committee was unimportant. This is always the case when you've got the White House. Johnson was going to run the campaign. He was going to do the scheduling. . . . He never lets go of anything. I've learned that he's like all politicians: he keeps the reins in his hands.

In these early months of 1964 the President evolved a pattern of relationships through which he "kept the reins in his hands," and which he was not to alter markedly for the remainder of the campaign. It was a pattern of direct contact with a substantial number of individuals immediately in charge of some particular aspect of the campaign—Carter (state coordinators), Moyers (television and radio), Maguire (money)— during this early period. Later, other names, such as Wilson McCarthy (scheduling), Lawrence O'Brien (state party organizations), and James Rowe (citizens groups), would be added. Still other individuals, including Jack Valenti, Walter Jenkins, Abe Fortas, Myer Feldman, and Mrs. Johnson, played key roles in transmitting the President's wishes to operating leaders.[2]

The participants in February White House meetings with the President felt that campaign strategy was well in hand and reported little disagreement except over who the Republican candidate was likely to be.* It was a decision-making situation of unusual equanimity for a political campaign. The reasons for this calmness are not hard to find. First, Johnson leaders were veteran politicians. Within their experience, the "logic of the situation" left little room for alternative strategies. The unwritten rules of campaigning were quite explicit for incumbent presidents, and the potential Democratic vote among the unregistered poor and Negroes was equally apparent. Very few of the innumerable alternative strategies were seriously explored; available knowledge and information confirmed the wisdom of the strategy selected. There was no need to search further. Second, this strategy grew out of programs already begun, offices already in place, and conditions known to exist. Third, disagreements about scarce resources and tactical implementation had not yet occurred or were far down the line of authority. These disagreements were destined to become increasingly important, but in February they were still "submerged" as far as White House strategy-makers were concerned.

We have discussed this early pre-campaign period in some detail in order to show that while Lyndon Johnson moved vigorously to organize both decisions and decision-makers, neither the people nor the plans sprang full-grown from a few Comprehensive decisions. In the face of widespread expectations of a "Texas takeover," the President acted gracefully to keep the best of the Kennedy leaders and to introduce his own in a very piecemeal fashion. Clifton Carter came to the National Committee as Executive Director in February, but rather than "take over," he shared operating leadership with Bailey and Maguire. At the same time Kenneth O'Donnell and Lawrence O'Brien—experienced Kennedy men—were being integrated into the decision process; both were later to have offices in the Committee (although O'Brien never used his).

---

*It is worth emphasizing this point, first made on p. 2, above. Until the California primary, very few Democratic leaders could bring themselves to believe the Republicans would actually nominate Senator Goldwater. In the words of one of their top men, a distinguished professional, "I had said we wouldn't be so lucky as to get Goldwater. He would be their weakest candidate."

Hence the President had not one but many direct contacts with what was going on at the Committee and with the operating aims of the developing campaign. Strategic decisions were indeed made by a relatively small group of individuals meeting with the President. Their strategic choices reflected an adherence to existing programs and to traditional patterns of campaign operation, not an exhaustive review of alternative possibilities. And their frank uncertainty about their opponent's identity was "absorbed" by plans which would work "for any Republican candidate."

Coordination at the Democratic National Committee

The months of March, April, and May saw an accelerated build-up of campaign staff and facilities through the elaboration of existing programs and the launching of several new projects of major significance. With the consequent expansion in the number and diversity of decisions, there was a clear need for coordination. Since the campaign was to be "run through the National Committee," it seemed logical to set up specific adjustment devices there. The President made continuing and aggressive efforts to keep important matters within his immediate grasp, so one of the first objectives was to coordinate the National Committee and the White House. The resulting arrangements had mixed success. Some worked as planned. Others worked well, but in ways that had not been anticipated. A few failed. Finally, there was coordination that occurred without conscious design which we think was particularly important. Nonetheless, the formal, visible mechanisms made a deep impression upon Democratic leaders who had participated in previous campaigns and found this one a masterpiece of wisdom, coherence, and harmony.

Perhaps the most important of these formal coordinating devices were the weekly staff meetings, held every Monday morning in Chairman Bailey's office, and attended by Division chiefs and heads of other major operations. As spring advanced, these meetings proved to be effective occasions for middle-level communication, quick minor decisions, information from the White House, and feedback to the President from program heads through O'Donnell, Carter, or others. Regular participants were enthusiastic about the effectiveness of the sessions in providing information and expediting decisions. Presided over by John Bailey, they were informal yet to the point. They were exceptionally useful in giving operating leaders a place to ask questions or express discontent before their problems became unmanageable. And they gave their participants a sense of familiarity with the campaign as a whole.

Another formal device was less successful. All hiring and salary decisions were to be made by Bailey, Carter, and Maguire together—a triumvirate generally recognized as governing the National Committee. This arrangement worked quite well for the first six months of the year but broke down as the campaign heated up and the three men became increasingly occupied with other matters.

A less explicit coordinating mechanism was Richard Maguire himself. Theodore White calls him "one of the most silent and most important men in America's politics, as inscrutable as he is efficient."[3] An experienced, strong-minded politician from the Kennedy campaign, Maguire participated personally in all matters of finance. Unless the White House intervened directly, he was able to veto or at least delay any decision that involved the raising and spending of money. He was not easily intimidated. One man who worked closely with the White House on the controversial advertising program remarked:

[Maguire's] the man who had the guts to say that even though the President approved [of a project], he wouldn't go for it. He would go to the President himself.[4]

This added to the late arrival of substantial segments of the budget, led to repeated cases in which authorized programs were delayed or altered by the Treasurer's intervention and the lack of funds. Money, of course, is an endemic problem in political campaigns, but its impact upon Democratic decision-making in 1964 is of greater interest than is usually supposed. From the White House down, the budget was recognized by Democratic leaders as a potent instrument of central program control. But the budget became in fact a pervasive resource of bargaining and mutual adjustment in the hands of the Treasurer. Instances of Division and program chiefs negotiating with Maguire for funds occurred almost daily. A number of such instances will be evident as we describe the campaign, and we shall return to the coordinating effects of this process in Chapter 11.

Another early device of decision coordination was the *Political News Summary* prepared by the office of News and Information, headed by Wayne Phillips. The *News Summary* was written during the night and distributed each morning throughout the Washington campaign organization. Its two to four pages of accurate, pungent, and witty reporting kept the Democratic staff abreast of campaign developments, with emphasis on the thrusts and parries of the opposing presidential and vice presidential candidates. Its avid readership testified to its sustained quality. Measurements of its specific influences on campaign decision-making remain impossible. But there were many indications that the *Summary* provided a sense of community and a base of information for staff members at every level.

The weekly staff meetings, the Bailey-Carter-Maguire triumvirate, and Maguire's exchequer, were three National Committee mechanisms consciously designed to impose order and direction upon Democratic decisions early in the campaign. Their way was to be eased and smoothed by the *News Summary*. Overshadowing everything else was the President. His desire to control campaign events directly and in detail was sensed by everyone. Sometimes his efforts to exercise personal overhead coordination seemed to match this desire. As such they introduced distinct Comprehensive elements into Democratic decision-making. The results—often unanticipated—may be seen in early choices concerning TV advertising, political research, and the "Great Society." Together, these were to have interesting effects upon both the content and procedures of the subsequent campaign.

To Create the Image

The advent of Doyle Dane Bernbach

Perhaps the most interesting set of early decisions involved the use of television.[5] In September 1963, John Kennedy, already impressed by the advertising work of the Doyle Dane Bernbach agency, asked his newly appointed campaign director, Stephen Smith, to talk with the agency about taking the Democratic account for the forthcoming campaign. Kennedy liked their ads for commercial products and thought they might be equally good in politics. "He saw a Volkswagon ad with the headline, 'Think Small.' It was the kind of thing that appealed to his sense of humor."[6] Doyle Dane Bernbach (DDB) was strongly Democratic. Its leaders were attracted by the challenge of a political account, and they got along famously with Smith.[7] By February 1964, however, as Johnson began to organize his own campaign, serious opposition to DDB had developed within the Democratic Committee, particularly on the part of such veteran politicians as Maguire and Bailey. Over the years, in a very Incremental fashion, Democratic party leaders came to accept the use of an advertising agency, but they were accustomed to agencies which were unassuming and inexpensive. DDB was neither. An immediate issue was production costs. Past Democratic agencies had absorbed them; DDB would not.[8] In the words of one participant in the discussion:

Some people in the Committee were disgruntled. After all, there were other agencies less expensive than DDB . . . and they had friends on the Committee. . . . I came in when the survey was being made. There were three agencies left at that point. . . . It was [Lloyd Wright's] judgment that the agency which offered to absorb some of the production costs, etc., could not do the job. So [he] made a strong recommendation for the agency which was hired. There was some disagreement with this.

The manner of reaching the decision to retain Doyle Dane Bernbach set a pattern that would be repeated throughout the campaign. The President had designated his White House Assistant, Bill D. Moyers, to be in charge of all his media and speech coordination in the campaign. Moyers in turn suggested Lloyd Wright as Media Coordinator for the Democratic Committee and the White House. Moyers had worked with Wright in the Peace Corps, and the two young men liked and respected each other. Wright reached the Committee in March just in time to review the agencies being considered and to plump for DDB. He made this choice on the basis of what he saw as their clear superiority in advertising quality. Wright argued that "you get what you pay for." DDB, he said, was respected among the mass media, and had "the knowledge of what media delivers what audiences at what time, and . . . the creative ability to present materials."[9] For their part, Committee and many other veteran campaign leaders felt that the price was too high, especially in view of the shortage of money and the lack of any pressing need for highly sophisticated advertising. After all, "an incumbent President commands full television coverage" anyway. One leader who shared these views was particularly important: "Dick [Maguire] felt the election was so secure that he didn't think we needed to spend the money . . . money that would be hard to collect."

Here was a decision-making situation in which values and perceptions of reality were clearly in conflict. For Wright, "creativity" was worth paying for. He felt it was needed to increase the President's vote and to raise the educational quality of the campaign. For the party leaders, creativity in advertising was overrated, and was certainly less important than other facets of the campaign, some of which would have to be sacrificed because of the high cost of DDB. They were dubious about the political impact of the agency's unusual plans, and in any case they saw little need for additional public support that would have to be purchased at such an "outrageous" price. For Lyndon Johnson the promise of more votes was compelling; he backed Wright. A process of decision initiated by John Kennedy had produced a choice, but its effects were just beginning. The use of TV and radio, and of advertising agencies to manage the programming, had been an accepted part of Democratic campaigns since 1952, but until now program content had been the province of the political leadership. Indeed, no less than the "O'Brien Manual" insisted that an agency might well handle production, but only political leaders should determine the content of campaign advertising.[10]

Wright began in April to work closely with the DDB staff on campaign "themes and story lines." He had to spend considerable time in New York City, where DDB had assigned about forty people to the Democratic account. Their aim, concurred in by the White House, was to "draft a definite plan for the campaign on how to get through to the public." It was a vaulting, Comprehensive-type ambition, inviting vast amounts of research, complex decisions, and detailed coordination of a burgeoning campaign apparatus. Wright found this appealing, but some of his operating problems began to emerge at once. He described one of them in the following words:

> When I came in I understood my assignment as being responsible for TV and advertising. At a cocktail party in Bailey's apartment, some . . . person made a reference to the Monday morning staff meetings. I hadn't known anything about them. At that point Cliff [Carter] said he would depend upon Wayne [Phillips] to represent me. But it was obvious that I could not effectively coordinate this important aspect of the campaign while isolated from the political leadership. I asked to be included in the meetings.

Wright had been accustomed to clear lines of administrative authority and felt they must be established in the campaign if the media objectives were to be achieved. He also felt that he needed to work closely with people like Carter and Bailey, but "I found it almost impossible to meet with them because of the hectic pace." One factor was Wright's need to stay in daily contact with DDB in New York. A second was his physical location and his tiny staff. With one secretary, and an office at 1907 K Street rather than at the 1730 K headquarters, he was just far enough away from Maguire, Carter, Bailey, and O'Donnell to impede direct personal contact. What is more, each of these Committee leaders seemed to be continually on the go or on the telephone. The traditional pulling and hauling and free-wheeling administrative practices of the Committee leaders made even the staff meetings a disappointment for Wright. He responded by resorting to the White House and direct contact with Bill Moyers. Since Wright was seeking decisive, positive, coherent action, his frustrations with the National Committee are not surprising. Neither is his decision to cut through the Committee thicket by using his personal contacts at the White House. Partially freed from opposing considerations, the developing plans of DDB found the sympathetic ear of the President. Meanwhile, the breakdown of a continuing interchange between the agency and Wright on one hand, and the party "pros" on the other, widened the gulf of experience, functions, and viewpoints which separated them. As a coordinator between the National Committee and the White House, Wright failed.

The relationship between persons responsible for mass media publicity and other campaign leaders during this February to May period was to have profound effects upon decision-making later in the campaign. The relationship had begun with conflicting values and developed with each side adopting sharply different patterns of decision. DDB and Wright promoted a Comprehensive-type plan for campaign advertising and treated Democratic party leaders as part of a Comprehensive structure. Thus the agency concentrated on White House approval rather than on trying to generate extensive support from the "pros" of the National Committee and elsewhere. The "pros" were accustomed to Incremental patterns involving consultation, bargaining, and a search for agreement. Some of these political leaders were opposed to DDB from the start, but many more became offended when they found themselves bypassed and ignored.

Interestingly enough, both of these patterns of decision found a place within Johnson's practice, clearly in evidence by April, of creating multiple and compressed hierarchies of authority radiating—not descending in a pyramid—from the White House. Responsibilities for campaign operations were handed to men with the understanding that their programs were to be formulated in consultation with the President. As this pattern of decision was conceived, Lyndon Johnson was the only agent of coordination. In the case of many decision-makers a great deal of mutual interaction occurred both in and out of the White House. In the case of Wright versus the "pros," however, there was very little of such interaction, and the basic concept of presidential coordination was given a direct test.

Numerous variations of this Johnson approach to central coordination occurred during the campaign. Two examples are the sets of decisions involving campaign information and research and the Great Society. [11]

The deployment of research

To fill his research needs, Lloyd Wright turned not to the National Committee's Research Division, but to Paul Southwick at the White House and the men of DDB. This illustrates both the low status of the Research Division and the common tendency for each campaign operation to do its own research. The result was a considerable amount of proliferation and redundancy and a generally low level of research sophistication within the DNC. Indeed, virtually all the "strategic" research for the campaign was done at or directly for the White House. Although by late spring the National Committee had a sizeable research staff, for the most part its work was limited to compilations of the administration's record, the votes of Republican congressmen, and speech materials for Democratic congressional candidates. Much of this was brought together in the *Democratic Fact Book,* which took months to draft as it passed back and forth between the Committee, the White House, and various government agencies that had pertinent data. Since what the Democratic party had promised in 1960, and what the Kennedy-Johnson administrations had delivered in the years that followed, were matters of considerable interpretive leeway, and since the *Fact Book's* multiple authors consulted at a distance, and then often by notation, there were intense irritations and frustrations on every side.

Committee researchers felt that their tasks were far removed from considerations of campaign strategy, and they were almost totally in the dark about what, if any, studies were being made of relevant public sentiments or electoral behavior. The "white backlash," for example, was being widely touted as a Democratic problem. It was a matter of keen interest to most members of the research staff, numerous Democratically-oriented social scientists in the academic community, and various concerned organizations. Yet there was no clue that systematic investigations into the scope or depth or political consequences of these backlash attitudes were even being contemplated. As far as the Research Division was concerned, the party leadership was indifferent to the problem and definitely not about to finance the complex opinion surveys that would be needed for a competent analysis. All this was at a time when these very surveys were being repeatedly commissioned and analyzed by the White House![12] Newspaper reports of Lyndon Johnson's fascination with opinion polls appeared almost daily, but the frustrated researchers had no way of appraising the quality of the polls being bandied about on the White House lawn.

The Research Division had long been the "sick man" of the Democratic National Committee, but it now suffered immediately from a lack of contact with the men at the top, specifically the President. The departure of William Keel as Director of Research in the second week of June gave the President an ideal opportunity to strengthen the Division at the top with a man of his own. To fill the position, Bill Moyers was instrumental in recruiting Frederick Dutton from the State Department. No political neophyte, Dutton had been Assistant Secretary of State for Congressional Relations, number two man to Byron R. (Whizzer) White in the 1960 Citizens for Kennedy and Johnson, and before that a top assistant to Governor Brown in California. He was an experienced and vigorous political campaigner and administrator. He also had direct access to the White House and was quite prepared to use it.

Sensing a new opportunity of their own, and reinforced by lieutenants that Dutton had brought with him, researchers in both the Committee and the academic community pressed proposals for systematic studies of voter attitudes and campaign issues (such as those relevant to the increasingly talked about backlash). Dutton was sensitive and generally sympathetic to these ideas. Johnson, however, demurred unequivocally, for this research was well underway at the White House. Not only that, but until September, Dutton was to be a very part-time Research Director. His first and major responsibility was to work directly through Moyers in drafting the party's platform for the Atlantic City Convention.

It was now clear that Johnson wanted the major substantive elements of campaign strategy to be formulated in the White House. Information which he thought could provide clues to what this strategy might be was kept strictly confidential. Even its existence went unrevealed. Cut off from information from above, various campaign operations sought to collect their own. Within the National Committee, research efforts were mounted by the Congressional Relations, Professors, and Special Registration programs. Each concentrated on its own needs. The same was true for the Democratic Congressional Campaign Committee and national labor organizations. In addition, various other operations took the easy way out by consulting Richard M. Scammon of the Census Bureau for voting data and technical advice.

During the first seven or eight months of 1964, the fact that the party organization had no strong, central research program caused painful irritation and discouragement in some quarters, yet it also contributed to an Incremental pattern of campaign decision-making. As various divisions went about collecting and analyzing their own information, they were able to use their findings as a basis for action and bargaining. Thus a certain amount of serendipity flowed from the weakness of the Research Division and Johnson's practice of monopolizing information where he could. Nevertheless, the President's secrecy had the effect of denying useful information to many campaign decision-makers, which led to both anger and wasted effort. Secrecy was a device of central control which hamstrung, but did not eliminate, the remedial and mutual adjustment elements of Incrementalism. What it did not achieve was central coordination.

Defining the Great Society

As early as February it was decided at the White House level that Lyndon Johnson was to be pictured as responsible, experienced, and firmly in control of the nation's military and governmental machinery. Formulated primarily by Kenneth O'Donnell, this "image" was subjected to no basic disagreement, mainly because no one conceived of an incumbent American President trying to look otherwise. As a theme of wisdom and responsibility, it emerged less from an exhaustive evaluation of alternatives than from converging "self-evident" traditions of election politics. It was strengthened further by issues of military irresponsibility being raised in the Republican primaries and the seemingly distant possibility that Goldwater would be the Republican candidate.

The selection of program issues, however, was more difficult, particularly because of the President's determination to find a distinguishing political position of his own—"a body of ideas that bore an LBJ brand,"[13] He and his speech writers, Richard Goodwin, Paul Southwick, and Bill Moyers, looked long and hard for a phrase and a set of ideas that would lend distinction and direction to his campaign and subsequent administration. Accepting an explicit commitment to the Kennedy and Johnson "record," they made no attempt to examine every possible alternative, or even all the consequences of a few alternatives. But many refinements of the basic themes of Democratic administrations reaching back to Roosevelt were tried out during the spring, both in private discussions and in a series of speeches and statements. The phrase, "better deal," was tried and dropped when it didn't seem to draw a response. On March 4th, Richard Goodwin drafted a speech which was never used, but which included the phrase, "great society." The President liked the concept and used variations on the phrase in a number of speeches in March and April. According to one count, he mentioned the "great society" in sixteen different statements during late April and early May,[14] assiduously gauging the feedback from the audience and the press. The result was the Great Society speech delivered at the University of Michigan on the 22nd of May. In describing the tortuous process of decision leading up to this speech, Theodore White remarks:

To appreciate both the phrase "Great Society" and its meaning, one must appreciate that exquisite process whereby ideas, maturing over decades of thought and stimulated by decades of change, first find form in the words of thinkers and scholars and then, slowly as they ripen, come to The King's Ear. . . . The decisions can be dated—but no one can say precisely where in the long flow of thinking any idea is born.[15]

The content of the Ann Arbor speech reflected a high degree of craftsmanship and eloquence. It also showed the results of the extremely Incremental process whereby the ideas were brought together. Concepts of progress, equality, justice, freedom, imagination, vigor, and opportunity were included. The speech integrated themes from the three preceding Democratic administrations—the New Deal, the Fair Deal, and the New Frontier—and from them set forth dramatic new goals to be achieved "in the cities, in our countryside, in our classrooms." And the values of beauty and excitement were articulated as public responsibilities. For the nation as a whole:

The Great Society rests on abundance and liberty for all. It demands an end to poverty and racial injustice, to which we are totally committed in our time. But that is just the beginning.

The Great Society is a place where every child can find knowledge to enrich his mind and to enlarge his talents. It is a place where leisure is a welcome chance to build and reflect, not a feared cause of boredom and restlessness. It is a place where the city of man serves not only the needs of the body and the demands of commerce, but the desire for beauty and the hunger for community . . .

For the cities:

. . . In the remainder of this century urban population will double, city land will double, and we have to build homes, highways and facilities equal to all those built since this country was first settled. So in the next 40 years we must rebuild the entire urban United States.

For the countryside:

. . . we have always prided ourselves on not only being America the strong, America the free, but America the beautiful. Today that beauty is in danger. The water we drink, the food we eat, the very air we breathe, are threatened with pollution. Our parks are over-crowded. Our seashores over-burdened. Green fields and dense forests are disappearing.

For the classrooms:

A . . . place to build the Great Society is in the classrooms of America. There your children's lives will be shaped. Our society will not be great until every young mind is set free to scan the furthest reaches of thought and imagination. We are still far from that goal. [There should be] for every child a place to sit and a teacher to learn from.

The ills deplored and the goals announced in the Great Society speech dovetailed neatly with the "achievements" of the Kennedy-Johnson administrations as set forth in the 1964 *Democratic Fact Book*. We have described how the *Fact Book* was begun by the National Committee's Research Division early in the spring, and then progressed painfully back and forth between government departments, White House advisers, and the Research staff, until it emerged in midsummer. Just as the Great Society speech was constructed Incrementally and reflected the Democratic "record," the *Fact Book* exhibited the concerns of the Great Society. Together, the speech and the *Book* served effectively as substantive campaign doctrine. They represented the knowledge and interests of many parts of the society, not to mention of the party and government. They provided an accessible, adaptable, and secure basis for all Democratic speeches and publicity materials.

It is hardly necessary to emphasize the contrast between the foregoing process of issue or position formulation and that pursued by the Goldwater leadership. Democratic decision-makers were intensely concerned with purposes and goals, but they showed little interest in defining or defending "first principles." The many goals presented were not deduced from a few superordinate values. They were drawn instead from overlapping themes—progress, justice, beauty, abundance— that covered the expressed needs and wants of diverse individuals and groups in the society. They were given urgency to the extent that certain needs were immediate and unfulfilled. Any group or interest, and especially those most deprived, could thus be mollified without sacrificing "principle." For the decision-makers, questions of what public policies to propose were answered by distributive, empirical evidence of who wanted what, how badly, and at what cost.

The Great Society speech and the *Fact Book* were accepted without question and variously elaborated. They formed a unifying source of positions and arguments for the different campaign programs operating out of Washington, and they were soon reflected in the party platform being drafted by Frederick Dutton from a White House vantage point. Only the advertising agency did not rely on this material almost in its original form. Doyle Dane Bernbach started work earlier and attempted to be more Comprehensive in its development of campaign themes. Thus the stage was set for divisive conflict within the Democratic campaign staff, when the two styles of decision-making would collide.

Notes on Chapter 10

[1]See Stanley Kelley, Jr., "The Presidential Campaign," in Milton C. Cummings, ed., *The National Elections of 1964* (Washington, D.C.: The Brookings Institution, 1966).

[2]Theodore White describes Johnson and his campaign leaders as "organized . . . on a radial, not a pyramidal model," with five "teams" radiating out from the President, each in close and direct touch with him on campaign tactics and strategy. *The Making of the President 1964* (New York: Atheneum, 1965), p. 348. Other important and marginally different descriptions of Democratic organization and the people close to Johnson may be found in: *Congressional Quarterly*, 22 (Oct. 16, 1964), 2447-2454; Ben Bagdikian, "The 'Inner Inner Circle' Around Johnson," *The New York Times Magazine*, Feb. 18, 1965. pp. 21 ff.; Rowland Evans and Robert Novak, *Lyndon B. Johnson: The Exercise of Power* (New York: The New American Library, 1966), esp. Chs. 20 and 21; Harold Faber, ed., *The Road to the White House* (New York: McGraw-Hill, 1965), pp. 135-140; and for one that is only peripherally related to the 1964 campaign, Charles Roberts, *LBJ's Inner Circle* (New York: Delacorte, 1965). Ben Bagdikian, "The 'Inner Inner Circle,' " mentions additional names but these were not repeated by our informants. The President, of course, met with other campaign leaders, too, but they were of a somewhat lower status at this point in campaign decision-making.

[3]*The Making of the President 1964*, p. 258.

[4]Shirley V. Robson, *Advertising and Politics: A Case Study of the Relationship between Doyle Dane Bernback, Inc., and the Democratic National Committee, during the 1964 Presidential Campaign* (M.A. thesis, The American University, Washington, D.C., April 1, 1966).

[5]We are particularly indebted to Shirley V. Robson for her work in *Advertising and Politics*. The evidence from her original research was in almost all respects consistent with our own information.

[6]Peter Hamill, "When the Client is a Candidate," *New York Times Magazine*, Oct. 25, 1964, p. 31.

[7]Robson, *Advertising and Politics*, pp. 2-3; and personal interviews.

[8]The Democratic party's gradual development of professional publicity in its presidential campaigns can be seen in Jack Redding, *Inside the Democratic Party* (New York: Bobbs-Merrill, 1958); and Stanley Kelley, Jr., *Professional Public Relations and Political Power* (Baltimore: Johns Hopkins University Press, 1956). Robson draws from these accounts and adds material of her own in *Advertising and Politics*.

[9]Robson, pp. 5-6; and personal interviews.

[10]"[An] agency should not be expected to determine campaign policy and strategy." *The Democratic Campaign Manual 1964* (Washington: The Democratic National Committee, 1964), p. 14.

[11]While it differs in some specifics, the detailed picture of Johnson's campaign staff and organization presented by Theodore White, *The Making of the President 1964*, pp. 347-356, is essentially the same as ours and supports the analysis of decision-making being made here.

[12]White, p. 257.

[13]White, p. 390.

[14]Evans and Novak, *Lyndon B. Johnson*, p. 426.

[15]White, *The Making of the President 1964*, pp. 387 ff.

11

Incrementalism in Action

Expanding the Campaign Office Space

Although the decision to run the campaign through the National Committee was made very early, at no time was there a Comprehensive blueprint for office space, equipment, personnel, or even major budgetary allocations. By January, the existing headquarters at 1730 K Street was clearly too small.* It was decided that rather than move the entire Committee, another building would be leased. This was about two blocks away at 1907 K Street. Several operations, especially News and Information, Research, and the Library, were moved there early in the spring. In April it was found that more space was needed, and another building, again about two blocks away at 1630 L Street, was occupied in May and June. Various printing and materials operations were moved in first, followed by others as more space was re-

---

*The DNC offices took up part of the 7th floor and part of the basement of the building, for a divided and very modest amount of total floor space. The 7th floor area was laid out, moreover, in the shape of a horseshoe, and not divided to accommodate the maximum number of people or different operations.

quired. Finally, in August and September, still another large building was gradually taken over, this one at 1025 15th Street, four blocks distant from the main headquarters.* The size of the total staff increased from less than one hundred in April to roughly five hundred in October.

Every decision to move was remedial. The cues tended to be the existence of leaders without offices or staff without desks. From many sources pressing demands for space would gradually build up to a point where "something had to be done" and a decision would be made. Richard Maguire, Clifton Carter, and usually John Bailey, helped choose the new buildings to lease; but almost every Committee leader played a number of day-by-day parts in reaching decisions about who was to be located where. It was always understood, whether true or not, that some locations, particularly those at 1730 K Street, were more desirable than others. The lack of long-term planning, together with such diverse pressures for space and facilities, resulted in a vast amount of moving and changing, both between buildings and within buildings. A majority of the staff made a half dozen moves between May and October. Each move in turn required a host of lesser decisions—which room, which desks, which typewriters, which phones—that seemed irritatingly remote from the central purposes of the campaign.

The focal point for these decisions was David North, whose formal title, Administrative Assistant to the Chairman, obscured the fact that he was immediately under Maguire. He ran the "housekeeping" operation with one regular assistant, two or three clerical aides, and a couple of volunteers. They were overwhelmed by detail. The decisions to lease the new buildings—the responsibility mainly of Maguire, Carter, and Bailey—"were reached fairly early; there was a lack of internal squabbles, and decisions were made more or less on time. It probably would have been better to arrange for the space earlier than we did, but it went all right."

Aside from the administrative overloading of his own staff, North's problems grew out of the fact that Committee leaders assigned him a central coordinating function without incorporating him into the decision-making process wherein he could gain information about general plans and strategy.

---

*Speech writing and major research were done at the White House, as was the work of the secret, *ad hoc* groups, loosely headed by Myer Feldman, whose function was to think up schemes to embarrass Goldwater and upset the Republican campaign. Mass media programs were formulated at Doyle Dane Bernbach in New York City; Republicans, Scientists and Engineers, Educators, and District Attorneys (all citizens groups) were close by in two buildings; some of the minority groups were decentralized to New York City; and the National Independent Committee for Johnson and Humphrey, organized by Rowe and Joseph Fowler, often worked directly from the White House.

Surrounded by a multiplicity of decision-makers, North lacked the time and status to exploit the coordinating potential of bargaining and mutual adjustment. Men such as Maguire and Carter could have helped him, but they were themselves desperately pressed for time. The seeming triviality of housekeeping decisions made them easy to delegate. To the director of a program, however, the need for staff, room, or equipment was not trivial at all.

Fred Dutton, for example, was dissatisfied with his location and resources. Committed to building a high-powered campaign research operation, he used White House support and pushed hard within the Committee for more office space, more staff, and more money. In so doing, he irritated other leaders, particularly Richard Maguire, and some of the cool personal relationships which resulted lowered the cooperation Research both received and gave. Registration, Citizens, and the placement of Media Coordination illustrate how even a short distance from headquarters could limit a leader's mutual interaction with other leaders. Under the pressure of time and events, those in another building would miss more meetings and exchange less information. Separation always produced "go it alone" tendencies, although no two cases were precisely the same due to varying functions, political experience, and contacts with the White House.

We have already noted that some of the same problems which the Democrats were facing plagued the Republican headquarters. Both campaigns set out to keep their operations in close physical proximity—to remain "under one roof." When this became impossible, fragmentation increased and collective decision-making became more difficult. But similarities between the two cases of decision-making are less striking than differences. Republican decisions were quicker, more orderly, and more centralized. It is likely that in terms of moving time, service and rental charges, and the location of personnel, the Republicans were also more "efficient." Yet the Republican decisions imposed high *political* costs, which the Democrats largely avoided. Democratic irritations and frustrations were many, but almost never profound. Location and staff shortages did offend some Democratic leaders. For some, the placement of their offices made interaction more difficult. But the relevant decisions were never interpreted as ideological, and rarely as basic threats to authority.

Indeed, unlike their Republican counterparts, Democratic campaigners never saw an organization chart. None existed. Authority could be discovered primarily by trying to make decisions, and this was an Incremental process. Though burdensome, the tasks of moving equipment and staff within a framework of Incremental decision-making were not hopeless or impossible. The processes of discussion, bargaining, and mutual adjustment went on. There were no feelings of isolation and alienation comparable to those of Clif White and his Citizens group on the Republican side. The Democrats had no Ab Hermann, whose skills were lost within the rational hierarchy constructed by Burch and Grenier. Perhaps the closest Democratic parallel to the widespread disruption occasioned by Republican reorganization was Lloyd Wright's sense of frustration at being unable to reach Committee leaders, and we have noted that Wright leaned toward decision-making relationships that were Comprehensive in character.

Citizens for Johnson-Humphrey

The Citizens organizations of the two parties provided another contrast. We have observed that Clif White's separation from central Republican headquarters contributed to harmfully fragmented decision-making, unbridged by mutual adjustment. A comparison with the organization of Johnson's Citizens shows, however, that separation alone need not destroy coordination. In fact, separation might be chosen as beneficial. Such was the case of James H. Rowe, Jr., another June appointment. He was brought in personally by the President. A veteran of presidential campaigns since 1940 ("In the 1936 campaign I was just a water boy"), Rowe explains how he came to head the Citizens groups and the pattern he followed:

[The President] told me to "get that Committee organized." I came over here (DNC headquarters) and just took over the Citizens. I knocked around here a couple of weeks. I wanted to do something, but I wanted to get away because I run my shows better without minute direction. [Besides] the people here were snowed under . . .

I tried to set up a parallel organization and stay out of the hair of the party. . . . Every once in a while I would talk to Walter Jenkins before doing something—it was more of a feeling-out-process. He would say, "It's up to you," or "That's all right," or, "I'd better check this."

As much as I could, I let them (the heads of the individual groups) run things . . . Once a week we would have a staff meeting. A lot of people wanted to work with us, and they would take over from me the operation of a specific group.

The 60-odd Citizens Committees were diverse and "naturally" independent of the party organization. Where practicable, they were set up on a regional basis, coextensive with the Democratic Committee's seven regions. To a considerable extent they had their own money, interests, and leadership. The Scientists and Engineers, Senior Citizens, and Professors, for example, each had a distinct interest in the election and policies of Lyndon Johnson and drew their leadership and operating funds largely from their own ranks. Such independence, added to Rowe's philosophy of campaign leadership, made the process of decision-making, even within the Citizens, exceedingly fragmented. Although he operated with a small personal staff of two secretaries and one assistant, John Stillman, Rowe had his "own men" at the head of most of the Committees. This direct understanding between Rowe and his operating leaders enabled him to "run" the Citizens with a staff that was utterly incapable of maintaining day-to-day contact with all the far-flung organizations. For most of these groups, Rowe's (and Stillman's) mode of operation was almost entirely remedial in character. He usually ignored a group's activities unless they were thrust upon his attention by the Republicans, the White House, or the demands of the group itself. For a few Citizens Committees, such as the National Independent ("Big Business") Committee, this was not true, but these leading cases drained Rowe's attention away from the others. In his own words, "The fact is that if you have 50 or 60 organizations like this, they *never* get supervised."

Yet there was actually much more coordination with other campaign decisions than the foregoing suggests. It grew in some measure from Rowe's intimate contact with the White House, where he was a member of Johnson's "inner, inner circle."[1] Coordination also developed from forced interaction between DNC leaders and those of individual groups. At least at the start, many of the groups needed money.

> Because Maguire had to give us money at first, I would consult with him . . . I would come to see [him] and . . . get the checks right there and have them signed. Oh, he would scream a little. But there were no delays. I handled the money end. On some of them, like the Scientists and Engineers, I would sit down with Maguire [and them] and we would give them a budget . . . The only real coordinator was Maguire.

Rowe used money as a coordinating device himself. But this success was limited. The Scientists and Engineers are merely one example:

> I tried controlling them by money and cut their . . . requests to a third. But they went out and spent the money anyway even if they didn't have it. It is true that they raised most of their money themselves, but they left me with a $20,000 deficit.

Between Rowe and the leaders at his level there were other patterns of coordination. "Joe Fowler and I wanted to do X, and the President wanted to do it. But O'Donnell said there was a conflict. So I yielded." or, "Walter and I wanted to do Y, but Cliff [Carter] kept us from doing it." All the participants agree that many ideas percolated among the political leaders surrounding the President—and were disposed of through an endless process of discussion in which they would be modified, cast aside, reintroduced, and so on. James Rowe did go his own way, but his decisions were confined within subtle limits of common understanding and personal discussion with other top leaders.

One part of the explanation for this outcome lies in Rowe's selection of strong like-minded leaders for his Committees. Another part takes us back to the physical setting of the Democratic organization. The early decision to run the campaign through the National Committee began a series of decisions placing all but a handful of groups and programs under the Committee's roofs. This meant that telephones, materials (brochures, buttons, etc.), printing, mailing, office location, and to a large extent budgets, were relatively centralized operations. The tendency for each group or program to have its own distinct brochures, for example, was in many cases limited by the need to get a budget allocation from Maguire and by the ease of using the general brochures already available at 1630 L Street. It was cheaper (in time, money, and trouble) for a group to use more of the common rather than more of their own specialized materials. The consequence for the campaign was less dispersion of images and issues.

It was perhaps the proximity of various groups and operations to each other that had the greatest effect upon the character of decision-making. Campaign leaders could "take a cab to the White House," or walk over to another office, in the space of a few minutes. Since the location of other leaders was generally known, even telephoning was easier. This easy ability to get together for lunch or a quick meeting was also true for middle and lower level staff. The strong verbal element in political communication and decision-making was thus greatly facilitated. The coordination of decisions resulting from such proximity and ease of contact was of course not complete; communications did break down, and decision-makers did develop specialized concerns and personal animosities which crippled the subtle process of mutual accommodation. Yet when measured against other presidential campaigns, these disjunctive factors were minimized in 1964. The fact that almost all of Lyndon Johnson's national campaign organization was within a three block radius in Washington, and tended to stay there rather than move around the country in a plane or train, was seen by every veteran campaigner as an important factor in its superiority over previous campaign organizations.

A middle-level Committee leader described the process as he saw it during the spring and summer:

Actually, there weren't many discussions about strategy . . . Never did I have a meeting with the six top people . . . The decision-making was a lot less formal than one would think. I would see Maguire in the men's room or elevator and ask him about something, and he would say, "Ask my secretary for this" . . . Decisions aren't really made. You talk and talk and talk, until the last thing you talk about happens.

Assessing the Early Stages of the Democratic Campaign

Decision-making for the Democratic presidential campaign began formally in November 1963, with the 1960 "Kennedy team" meeting to project a design for careful systematic planning and organization. Most of these same men had leading parts when Lyndon Johnson began his own campaign planning early in 1964. Johnson's determined efforts to achieve continuity in both programs and leadership thus had the effect of reinforcing an Incrementalism already present when Kennedy was in command. Electoral support programs aimed at Negroes, women, and the public as a whole had been operating for years at the National Committee. Organized efforts were being made to register voters, to "keep book" on Republican congressmen and presidential aspirants, to prepare for the 1964 convention, and to raise money. The men and women in charge of these operations were old hands at campaign politics. Like O'Brien and O'Donnell, they knew the existing centers of political power, the accepted ways of doing things, and each other. Everyone was in favor of better planning and organization for the forthcoming campaign, but no one advocated Comprehensive rethinking or radical changes in form. This was as true in February 1964, as it had been in November 1963.

Compared to their situation in 1960, or that of the Republicans at the moment, Democratic decision-makers could luxuriate in time and knowledge during the spring and summer of 1964. They had their candidate. He was the incumbent. They were undistracted by the work and conflict of primaries and state conventions. Much of their organization was in place, and their finances were strong. Yet in these chapters we have seen that even in these "easy" months, few Democratic leaders actually attempted Comprehensive planning or organization. The few that did were in the White House or the Doyle Dane Bernbach advertising agency. Why was it that despite the tempting availability of time, skill, and presidential power, Democratic decision-making rarely reflected or imposed Comprehensiveness?

Any number of answers to these questions have been suggested as the organization, processes, and *dramatis personae* of precampaign decisions were described above. Certainly a major part of the answer lay in the personality and style of Lyndon B. Johnson. But it was a factor that cut both ways. By recruiting a large set of experienced, able, self-reliant, and diverse campaign leaders, especially from on-going operations begun by Kennedy, and associating them directly with himself, Johnson laid the foundation for important elements of Incrementalism. As decision-makers, his leaders tended to build upon the existing program, to exercise a good deal of independence, and to focus on the needs of their own operations and clientele. They sought supporting resources through direct contact with each other and Johnson. They selected goals consistent with available means and the usages of campaign politics, and chose subordinates who would do the same. Virtually the entire structure of Incrementalism was incorporated in the relationships and behavior of these leaders, all of which was fostered by their proximity in Washington.

On the other hand, it is quite clear that Johnson was aiming for as much exhaustive analysis and personal control as he could get. Both were most closely approximated in the work of his advertising agency, and in his use of the confidential opinion surveys carried out for the White House, mainly by Oliver Quayle. In this precampaign period, DDB set out to formulate a synoptic plan for campaign publicity. Their research was designed to be exhaustive; their purpose was to produce not a sufficient plan but the best. The President was attracted by this goal just as he found his professional pollsters providing information that would help him direct a masterful campaign from the White House. Here, then, was an instance in which Comprehensiveness was nearly achieved. What were the political results?

It is evident that as Johnson tried to impose central, overhead coordination there were outbreaks of political disagreement and bitterness within Democratic ranks. Johnson's close-to-the-vest secrecy regarding the findings of his opinion polls hardly had the effect of keeping valuable information out of Republican hands (their pollsters had uncovered the same public attitudes), or of enabling him to unify Democratic campaign research (we have seen that just the opposite was the case). It did cause many researchers to spend days struggling fruitlessly to obtain opinion data needed by their particular operations, or which they feared was not being professionally collected by Democratic strategists at all. The point is not a criticism of White House research, or of its strategic use, but of treating the information as the sole province of a very few top decision-makers. The assumption that only these top few should make decisions seems clear. And it also seems clear that the results, though by no means crippling, were not benign.

In contrast, the President's efforts to incorporate the Kennedy staff, to build an "image" and a platform, to gain support from diverse elements of the political community, and to activate a wide variety of campaign operations, may be taken as almost pure cases of Incrementalism. Many at the time wondered at the lack of overhead direction and considered the accompanying uncertainty, delays, and openings for initiative, as challenges to be overcome. From our present perspective, the results appear impressive. In their midsummer formative months, James Rowe's Citizens Committees demonstrated a remarkable amount of vigor, ingenuity, and effectiveness, although many of their participants felt they were entirely at loose ends. During this period, political groups and leaders ranging from disgruntled Republicans to disgruntled liberal Democrats were drawn into Johnson's campaign organization. Instances of groups leaving the campaign because of disagreements with decisions or decision processes were notably lacking. Similarly, for the first eight months of 1964, we did not find acute dissatisfaction or dissent within Johnson's political staff arising from Incremental decisionmaking.

The American people gave no indication of turning away from Johnson because of his political decisions during this precampaign period. Between December 1963, and June 1964, the proportion of the public approving "of the way Johnson is handling his job as President" began at 79 per cent and ended at 74, with 10 per cent more disapproving in June than in December.* Given the context of his unusually high initial support and a developing Republican effort to find fault, these national survey data indicate that Lyndon Johnson's political decisions did not offend many citizens who were not so predisposed.

*"Do you approve or disapprove of the way Johnson is handling his job as President?"

	Approve	Disapprove	No Opinion
	%	%	%
December 1963	79	3	18
January 1964	80	5	15
February 1964	75	8	17
March 1964	73	9	18
April 1964	77	9	14
May 1964	75	11	14
June 1964	74	13	13

(Source: *Gallup Political Index*, 2 (July 1965), p. 3)

If adherence of political leaders and social groups, ability to carry out administrative operations, and reception of a high level of public approval are measures of political effectiveness, then the opening months of Democratic Incremental decision-making in 1964 must be judged a success. But the crush of the National Convention and the formal campaign lay ahead. The pressure of events was bound to increase. And above all there loomed a President determined to avoid mistakes and to control his party's campaign.

Notes on Chapter 11

[1]Ben H. Bagdikian, "The 'Inner Inner Circle' Around Johnson," *The New York Times Magazine* (February 28, 1965).

12

Incrementalism Challenged and Ascendant

The Democratic decision-making situation in mid-summer 1964 was dominated by two sets of events. The first was the California Republican primary and the Republican National Convention which followed it; the second was the Democratic Convention held in the last week of August. The first set served to diminish and then remove lingering uncertainties about the identity of the Republican presidential ticket and the "image" it would project. Before San Francisco, Democratic decision-makers absorbed uncertainty about the character of the opposition by continuing programs which would bolster their organization and electoral strength regardless of whom the Republicans might nominate. Democratic attention was widely dispersed among a variety of registration, finance, facilities, and special group projects. As Goldwater's nomination became apparent, however, Democratic decision-makers sharpened the focus of their attention. Tempting thoughts of Comprehensive strategies crossed the minds of many but were discarded as the Democratic National Convention accelerated and fragmented the process of decision-making.

The Impact of the Atlantic City Convention

National conventions normally defy the Comprehensive Ideal, and the 1964 Convention in Atlantic City was no exception. Without recounting the bewildering hodge-podge of decisions required to plan and manage the convention, we want to concentrate on some of its many effects on campaign decision-making as a whole. These were mainly disjointive; virtually all contributed to Incrementalism. Casual observers of the political scene often forget that every national convention poses massive problems of logistics and human organization—problems that the comparatively small, inexperienced, and unspecialized party staffs are ill-equipped to handle. It is probably true that the 1964 Democratic party was uncommonly well-prepared in terms of time, money, experience, and technical skills to cope with the requirements of convention organization. Yet the supply of resources never seemed to equal the demand.

J. Leonard Reinsch, manager of radio and television for Kennedy in 1960, was selected as 1964 Convention director. He demonstrated unusual know-how and experience. Reinsch was able to start work long before August, to draw heavily upon the resources of the National Committee and White House, and to get authoritative guidance about who would attend and what was to be done at the Convention. All this enhanced his chances of helping to make it into a smooth, businesslike operation. Yet the familiar picture of the Democratic Convention as an elaborate charade, acted out by puppets on strings held by the White House, is quite misleading. It diverts attention from the enormous costs in time, money, and organization that had to be paid both before and afterward. It also gives a mistaken impression of complete design and control. The Convention was unusually late, the vice presidential nominee was not known beforehand, virtually the entire campaign staff was engrossed for months in preparing for the occasion, and the actions of the Mississippi Freedom Democratic Party (MFDP) were certainly not directed from the White House—all these facts had a sharply distracting influence upon campaign decision-making.

The decisions, emotions, and events which constituted the Freedom Democratic Party's dramatic challenge to the seating of the regular Mississippi delegation at the national convention were far too complex to be detailed here.[1] Yet the situation of ideological conflict was in important ways analogous to that at the Republican convention. We have seen that Goldwater's responses there tended to aggravate disagreements within the Republican party. In contrast, the pattern of Democratic decision-making served to soften the emotional stridency and the lines of division separating the different sides; the resolution was predominantly Incremental. The character of decisions could be observed in many of the "confidential" proceedings and conferences devoted to the problem at the Convention. Throughout, there was no lack of White House determination to exercise control and to smooth over the controversy.

The basic challenge of the MFDP had of course been foreseen. It presented the spectre of civil rights discontent, and ensuing political consequences, far beyond the confines of Mississippi. Indeed, the MFDP strategists made no secret of their intention to rally support from civil rights activists wherever they could be found and to bring concerted pressure to bear upon the Atlantic City Convention. White House and party leaders saw this as a major threat, for it would play directly into the hands of Goldwater's lawlessness and crime-in-the-streets themes and undermine Johnson's identification with stability, order, and consensus. Over the summer, various government agencies and National Committee operations (such as Louis Martin's Minorities program) moved to forestall disruptive agitation by urban Negroes.

As the convention drew near, elaborate plans were made to cope with the anticipated trouble. For one thing, precautions were taken against the threat that thousands of Negro demonstrators, fresh from rioting in northern cities, would descend upon Atlantic City. For another, members of the Credentials Committee, formally responsible for hearing the MFDP challenge and recommending a decision to the convention, were contacted so that a prepared "compromise" solution would be quickly accepted. This solution was a patchwork. It had been pieced together by Lyndon Johnson and his lieutenants as a package of marginal gains and losses for the contending factions.* They knew it would satisfy no one, but calculated that it had the best chance of avoiding an embarrassing southern walk-out, a liberal floor fight, or Negro demonstrations on the Boardwalk.

The process of arriving at this official compromise lacked the elements of bargaining and mutual adjustment among contending decision-makers. While many persons had been consulted, very few felt they had participated in deciding. To make the decision "work," Johnson resorted to administering it from above. A variety of devices were used, including the on-the-spot leadership of Hubert Humphrey and David Lawrence, Chairman of the Credentials Committee.[2] In short, detailed plans were made to achieve overhead coordination of the many other decisions—ranging from those of the Credentials

---

*The "official" compromise would have (1) seated the regular Mississippi delegates who pledged to support the party's ticket, (2) given the MFDP floor privileges but no votes, and (3) revised official party rules to require that Negroes henceforth have full rights of membership and participation in Democratic parties of the South.

Committee to those of southern delegates—required to make the White House compromise effective.

But there were too many uncontrollable factors: the emotional impact of MFDP testimony (nationally televised) before the Credentials Committee on the preceding Saturday; the vigor, skill, and commitment of MFDP leaders, such as Robert Moses and Joseph Rauh; the personal beliefs of many people, including other and more radical leaders of the MFDP and members of the Credentials Committee; the sources of MFDP support, especially in urban centers of the north; and simply the great number and diversity of the decision-makers. A number of Committee members were irritated by pre-convention pressure to support the official compromise, suspecting a White House scheme to muffle the legitimate demands of the MFDP, and they organized against the leadership.

Their first meeting (on Monday) showed the Credentials Committee sufficiently split to produce a minority report, which in turn would have moved the debate to the Convention floor—a prospect that the Johnson leadership wanted to avoid at all costs. It was a situation of unexpected difficulty and confusion. As the initial administration strategy faltered, uncertainty mounted among the leaders of each side. Local negotiations and bargaining were intensified and dispersed. Groups of leaders milled about and lost contact with each other.

To retrieve initiative and control, the leadership team—including Humphrey, Walter Jenkins, and Tom Finney (a close associate of Clark Clifford), augmented by Walter Reuther, who had been called in from Detroit—labored all night for a workable solution. They sought to meet the most imminent dangers, not the least of which was to Hubert Humphrey's chance to be vice president.[3] But now the Credentials Committee needed more time before making its report, and modifications were required in the Convention schedule. Each modification required others, and an increasing number of factors and interests had to be considered. Some of the factors were inflexible deadlines. The times for the presidential and vice presidential nominations and the eulogy to John F. Kennedy were set. To change them now was unthinkable. Facing these deadlines, the leadership came under rising pressure to move further toward the MFDP position. They did. In the final solution, (1) the MFDP received two delegates at large with full voting rights, (2) the other MFDP delegates were accepted as "honored guests" of the Convention, (3) no regular Mississippi delegate could sit until he pledged to support the ticket, and (4) there was to be a new rule at the 1968 and following conventions, that no delegation would be recognized from a state where the party process excluded citizens for reasons of race or color.

It was a great victory, but achieved through such an Incremental process that many uncompromising victors did not recognize what they had won. No one ate crow. And the party leadership succeeded in restraining the controversy and achieving a resolution within the bounds of its campaign purposes. The White House had made a determined effort at central coordination of convention decision-making, but the results were produced by a much more fragmented process of mutual adjustment. Even though the initial "compromise" solution had been carefully devised to pacify the contending groups, its failure to do so, and the tendency of central influence to irritate decision-makers it was designed to mollify, was a classic example of the difficulties of overhead, reasoned coordination under conditions of conflict.

The National Convention was, of course, planned as an integral part of the presidential campaign. Indeed, Democratic politics did not await the Convention before becoming campaign politics. We have treated decisions as part of the campaign if they were consciously directed at the 1964 election, regardless of when they were made. There is a point to be added, however. While no decision-maker (to our knowledge) believed that the President's campaign should or did begin only after the National Convention, the suspicion lingered that someone might be offended if Lyndon B. Johnson acted as if he were the candidate before the delegates, in their independent judgment, chose the party's ticket. This notion, plus the traditional Labor Day starting date, exerted a real restraining influence. Many decisions—about scheduling speakers, printing materials, organizing groups, spending money—which had been talked about for weeks and months, were deferred until after Atlantic City. Naturally, the formal nicety of the party's mantle-bestowing was not the only reason for this hesitancy. More tangible factors were also involved. Materials could not be fully prepared before the vice presidential candidate was known. Certain financial allocations to other programs depended upon what the costs of the Convention would be. And, above all, Atlantic City monopolized the time and attention of both leaders and staff.

As part of the campaign, the Convention was used to project images of Goldwater and Miller, and Johnson and Humphrey. Associations were made with the Kennedy legacy, thus mobilizing the party and drawing the public around the Democratic cause. Intensive nuts-and-bolts sessions were held between top experts on campaign organization, themes, and techniques, and state and local leaders, especially including Johnson's state "coordinators." Perhaps never before in convention history have party leaders, fresh from a night of parties and politics, been roused to attend working sessions lasting from 8:00 to 10:00 every morning. Convention organizers boasted that "almost 95 per cent of the state leaders invited showed up." While doubtless inflated, this assessment reflects the widely-felt satisfaction with the campaign uses of the Convention.

Lyndon Johnson's own decision-making was distinctly Incremental; yet he strove for close coordination of the decisions of others. We have seen this pattern in his attempt to produce a solution for the problems raised by the Freedom Democratic Party. It was also illustrated in the careful though comparatively rapid construction of the party's platform. Managed for the President by Fred Dutton, the platform was drawn up to capitalize on the Democratic record, the demands of many interests, and the vulnerability of Goldwater. Its development resembled—and was expedited by—that of the Great Society speech discussed in Chapter 10. The coordination of platform decisions was comparatively systematic and centralized, yet attention was focused on disparate views, the refinement of existing policies, remedies for immediate defects and ills, and the distributive needs of many different population groupings. Strategic coherence was given to the platform's many themes by its title, "One Nation, One People"—a deliberate contrast to the exclusiveness associated with the Goldwater position.[4]

Behind the façade of the National Convention's Platform Committee, chaired by Representative Carl Albert, Lyndon Johnson thus operated to construct an instrument of his presidential campaign. That an incumbent president should do this was an accepted tradition of American politics. When added to the soothing contents of the finished product and the well-publicized contretemps of the Republican Convention, this tradition helped to make the Democratic platform remarkably free from criticism. Its formulation and adoption provide another example of how Johnson seized every opportunity to "run his Convention." Descriptions by many observers indicate that the thoroughness and artistry of his efforts may be unmatched in American politics.

But these efforts were definitely not Comprehensive. Few events of the Convention were the direct products of smooth, centralized planning. Johnson's attempt to manage the Freedom Democratic Party controversy was overshadowed by Incrementalism, with brilliant results. Each event of the Convention had, of course, its own history of decisions. Yet last minute changes, unexpected demands, and failures of communication, seemed to characterize them all. Faced with a very confusing situation, convention leaders followed a strategy of almost classic Incrementalism, concentrating on decisions of overriding importance (i.e., those directly affecting events under public or presidential scrutiny), and ignoring the rest. The result was a Convention of impressive main events within a context of mistakes, discomfort, frustration, and outrage over many other events.[5]

The case of the vice presidency exhibits yet another facet of decision-making affecting and affected by the Convention. Here, Johnson exercised more complete control, and the effects were also in the direction of Incrementalism. Since the presidential candidate's "right" to select his running mate is accepted as a rule of the game, Johnson's effort to influence the Convention's vice presidential choice was uncomplicated by opposition. In making his own choice, however, the President was acutely sensitive to his relationship to the Kennedys. This blossomed into the so-called "Bobby Problem." Wanting to free his own reputation from that of the Kennedys, yet afraid of alienating Kennedy admirers by some precipitous act, Johnson searched relentlessly through the first seven months of 1964 for a safe way to eliminate Robert F. Kennedy from vice presidential consideration.[6] Finally, on July 30th, after fits and starts in other directions, he solved this problem by the expedient of excluding "any member of my Cabinet or any of those who meet regularly with the Cabinet." Having reduced the number of men to be considered, Johnson still had to choose the one he wanted.

It would be difficult to conceive a more tortuous path of decision than that followed by the President before he presented Hubert Humphrey to the Convention on August 26th. He considered many alternatives. He sought advice from innumerable politicians, reporters, and personal friends. He made an involuted series of small, often tentative, decisions which not until a day or two before Humphrey's nomination had gradually eliminated everyone else. It was typical of Johnson's reaching for certainty through Incrementalism, and the entire episode was an excellent illustration of his approach to decision-making. It emphasizes, too, the sharply different approach taken by Goldwater in his selection of William Miller, which we have described in Chapter 5.

But the President's indecision was also strategic. It focused attention on him and provided an additional mechanism of convention influence. He used it with skill and success. But the price was high in terms of coherent organization of the subsequent campaign. Neither Humphrey nor the National Committee had been able to make any preparations for the vice presidential candidate's participation. There was no office space for Humphrey's staff at the Committee. Indeed, there was no Humphrey staff. All his schedulers, advance men, and speech writers had to be recruited. They had to be organized and given facilities and resources. Their logistic needs alone were of vast proportions. Committee leaders, especially Carter and Maguire, had foreseen vice presidential needs, but the lack of effective physical preparations was striking. What took place is indicated in the following comments by staff leaders of the Committee:

... None of these people [the National Committee leadership] thought we were going to have a Vice President!

We had not made adequate plans. Maguire was talking about a Vice President's desk. It was finally resolved by squeezing the Speakers Bureau into a smaller space.

Humphrey said, "I've got to have room." After a bit, the Vice President said to his people to just get out if space wasn't found, and space was found.

As August and the Democratic Convention ended, there were no appropriate materials (brochures, buttons, bumper stickers, and so forth) for the Johnson-Humphrey campaign. There was almost no organization of the vast range of special groups, such as Nationalities. And great gaps existed in the speaking schedules. Many of the party leaders were exhausted, and some were still occupied with the chores of dismantling the Convention. The Convention was indeed an integral part of Lyndon Johnson's election campaign; but its organizational demands, its traditional functions, its late date, and its burdens of operation and management, all served to delay programs and interrupt and fragment campaign decisions.

This erosion of Comprehensive type planning and coordination was not for the lack of trying. Advertising materials had been designed before the Convention with blank spots for the vice presidential nominee, very careful plans had been made to fit the Convention into an overall publicity campaign, and enormous amounts of energy had gone into the calculation of Convention spending (and income) as part of the campaign budget. The compelling point is that Democratic decision-makers tried hard to make their National Convention a finely-machined part of their campaign. Their planning was not a model of Comprehensiveness, but there was no intention to be makeshift or haphazard. With strong pressures for coherence and coordination from the White House, leaders tried to exercise close control over their Convention responsibilities. These men were not amateurs. Yet their knowledge was insufficient to foresee the actual contingencies that developed. Careful plans were disrupted and salvaged only by remedial and disjointed decisions as events drew near. Ironically, where presidential authority intervened directly and late, such as in the person of J. Marvin Watson[7] or Lyndon Johnson himself, fragmentation was sometimes increased. Coordination was characteristically achieved by follow-ups of mutual adjustment.

Fragmentation and Adjustment in the Opening Campaign

Early in September there was a massive burgeoning of campaign organizations and activities, while only marginal changes took place in patterns of decision. By any definition, the campaign had now begun. Innumerable decisions about scheduling speakers, printing and distributing materials, establishing organizations and recruiting their leaders and staff, collecting and spending money had been under discussion for weeks and months. They had been deferred until after the Convention and now were urgent. These decisions were made, first, by doing what had been done in previous campaigns, and second, by recruiting people who had done it and then trusting them to do it again. Diverse operations got under way, and as they did, the fragmentation of decision-making increased sharply. Citizens and Nationality groups, for example, were created in a matter of days or even hours as a result of decisions at the top, bottom, and middle of the campaign hierarchy. In the post-Convention rush, men near the top, such as Clifton Carter or James Rowe, usually took time to decide only (a) if a group should be organized, and (b) under whom it should operate. Few of these organizations preceded the Convention, and some were established just four weeks before the election. Since only a handful had no precedents in 1960, and since various 1960 leaders were "available" in party or governmental positions, the range of choices actually considered was relatively narrow. The critical effect of campaign traditions and available experience upon the decisions was emphasized by many leaders. One remarked:

A lot of organization is stereotyped. You have organizations for women, for example. How much they accomplish, no one knows. In this campaign they helped in fund raising. . . . A lot of these organizations might not have been needed, but who can say.

An illustrative case was that of Craig Raupe. Between the Convention's end and September 1st (four days), he was pulled out of the Agency for International Development and set up at the 1025 15th Street building as "National

Coordinator" of the All-Americans Council. He immediately recruited operating heads for Spanish-American, Italian, Polish, Chinese, Greek, and other groups, often from relevant governmental jobs,* and almost always with previous political experience. Most of these hastily-selected group directors joined Raupe at 1025 15th Street although a few remained in other cities, such as New York and Philadelphia. They were faced immediately with all manner of large and small decisions, and the need, as one of them put it, to act "the day before yesterday." Raupe was directly under Louis Martin at party headquarters and met with him each day. But the needs of his groups were so specialized, detailed, and pressing, that the already harried top leadership gave only the most general directions. One of Raupe's group directors expressed the situation this way:

> The likelihood was that there was very little control [from the White House]. We got guides from newspapers, radio, the Convention . . . but I can't recall a single instance where I got specific guidelines from somebody higher up . . . The content of advertising in papers, radio, and so forth, was pretty much left to us. We received I suppose as much freedom as you could possibly have and still have organization . . . Craig Raupe did not get any strategy either. . . . Things happened. A statement was made. There was no overall strategy . . . , which was fine. It was what I liked. The strategy was only as I thought, or Craig Raupe thought.

This pattern of last-minute decisions at every organizational level, under conditions of considerable uncertainty and great pressures of time, was considered quite "natural" by a large majority of the leadership. A few, however, found that it impeded their operations. One leader remarked:

> There's a disease at the Committee and the White House that a campaign can be planned, mounted, and carried out in a period of weeks rather than months. [For my program] one of these top people suggested . . . that we get one man in each precinct, and that would do it! They don't respect enough a job of doing something.

The production and distribution of campaign materials nicely illustrates the decision-making situation during the last two months of the campaign. In contrast to much of the special group organization, basic decisions about materials and TV advertising were made early and with considerable time and care. But this statement is relative; for the "final" decisions resulted from

---

*Two of the most frequently heard phrases in Democratic campaign patois were "hatched" and "unhatched," indicating the speaker's status under the Hatch Act, which prohibits certain political activities by federal employees. With a few minor exceptions, the Democrats were quite careful to stay within the formal definitions of that law while vigorously recruiting campaign staff from governmental personnel.

repeated reviews, quick remedial changes, and countless modifications in individual cases. Nonincumbent congressional candidates, for example, unable to get materials through the regular channels, would often make vigorous efforts to get them in any way they could. Their success depended on their direct and indirect contacts in the Washington organization and the short circuiting of the planned procedures. Moreover, some rather obvious basic alternatives were either not considered at all or given very short shrift. One leader remarked: "Maybe you don't need a lot of this campaign literature, but I'll be damned if I'll recommend [that it be dispensed with]." The ad agency and Lloyd Wright did make this suggestion, but Committee leaders could not bring themselves to depart so radically from traditional campaign devices and rejected the suggestion out of hand. In any case, the factors that went into the decisions were widely understood among the campaign leadership.

Consistent with the early and fundamental decision (made at the White House) to conduct a short campaign, and with the subsequent late Convention, adjournment of Congress, and vice presidential nomination, it was decided to hold back all materials until after Labor Day, and then to order and distribute them from a central point at 1630 L Street in Washington. State parties were to purchase their materials from this source and redistribute them to fill the particular needs of their various candidates. The reasoning behind this plan was simple: materials sent out earlier "wind up in a closet someplace," and thus would be stockpiled and wasted; if local campaigners "are hungry for [the materials], and bitching and fussing, when they arrive they are really used"; and great economies (for the national campaign) could be achieved by centralized purchasing and by passing costs along to state and local units. Great demands were anticipated, and painstaking preparations were made for the post-Convention deluge.

But the intensely felt needs of state and congressional candidates had been building up all through the summer. They were now acute. To their pressing demands were added new and diverse requests from the growing host of campaign operations, such as the Nationality groups, centered in Washington. It was time for materials to be ready, but there was a shortage of money. A campaign leader, who had been intimately involved in the decision to withhold materials until after Labor Day and had been its most active defender, expressed it this way when he was asked why it was decided to put off material distribution so late: "It wasn't decided. There was the little item of money!" Another leader said much the same thing:

The materials people had some of the same problems I had. No budget. The day before the election they got some of the stuff in for my election-day effort, and I told them to ***. But it really wasn't their fault; it was a problem of money.

Added to everything else were fundamental disagreements and misunderstandings between Lloyd Wright and DDB on one hand, and Committee leaders like Bailey, Maguire, and Price, on the other. These disagreements had been quietly simmering since May and now reached the boiling point. Hence the decision and administrative system which had been constructed to handle materials was overloaded by unexpected demands and conflicts.

As Johnson's state coordinators, then his advance men, and then the President himself, moved out into the field in September, they often found a dearth of materials and local politicians in a state of outrage. A number of the more experienced campaign leaders viewed the situation quite philosophically; indeed, as quite normal. One expressed it this way:

> My experience is that no matter what system is adopted, and no matter how many principals agree to it, unless the candidate sees billboards and posters at every stop, and unless not one single simpleton who has a ton of unopened materials at his headquarters does not tell the candidate, "We're not getting anything from headquarters," the plan is going to go out the window and top priority will go to making sure that the candidate sees his face on billboards and posters at every stop–à la our Russian friend who put up movie set façades for his Czar.

A strong candidate's direct intervention is expected to upset the best laid plans and to replace them with a patchwork of remedial adaptations. It also, we note, provides a safety valve for those plans which have gone awry, for local situations which have somehow missed out. Among the Democrats, when the widespread and intensified demands for materials were not speedily met, tensions, misunderstandings, conflicts, and fragmented solutions increased abruptly. Women's, Nationalities, Citizens, and Labor operations began contracting for materials directly with suppliers outside the established system. How effectively this could work and how smoothly content coordination was achieved is suggested by a Nationality director as he described the design and ordering of special brochures:

> You'd make it up [the design and content] and run it through Craig Raupe–he had one man who was very good at all languages–and after that was done, somebody–I suspect it was Wayne Phillips–would check it. A runner would take it over and back. I could sit down and say to Craig Raupe that I needed 20,000 brochures. He would say "go." There was no more time to quibble. Where the stuff would be placed was up to us . . .

Too much should not be made of the dispersive aspects of the above situation, especially since we have indicated earlier that the comparative easy availability of common materials in Washington served a coordinating function in the campaign. It is more important to observe the adaptability of this disjointed organization. The point was elaborated by another leader, as he described how the Citizens groups coped with the problem of materials:

> We wrote our own. I tried to get them to start early. I told them it would be all messed up. But Carter gave me a 15-minute speech, and almost convinced me; and it was bad! Carter was so persuasive, I thought it was solved at last, but it wasn't. My people couldn't get [materials] through the Committee, so they got [them] done outside, and cheaper!

There were indeed ample frustrations and irritations over materials, but even on the hustings, where the irritations were immediate and intense, there was relief. Special shipments were sent out on personal orders from Johnson, his advance men, Charles Roche (for congressional candidates), and other campaign chiefs to whom certain candidates and state party officials had "indirect lines." And finally, when in October the regular pipeline still had not supplied materials to many localities, the DNC made large shipments to all the states without charge. The end result was that substantial amounts of materials reached their destinations just in time for election day.

In response to these tendencies toward fragmentation and the need to make quick and coordinated decisions, following the Convention the weekly staff meetings were converted into daily sessions. They began each morning at about 9:30. Still chaired by Bailey, and in his frequent absences by Carter or O'Donnell, these meetings performed information and decision functions even more effectively than their weekly predecessors. A somewhat expanded group of the top campaign leaders attended (Robert Short of Senator Humphrey's staff was included), and the sessions were "wide open" for discussion, with "no one feeling restrained." They were unusually successful in bringing together information gathered by every operation, and in facilitating fast decisions—especially reactions to Republican moves and campaign "crises." The President was informed—separately—of what went on by Carter, O'Donnell, and Feldman. Johnson, in turn, would meet almost every evening with a few advisers like O'Donnell, O'Brien (when he was in town), and Moyers to consider campaign events, especially from a more strategic point of view. This high number and frequency of both regular and irregular meetings between virtually the entire leadership set was facilitated by the presence of so many of them in Washington, with offices close at hand. It was further encouraged by the commanding lead that Johnson was maintaining over Goldwater. The growing conviction that the outcome of the campaign was not in doubt soothed feelings of desperation that might have drawn these leaders back to their desks or out into the field.* The meetings, and the "indirect lines" that almost all of them had to the White House, gave these leaders a strong sense of knowledge, confidence, and control concerning the mechanisms and results of the campaign.

But these meetings were hardly the scene of Comprehensive decision-making. Incrementalism flourished. Those who participated were reassured that they knew or could readily find out what was going on. One leader gave this answer when asked how he managed to keep informed:

> Basically through our [morning] meetings. There was nothing I had to know that I couldn't find out about. [If not in the meeting] I could just pick up the phone and call O'Donnell . . . or I could just go next door and see him.

Of course, information flowed both ways, and these Democratic leaders were quite aware that the President could easily discover and judge their own activities. This easy access to the White House and each other, and the willingness of those above (including the President) to have those below initiate action, encouraged decisions that were fast, Incremental, serial, and fragmented. But there were built-in restraints on the amount of fragmentation. As a top Johnson associate put it: "Everyone went out and did what he wanted, and if he made a mistake he got the hell kicked out of him."

---

*This is not to imply that Democratic leaders were lackadaisical about their work. Other forces than simple victory motivated them. These included strong feelings of professionalism, a desire to crush "Goldwaterism," and the personal drive of Lyndon Johnson.

Notes on Chapter 12

[1] A brief but well-balanced account is given in Theodore H. White, *The Making of the President 1964* (New York: Atheneum, 1965), pp. 277-282. Equally interesting is Rowland Evans and Robert Novak, *Lyndon B. Johnson: The Exercise of Power* (New York: The New American Library, 1966), pp. 451-456.

[2] Analysts have also seen the use of Humphrey as an effort to test his ability to work with both factions and to raise his status in the eyes of the southern leaders. See Evans and Novak, *Lyndon B. Johnson*, and Paul Tillett, "The National Conventions," in Milton C. Cummings, ed., *The National Election of 1964* (Washington, D.C.: The Brookings Institution, 1966), pp. 24-25.

[3] Evans and Novak, *Lyndon B. Johnson*, pp. 452-454.

[4] Paul Tillett, "The National Conventions," p. 29. Tillett argues that despite its image, the Republican platform was "more moderate than the convention from which it emanated" (p. 28).

[5] A good illustration was the case of the badges or passes enabling leaders, staff, and various functionaries to enter appropriate parts of the hall. An elaborate scheme of changes in these credentials was worked out, mainly to protect the President from a conspiracy. Unfortunately, news of these changes continually failed to reach a large number of persons entitled to know. The result was a great amount of lost time and inconvenience for staff members—and outrage on the part of reporters and commentators who were denied entry at last and arbitrary moments.

[6] Details are presented in Evans and Novak, *Lyndon B. Johnson*, pp. 435-448.

[7] To many party leaders, Watson made his first appearance in Atlantic City. He had been named by the President to handle the convention's physical arrangements—a role that brought him into last-minute conflicts with many other projects and program organizers.

13

The Late Democratic Campaign

Advertising Through Television: The Fate of Comprehensiveness

Throughout the campaign a continuing controversy raged over the role of the advertising agency, Doyle Dane Bernbach. One of the early decisions was that in addition to TV and radio, DDB would also be responsible for designing materials. The first materials needed were billboards and pictures for the National Convention. Basic conflicts occurred almost at once. The agency began in April to devise an overall "image strategy" for the campaign—a strategy which would then be systematically implemented with concrete publicity designs and events. The initial decisions about this strategy were made within the agency after a careful study of public opinion (especially about the likely candidates) and briefings from electoral experts such as Richard Scammon and the White House researcher, Paul Southwick.

The agency's strategic decisions were reached in close consultation with Bill Moyers and Lloyd Wright. Other men, including John Hayes, Richard Goodwin, Kenneth O'Donnell, Clark Clifford, Abe Fortas, James Rowe, and Leonard Marks, were also involved to lesser and varying degrees. It is said that the advice of many political experts was sought in framing this strategic plan and designing the first TV "spots" to illustrate it. This was formally true, but the experts at the National Committee did not think they were being heeded or even heard. Throughout the entire campaign period, DDB leaders, such as

James Graham, maintained direct contact with the White House. Their tactics of influence were based on the assumption that Lyndon Johnson made campaign decisions and that members of his White House staff had the best access to him. Since the President had already designated Bill Moyers to head the speech writing and publicity components of the campaign, and Johnson did indeed try to review or make as many decisions as possible, these assumptions were essentially correct. They erred in oversimplifying the decision-making and authority structure of the Democratic campaign. Part of this misconception was reflected in the serious belief of Lloyd Wright and DDB that campaign decision-making and execution could achieve a Comprehensive form.

At first their assumptions were impressively sustained. In the face of strong DNC opposition, Moyers and Wright influenced the President to choose Doyle Dane Bernbach over its more traditional competitors. At the agency's initial meeting with Johnson, during which he was shown early versions of the "nuclear-responsibility" films,

> He asked a few questions, made the comment, "You know what you're doing," and left. The agency people—somewhat dumbfounded by his brevity . . . —were assured by Bill Moyers and Jack Valenti, another Presidential aide, that it had been a good meeting. "If he hadn't liked them [the films] he would have said so."[1]

Heartened by this success, DDB and its White House consultants proceeded to draft their "definitive plan for the campaign on how to get through to the public." The plan was ready late in July, revised three times, and accepted at the White House before the National Convention. It represented careful analyses of both political attitude formation and national opinion surveys.

The plan itself—to hit hard at first and put Goldwater on the defensive, to present a positive picture of Johnson by "letting him be President," and then to have advertising concentrate on substantive policy issues—came comfortably close to the overall campaign strategy worked out earlier by the party leaders. But at the National Committee's staff meetings, dissatisfaction with the agency's work was intense. According to a chief participant:

> Material development and TV and radio were the hardest to find out about. Others shared this feeling. We felt that another group was sitting with the President and making these decisions. Lloyd Wright seemed to have a split personality. They seemed to be making decisions at the White House without talking to the party. This was an area I was outraged about from the beginning. In May sometime the ad agency wanted to talk to me about [my program]. Then they came out with material that had to be thrown out. Every block was put in our way.
>
> It was the same for convention material. We would clear something (with the White House), and then they [DDB] would argue with me. They were supposed to be in charge of [the content] of material. Then they came out with this stuff . . . Bailey was apoplec-

tic. Maguire was surprised. We wasted so much time getting our material laid out—and they (DDB) didn't think it was important! They had a completely wrong concept. When they (certain pamphlets produced by the agency) came into the strategy meeting, there was a major explosion . . . I'd raise the issue [of whether these DDB materials should be used] in the meetings. It was agreed [that they shouldn't be used], and Lloyd would take it back; we'd make a decision, and it still went out . . . They seemed to think they were above the political pros.

We in the meeting were never consulted about those TV spots (showing the little girl and the daisy). I know the Chairman wasn't. Those shown at the Convention were supposed to be a rough sample [but weren't] . . . This to me was the biggest problem. They had little concept of political timing . . .

Antagonized by being ignored, believing that an agency's function was not to make strategy but to implement it, appalled by the high prices, convinced that some of the "radical" designs were politically harmful, and suspicious of the "hard sell" approach they detected, most of the campaign leaders at the National Committee lobbied against the agency's work. They had considerable success. DDB's definitive plan for campaign advertising involved "a whole package costing $9,000,000." Billboards and materials were included. O'Donnell, Maguire, and Carter opposed the billboards, and it was agreed to cut them from the budget. Materials were more complicated. As a compromise, they were to be the responsibility of a "troika" composed of Wayne Phillips, Sam Brightman (Deputy Chairman for Publicity), and Lloyd Wright. Wright describes what happened:

I was told (by the top leadership) to work on materials. Then a troika was set up: Wayne, Sam and me. This simply could not work, not only because of the difficulty in meeting as a group, but also because of the basic disagreements over the role of printed materials as a communication medium. We designed some brochures through the agency that pursued the educational goals . . . materials admittedly quite different from any previous campaign literature. They were designed to intrigue readership, to discuss campaign issues. If materials were in fact required, we felt they should do more than merely billboard the candidates. TV and newspaper exposure does that more efficiently and effectively. When it became clear that this type of approach to brochures would not be accepted, I finally called Wayne and suggested that he do the whole thing. The basic advertising effort demanded my full attention.

Thus the problem of materials we discussed above obviously had more to it than a late start and production and mailing breakdowns. These were largely mechanical in nature. The conflicts over design were, however, more complex and fundamental, and the fragmentation of decisions more difficult to alleviate than that involving distribution. Here was one aspect of campaign publicity that eluded DDB's definitive plan. A diverse menagerie of pamphlets, brochures, and other materials was ultimately produced, largely in response to the unhappiness of the campaign leaders who needed them.

But if DDB and Wright gave up on materials without a determined fight, it was because they considered them of minor importance compared to the mass media. DDB's opinion research showed that the public had a strong "wheeler-dealer" image of Lyndon Johnson. Agency strategists concluded that their television advertising should concentrate on the weaknesses of Goldwater and the strengths of The Great Society as a social program. Johnson was to contradict his image by acting as a man above politics—as President of the United States.[2] As DDB developed its initial plans with Moyers and Wright, the major substantive issues were to be nuclear responsibility and civil rights, and on this basis the agency proceeded to prepare TV spots. But the Republican Convention and subsequent opinion surveys led White House and agency leaders to decide that civil rights would take care of itself; that the backlash was overrated; and that social security, TVA, and Republicans against Goldwater should be added to the nuclear responsibility issue.[3] This Incremental change in strategy did not ruffle Committee leaders; it was billing the party for the unused civil rights spots—a normal operating procedure for DDB—that irritated Maguire especially. Seemingly trivial, this was confirming evidence for those who had opposed DDB from the start as an over-priced luxury.

The agency produced a total design for the Convention hall intended to launch the television "image" campaign. In place of bunting, balloons, and heroic portraits, they planned billboards depicting various facets of The Great Society. Convention television would thus pick up images of social concern rather than the traditional paraphernalia and hullabaloo which would "smack of old-time politics and might increase the wheeler-dealer image."[4] Along with this calculated departure from the traditions of convention imagery, DDB presented Democratic decision-makers with a striking lineup of TV spots giving operational expression to their overall strategy. Quite contrary to the apparent simplicity of the decision-making process at this point, we have found its details unusually complex. Few of the leading participants in this process shared the same view of what took place.

By August, the experiences of James Graham (in charge of the Democratic account at DDB) and Lloyd Wright had convinced them of the wisdom of reaching the President and his top advisers without having to gain the "parochial" approval of such National Committee leaders as Margaret Price, John Bailey, or Wayne Phillips. But their tactic of moving directly to the President through Moyers was partly undermined by the fact that others also had direct access to Johnson. It was one thing to circumvent the DNC staff meetings, but quite another to bypass all those who shared the views expressed in these meetings. At the White House level, the agency still had to cope with a diverse set of presidential associates, including Clark Clifford, Abe Fortas, John Hayes, and Leonard Marks. Each reacted in a different way to the issues of television advertising.

Then, of course, there was the President himself. Accounts vary, but it appears that a smooth compromise overcame the nagging doubts about the meager exposure the candidate was to receive at the Convention: DDB got its billboards; but two huge pictures of Johnson and Kennedy looked out over the delegates, and the President enjoyed a vigorous demonstration (placards and all) upon his nomination. Added to this were Lyndon Johnson's own efforts to insert drama and excitement into the Convention with last-minute personal appearances and manipulations involving the vice presidency. Obviously, the decisions which led to the actual projected image of Lyndon Johnson went far beyond the careful logic of DDB. Some decision-makers saw more conflict than others, but the evidence of early mutual adjustment, later fragmentation, and outright bargaining seems clear.

The TV spots, to become famous soon after the Convention, had been screened and considered for weeks, some for months. During this period, disagreements within the White House group were ironed out in a series of working sessions. Clifford was the most critical of the DDB creations, while Marks seemed able to find money to finance them if there was an unexpected shortage.[5] We have stressed the very close relationship between the campaign budget and these television decisions. Even at the White House level Richard Maguire would delay and threaten to withhold money from projects he thought politically unwise. He thought this way about a number of the DDB commercials and made strong cases against them. The other Committee leaders also tended to be critical of the spots when they had the opportunity to see them. For example, they generally objected to all the nuclear responsibility films, with the exception of the "hot line" spot.* The "daisy girl"** and "ice cream cone"*** spots were heavily criticized as being too "hard-

---

*The picture shows a special telephone marked "White House." While the phone rings ominously, a voice says: "This particular phone only rings in a serious crisis. Keep it in the hands of a man who's proven himself responsible. Vote for President Johnson on November 3rd. The stakes are too high for you to stay home."

**The picture shows a little girl in a meadow picking petals from a daisy. As she does, a background voice begins a countdown. At the end of the countdown, the scene dissolves into a nuclear explosion. A voice says, "These are the stakes: To make a world in which all of God's children can live or go into the dark ... "

***The picture shows a little girl licking an ice cream cone, while a motherly voice explains that Strontium-90 is a fall-out product found in milk, and that Barry Goldwater voted against the Test Ban Treaty.

sell" and dangerously overstated. One was shown on September 7th, the other on September 9th. They became famous overnight. These films had been previewed by most of the campaign leadership; they had been shown to party leaders at the National Convention ("and were applauded!"); yet it was apparent that Democratic decision-makers were as unprepared for the impact of these commercials as their Republican counterparts. Their embarrassment was personified by that of Hubert Humphrey, who, speaking on "Meet the Press," confessed that the daisy girl advertisement was "unfortunate." In contrast, one of the Wright-Moyers-DDB team expressed a much different view:

> On the little girl and daisy, everyone [in the leadership group] saw it beforehand, and I didn't expect the reaction. When the history of the campaign is written, I think it will be seen as a triumph. Our strategy was to . . . put [Goldwater] on the defense . . . This worked.

We know that this film, plus the other fifteen produced by the DDB for the campaign, were a calculated segment of a coherent and sophisticated image strategy worked out by the agency. We know, too, that both the President and the agency were at the outset enormously attracted to the appeals of Comprehensive decision-making for the campaign's mass media advertising. What is more, the number of decision-makers could be kept relatively small and centered at the White House. Lloyd Wright, whose job it was to coordinate media decisions made at the Committee, DDB, and White House, was personally dedicated to "clear lines of authority" and decisive action based on imaginative thinking. Thus the decision situation would appear more conducive to Comprehensiveness than most in the campaign.

Our descriptions have tended to abstract a situation in which the agency, Wright, and Moyers proposed, and the President and a small group of personal confidants disposed. If a single dominant pattern of communication and choice must be abstracted, this would be it. But we have already shown that other decision-making intervened. In particular, neither DDB-Wright-Moyers nor Johnson-Jenkins-Fortas-Rowe were a unified set. Wright, for example, was sincerely concerned to "utilize the [advertising] opportunity as an education medium on what issues are confronting the country." He was inclined to agree that the "daisy girl" spot gave a questionable impression of Goldwater and that the "ice cream cone" commercial bordered on dirty tactics.[6] Graham, on the other hand, argued that these films would be politically effective. It was Wright who rejected the "pregnant woman" spot,* which had been conceived and executed by one of the men in the agency. Thus, different viewpoints did exist within this group of decision-makers, and among the entire set of top staff and advisers at the White House. The characteristic patterns of decision-making emerged from a continuing series of viewings and discussions between different combinations of these people about the ideas and forms presented by the agency.

Almost from the start, however, conflicts between basic values and purposes—minimized elsewhere in the campaign—dominated the relationships between the agency and various political leaders. "In all the years I have spent in politics," said one of the President's closest advisers long after the event, "I have never seen money wasted more extensively than was done in the 1964 campaign for television."[7] Wright's and DDB's effort to neutralize this conflict by confining the decision-making process to themselves and Bill Moyers had some success, but it also served to heighten the sensitivity of the party leaders and then the President to the range and depth of the differences. The result was to expand the set of decision-makers, encourage additional bargaining, and fragment decisions.

The agency's strategic decision to avoid picturing the President in their commercials had been resisted by various Democratic leaders, and during July and August there were repeated suggestions for alternative uses of television. Most of these had been opposed by DDB, Wright, and Moyers. Now, after the Convention, pushed by criticism of the first two nuclear responsibility spots,[8] the White House decided to add TV programs featuring the President himself. Seven films were made, and all were shown toward the end of the campaign.** They cost approximately $2,000,000, and it was this addition to the television budget that helped upset the materials budget. The decision was clearly Incremental. Faced with uncertainty about the effectiveness of current programming, with divided counsel, with the desire to win more support, the

---

*The picture shows a pregnant woman walking through a park with a small child while a background voice depicts the dangers of fall-out to children born and yet-to-be born, and how President Johnson—not Barry Goldwater—supports the Test Ban Treaty.

**Four of the films were five-minute spots in which the President discussed foreign affairs, nuclear responsibility, domestic affairs, and economic policy. Three were half-hour programs in which he was interviewed by some young people, a group of ladies, and a group of businessmen. Only one of the 16 DDB commercials was longer than 60 seconds. This was the five minute "Young Republican" spot in which a Republican voter explains why he will *not* vote for Barry Goldwater and will vote for Johnson. "My party made a bad mistake . . . in San Francisco. And I am going to vote against this mistake on November 3rd."

President made *additions* to his television advertising which combined traditional elements and the thinking of DDB.[9] The consequence was to mollify some of his campaign advisers (but not the Treasurer!), to disperse decisions about materials, and to have more unplanned shifts of resources in the last month or two in response to state demands for more advertising and personal appearances. Thus, in this area of campaign publicity, where the President was in a relatively favorable position to coordinate decisions centrally, the use of DDB's Comprehensive-type planning led to sharp conflicts within the campaign organization, followed by Incremental conflict resolution.

The Personal Appearances of Lyndon Johnson

The inclination of Johnson to make last-minute changes in his speaking schedule affords a good illustration of how Democratic decisions were reached in the face of uncertainty and unexpected events. The original speaking schedule was hammered out after the Republican Convention by a group including Kenneth O'Donnell, Richard O'Hare, Bill Moyers, Jack Valenti, Richard Maguire, Cliff Carter, and Wilson McCarthy. They had the luxury of time and used it to devise a strategy of presidential appearances which would have the maximum political effects. The schedule emphasized the twelve most populous "priority states" and was constructed around invitations received from Democratic candidates and the recommendations of still other party leaders, such as John Bailey, Charles Roche, and Margaret Price. About half a dozen major commitments were made, with prime consideration given to population distribution and campaign timing. But this was just the start. Almost at once additional leaders had to be consulted—Paul Aiken, head of the DNC Speakers Bureau and, after the Atlantic City Convention, the principal assistants of Hubert Humphrey. Further meetings were held. Requests for the President multiplied, and his appearances now had to be coordinated with those of other notables, such as Mrs. Johnson, Hubert Humphrey, and members of the Cabinet.

Wilson McCarthy, chief advance man, struggled to maintain a firm three- or four-day schedule that would remain consistent with the "overall campaign strategy." His problems were considerable. To maintain control he met daily with O'Hare, Valenti, and Moyers, and together they ironed out the innumerable details. He also submitted a daily plan to the White House for Johnson's personal approval. "No decisions were made without consulting the President. The *President* decided where he would go."

Thus toward the end of the campaign, decision-making about the President's schedule was the work of a handful of men, and most of all of Lyndon Johnson himself. Their decisions were carried out by a staff of speech writers and advance men that was unusually small, but which made up in professionalism for what it lacked in numbers.*

Yet a large number of interests, baffling in their combinations, influenced the speaking schedule of the President. Almost every organized party operation wanted the President to say something, somewhere. Seeing their requests get lost in this maze of diverse and conflicting interests, vigorous candidates, in the midst of their own campaigns, contacted the White House directly. Johnson was sensitive to such appeals. He also was attentive to the reports of Lawrence O'Brien (who was touring the country evaluating political conditions in different states), and to the behavior of the crowds at his own appearances. One of the President's chief schedulers suggested some of the problems:

> At the beginning of the campaign (before the Republican Convention) we didn't know how popular the President was. We had polls, of course, but they really didn't tell us how popular he was. The first Poverty trip through the Midwest showed he was immensely popular ... [Later] he drew 400,000 people in Atlanta. It was really something.

Johnson's response was to expand his personal appearances. While persons such as Bill Moyers, Jack Valenti, Kenneth O'Donnell and Wilson McCarthy usually had a good idea where the President would be during the next few days or week, other campaign leaders were likely to be quite unsure. Even his closest advance men would have to make changes at the very last moment. "He'd often throw you off in time by making unannounced stops," was a common observation. The first trip to Atlantic City had to be planned in an hour and forty-five minutes.

Despite these many factors that kept the President's schedule in a state of flux, experienced Democratic campaigners agree that it was under very good control in 1964. The main reason was the ability of those who made the scheduling decisions to meet together quickly, and the fact that other leaders could find out what they needed to know. The number of decision-makers was small, they were closely located, and they were accessible.

*Wilson McCarthy and his staff of 37 advance men were exceptionally proud of their performance in the presidential campaign. Almost all the men had had experience in 1960 or before. They liked to contrast their effectiveness with that of the 167-man Humphrey operation.

Walter Jenkins

The case of Walter Jenkins upset the campaign organization at every level. Overnight, massive uncertainty was introduced into Democratic decision-making. What would be the political reaction of the American public? Was there more to the story, especially insofar as secrets of state were concerned? How would the expose be exploited by the Republican command?* The answers to these questions were shrouded in mystery, and as the Democratic leaders grasped for information, their responses were Incremental, remedial, and fragmented.

The story first became known within the Democratic hierarchy on October 14th, when an editor of the *Washington Star* phoned the White House seeking confirmation for a widely circulating rumor.[10] The President and much of his staff were campaigning in New York, and Jenkins himself took the call. Realizing his dilemma, he sought the help of Abe Fortas. Fortas, in turn, contacted Clark Clifford, and together these close friends of the President moved on their own to get Jenkins into a hospital and then to persuade the Washington papers not to publish the story. But it was too late. During the day, Johnson and his staff had heard snatches of the story as they campaigned, but it was not until evening, as it was about to become public across the country, that Clifford was able to phone the full account to the President in New York City. By this time at least two basic decisions had been reached in Washington. There, Mrs. Johnson made the first statement about the affair. It expressed her sadness over Jenkins' physical collapse and her hope for his recovery and the well-being of his family. Fortas, meanwhile, had gone to the hospital and obtained Jenkins' resignation from the White House staff. These two moves set the Incremental and remedial tone that other decisions would also take.

The uncertainty and alarm that swept through the Democratic organization when the Jenkins case became known were accompanied by innumerable discussions of how the problem might be handled and the consequences it would have. The President and his closest advisers, communicating largely by phone between New York and Washington, immediately embarked on an intensive consideration of alternatives and consequences. That night the President ordered an FBI investigation to answer the national security question, and aroused his pollster, Oliver Quayle, from his sleep for opinion data about the public's reaction. Quayle's organization began a telephone poll the next

*See above, p. 107, for Republican reactions.

morning (October 15th) and by late in the day had sufficient returns to buttress a decision to play down the Jenkins issue—a decision that was reinforced by news of Khrushchev's resignation and Communist China's first nuclear bomb explosion.[11] Quayle found that the publicity concerning Jenkins' arrest had little impact upon voting intentions. More systematic surveys followed and showed the same thing.[12] Voters were more impressed by the President's ability to cope with developments in China and the Soviet Union than by his association with Jenkins. When, on the 18th, Johnson addressed the nation about the meaning of international events, he played on this public reaction and the basic "responsibility" theme of his campaign.[13]

The Jenkins crisis passed almost as quickly as it had arisen. It disrupted Democratic decision-making, but only briefly. The extensive political experience of both campaign leaders and staff led them to interpret the event as a bad but in a sense "natural" part of politics. Almost all the leaders with whom we talked said they had "expected Republican moves" of this type, a perspective that softened the shock of the event itself. The meaning of such statements is difficult to summarize, since it ranged from beliefs that Jenkins had been deliberately "trapped," to assumptions that any campaign will turn out some dirty linen, and that the Republicans were not particularly responsible for its disclosure. Jenkins was widely known and universally liked among the campaign leaders. For most of these people the immediate personal tragedy of the case outweighed considerations of electoral consequences. Apart from the few at the top, Democratic leaders waited. The cues soon came. Jenkins was not to be condemned; he was to be treated with kindness and sympathy; he was to be firmly dissociated from the presidential office; and no further comments were to be forthcoming. The themes of the Johnson campaign were to be reemphasized.

We cannot calculate how much the success of this response owed to the coincidence of world events or the failure of Barry Goldwater to exploit the issue more sharply, but it smoothed the fears and drew the praise of many Democratic leaders. One respondent said:

It [the Jenkins case] couldn't have been handled better, as far as the President was concerned . . . We don't know how widespread homosexuality is in the population. Johnson didn't condemn Jenkins. He simply said, "In your position you make me vulnerable; so you have to quit." Sympathetic but firm.

Treating this new and uncertain situation by trying to say as little as possible, by seeking immediate knowledge of the state of public opinion, and by changing earlier policies as little as possible, Democratic decision-makers sought an Incremental rather than Comprehensive resolution of a problem that appeared to invite disaster.

Characteristic Patterns and Results of Democratic Decision-Making

The 1964 Democratic campaign was marked by more improvisation and omitted alternatives, more piecemeal and fragmented decision-making, and more coordination of decisions through bargaining and mutual adjustment than it has received credit for. It was, in short, highly Incremental. This Incrementalism was not for lack of desire for central planning or control. Before his death John Kennedy had begun systematically to develop campaign strategy and organization. There was a strong Comprehensive element in his intentions.

Yet Incrementalism was a hallmark of his organization. Kennedy's experienced lieutenants did not pull surprising strategies from new bags. Neither they nor the Kennedys were detached from previous decisions, continuing problems, or existing political usages. Their attention was focused on a small number of continuing problems, their search for alternatives was limited to a few, and they chose from these. Their decisions were refinements of what had been known and done before.

The accession of Lyndon B. Johnson brought distinct changes in campaign decision-making that, on balance, reinforced these Incremental tendencies. The new President moved cautiously. He held the Kennedy staff and built on Kennedy designs. His own decision-making was tortuous in its secrecy, piecemeal choices, and last-minute changes. He wanted direct control over decisions and programs. We have seen that Lyndon Johnson took over as a man of uncommon personal pride, vigor, and ambition. Out of this experience and his own inner resources, he developed skills of direct influence and group manipulation. His concern for a massive electoral triumph was matched by his determination to exercise personal control over the Democratic campaign.

To achieve these two goals, the President followed the practice of finding the best men for campaign jobs and attaching them as closely as possible to himself. He was to be the coordinator of decisions. He made a major effort to choose his top operatives personally. The integration of the "Kennedy team" into his own enabled the President to avoid the inevitable irritations accompanying a changeover in leadership and reassured party and group activists throughout the country who were watching for clues to Johnson's political intentions.

There were many decision-makers, and the direction of the campaign was influenced by countless decisions not made at the top. A surprisingly large group of leaders was within the President's immediate purview. He saw them often, even daily, seeking their views and giving them his. Their views and judgments were a rich source of feedback, enabling Johnson to respond quickly and relevantly to a variety of operational problems of the campaign. His judgments were taken back to a larger set of leaders and introduced into the bargaining process through which their collective decisions were reached. The impressive coordination of the Democratic campaign was the product not of dictation from on high, but of intense horizontal and vertical interaction among decision-makers trying to find practical answers to the problems facing their own operations. New ideas were exposed to numerous reviews before they became part of a major campaign program. And when introduced directly at the top, they were subjected to the innate caution of the President and his practice of seeking diverse judgments of others.

This type of decision-making had immediate implications for the type of decisions that were reached. The Johnson campaign set forth no new ideology. No radical programs were introduced. With the possible exception of the television spots and the major organization of the Republican and business groups, no tactical innovations were attempted. In the case of the television programming and the publicity material, what later turned out to be controversial in the political community as a whole had been subjected earlier to vigorous internal dissent. These DDB efforts were softened, moreover, by other, more traditional programs and material generated by other decision-makers. Richard Maguire served as an important agent of campaign coordination—not because he participated in Comprehensive budget-making, but because his tight grip on the purse strings generated bargaining and adjustments among other decision-makers. Programs were designed and modified to meet available finances.

Speeches, of course, could be delivered only by the candidate, and the prospect of making them an integral part of a Comprehensive campaign plan faded in light of the Johnson style. Considerable Incrementalism was apparent in the speech-writing process; and the duplication of effort meant that few ideas were missed or accepted without repeated challenge. Notorious as he was for last-minute changes of all types, Johnson's spontaneous speeches seldom betrayed unprepared positions. His deeply ingrained discipline and caution in matters of policy were not lost in the enthusiasm and quick arrangements of the September and October campaign. His off-the-cuff remarks served for the most part to translate carefully considered positions into a Johnsonian patois. By this time, Barry Goldwater's analogous statements were cautious and more controlled than Johnson's. But it was too late; Goldwater's efforts to soften his image as an erratic radical made little impression upon the voters.[14]

Most campaign operations, however, did not depend exclusively on the President for expression. The very strength of Johnson's lieutenants caused them to act for themselves and to coordinate with each other. Their "professional" experience gave them operating rules for conducting a campaign. These were dominated by Incrementalism, especially by the importance of remedial and marginal changes from what had been done before. Chairman John Bailey expressed it to us this way: "The main problem we had was to make no mistakes. It's like a football game. If you think you are ahead, you don't try any laterals." Mr. Johnson and his colleagues did not reject the Comprehensive Ideal—on the whole they admired it very much—but they treated the elements of Incrementalism as an expected and controlling feature of politics; they rejoiced that things were as coherent and orderly as they were. The prevailing mood was expressed by a 25-year veteran of presidential campaigns when he declared: "All campaigns are fouled up."

Notes on Chapter 13

[1] Shirley V. Robson,"Advertising and Politics: A Case Study of the Relationship between Doyle Dane Bernbach, Inc., and the Democratic National Committee, during the 1964 Presidential Campaign" (M.A. thesis, The American University, Washington, D.C., April 1, 1966), p. 61.

[2] Robson, pp. 27-28.

[3] Robson, p. 32.

[4] Robson, p. 29.

[5] Robson, p. 27.

[6] Robson, p. 36.

[7] The argument that Lyndon Johnson would have received excellent television coverage as President and thus hardly needed the services of a professional agency was not

limited to Democratic party leaders. See Charles A. H. Thomson, "Mass Media Performance," in Milton C. Cummings, ed., *The National Election of 1964* (Washington, D.C.: The Brookings Institution, 1966), pp. 114 ff.

[8]Robson, "Advertising and Politics," p. 40.

[9]The films satisfied more traditional viewpoints by focusing on the President, but at the same time reflected DDB's analysis that Johnson was most effective with small groups where his "personal warmth" would have a better chance to be shown.

[10]The best factual account of the occurrences of the Jenkins case may be found in Theodore H. White, *The Making of the President 1964* (New York: Atheneum, 1965), pp. 367-372. We present only those aspects of the situation directly relevant to our analysis of decision-making.

[11]Soviet Premier Khrushchev was deposed on October 14th-15th, and Communist China announced on October 16th that it had exploded an atomic bomb that day. In addition, the Labor party won (for the first time in 13 years) the British general election on the 15th, while the St. Louis Cardinals defeated the New York Yankees to win the World Series.

[12]Stanley Kelley, Jr., "The Presidential Campaign," in Cummings, ed., *The National Election of 1964*, p. 71.

[13]Kelley, p. 70; and White, *The Making of the President 1964*, pp. 371-372.

[14]Thomas W. Benham, "Polling for a Presidential Candidate: Some Observations on the Campaign of 1964," *Public Opinion Quarterly*, 29 (Summer 1965), pp. 191 ff.; and Kelley, "The Presidential Campaign," pp. 71-72.

[15]Rowland Evans and Robert Novak, *Lyndon B. Johnson: The Exercise of Power* (New York: The New American Library, 1966), pp. 466-467.

Part 4

Conclusions

14

Political Decisions and the Democratic Order

We now near the end of our analysis of two complex sets of phenomena: the Johnson and Goldwater presidential campaigns of 1964. These campaigns differed from each other in many ways, but we have pictured the most important difference as the contrast between two methods of making decisions. We have stopped short of depicting these contrasting methods as the classic "independent variable" of scientific analysis, for we have found that the decision-making characteristic of each campaign was interrelated with many other variables. The historical circumstances of the two political parties and the psychological states and political perceptions of the candidates and their subordinate leaders were among the most important.

We thus must ask, first, if we have isolated the process of decision-making completely enough to use our understanding of this process to explain better the political outcomes of 1964; and second, if the conclusions based on studying the events of 1964 are of a sufficiently general validity so that they may be applied to other campaigns and to other aspects of the American political system.

We have analyzed the decisional processes of 1964 from the viewpoint of two models of decision-making, but these models were not abstracted from the events of 1964 alone. They were constructed both inductively and deductively. As deductive forms, they are logical extensions of assumptions about the nature of rationality, social organization, and politics. Such forms did not originate with us. Other social scientists have formulated similar models, and these have been widely discussed in the professional literature. The study of decision-making, as a branch of organization theory, is more than a decade old in political science, and the models we used to guide our examination of the 1964 campaigns were based upon an accumulating body of both analytic elaboration and empirical research. Moreover, our modification of the models in order to relate them to the campaign situation was in large measure an inductive process through which descriptions of various political organizations and events by scholars, journalists, and practicing politicians were brought to bear upon existing theory. In short, the construction of our models from both axiomatic propositions and diverse empirical evidence suggests for them a relevance beyond the 1964 campaign.

The Models of Decision

The first model, which we have called the Comprehensive Ideal, combines classic forms of rational choice and hierarchical authority. The decision-maker knows his goals and ranks them in a coherent, transitive order. Choosing between conflicting or competing goals is then a simple matter of picking those of higher rank. The means for achieving the chosen goals, together with all their attendant consequences, are exhaustively surveyed, and the best means selected. Since campaigns are collective enterprises, within this first model the leaders agree on their priorities and then make policy decisions with a minimum of controversy. They can be confident that there are no better ways to achieve their purposes. From this unified, central command, appropriate coordinating directives are transmitted through the organization's chain of command to the thousands of other participants in the campaign. In this fashion all implementing decisions and acts are faithfully consistent with those of the very top leaders. Campaign policy is made in an orderly world of sure knowledge, through a process of rational choice, unified direction, and consistent execution. The Comprehensive Ideal combines what Charles Lindblom describes as "synoptic" problem-solving with central, overhead coordination.[1]

The Incremental model is designed for a world of uncertainty. It postulates that, in most political situations, the cost of perfect knowledge is exorbitant, if indeed it is attainable. To strike an effective balance between the need to decide and the costs of information, the individual decision-maker does not attempt an overall evaluation of his goals, or an exhaustive consideration of every alternative in order to find the best means for achieving some goal. He reacts, instead, to problems which press upon him—money which must be raised, staff which must be recruited, brochures which must be designed, speeches which must be written, attacks by the opposition which must be answered. He seeks remedies in "solutions" which depart in only small ways from things which have worked before, which may satisfy various goals simultaneously, and which may combine bits and pieces of several promising alternatives. His resulting course of action thus reduces immediate pressures, yet is only marginally different from the direction he has been taking already.

The model prescribes a multiplicity of decision-makers whose efforts are coordinated through a process of bargaining and mutual adjustment. Overlapping fields of authority are encouraged, so that no vital campaign function will be overlooked or altogether mismanaged, and there are numerous outlets for political ambition and energy. An active candidate intervenes at selected times and places to produce a high level of interaction between decision-makers and to subordinate other goals to that of victory. Among the decision-makers, devotion to the candidate is expected, but unanimity on ends and means is not. Vigorous proponents of diverse ideas and operations, who must compete for scarce campaign resources, help avoid drastic errors or inattention to viable alternatives. As they become more numerous, these decision-makers "mop up the adverse consequences of each other's inevitably imperfect decisions";[2] they call attention to problems others have missed, and bring new energies into the campaign. The model of Incrementalism represents a combination of Lindblom's problem-solving strategy of "disjointed incrementalism" and coordination through "partisan mutual adjustment,"[3] modified by the addition of a strong decision-making candidate.

Both models call for such a candidate, but they differ in the relationships they project between the candidate and other decision-makers. The Comprehensive Ideal places him at the head of a small, closely-knit group of top leaders. They direct the campaign. Their decisions impose central coordination upon its far-flung activities. Because these decisions are final and authoritative, great care must be exercised in selecting the men who make them. Their agreement on ends and means is essential. And the distribution of influence within the campaign organization must parallel the structure of decision-making. Delegations of authority must be precise, assignments of function clear, and competition between decision-makers discouraged.

Incrementalism, on the other hand, gives the candidate a position of pre-eminence among a large and extended set of decision-makers. They gain their roles in many ways and for various reasons. The candidate chooses some of his campaign leaders because they are personal friends; others because they have special skill, or are recommended by trusted advisers, or represent certain groups whose support he needs. Furthermore, many decision-makers enter the campaign by routes that are quite independent of the candidate's judgment. City and state party leaders, or officers of allied organizations, are in this category, as are a considerable number of subleaders whose selection is delegated to men nearer the top. In short, recruitment decisions are also Incremental. They are consistent with the significant characteristics of the organization of American politics: a pluralistic society, and a decentralized structure of political influence in the federal system. Such recruitment decisions are also made necessary by the severe shortage of time and uncertainty as to the best way to maximize the vote.

Since many of the decision-makers occupy independent bases of political influence, the relationships between them are subtle and impermanent. As a result, the candidate leads a mixed band of associates, all of whom are trying to serve partly self-defined values in the campaign. The candidate strives to mould these diverse motivations to fit the direction of his own purposes. He uses his unique resources of power to set forth visible issue positions and to choose among contending ideas and programs which are thrust upon him. Subleaders vie for his attention and approval, since they need these for both immediate success and future payoffs. The candidate remains as receptive as possible to messages from all echelons of the organization, but he has neither the time nor the information to check the decisions of subleaders nor, in many cases, the power to dictate their acts. To coordinate and promote this symbiotic relationship between decentralized decision-makers, Incrementalism calls for vigorous and widespread interaction and mutual adjustment.

In analyzing these models, we predicted that the Comprehensive style would prove inappropriate in the world of campaign politics. We predicted that both Goldwater and Johnson campaigners would begin the campaign period with some desire to establish Comprehensive methods of coordinating decisions, but that this would be abandoned in the face of campaign realities by the Democratic decision-makers. The Republican leaders would cling to their Comprehensive illusions much longer, for those illusions were bound up in the logic of Goldwater's candidacy: "A choice, not an echo."

This pattern indeed proved to be the basic one of both campaigns, although there was no single point in time marking a change in Democratic attitudes. The President and Doyle Dane Bernbach continued, even quite late in the campaign, to inject Comprehensive-type decisions into the Democratic structure.

The Impact of Decision-Making Styles

But what was the impact upon the two campaigns of their different styles of decision-making? To help clarify operational differences between the models, we presented decision-making not as a collection of unique events, but as a dynamic process of focusing attention, designing alternatives, and choosing courses of action. The process takes characteristic forms, conditioned by the attitudes of leaders and the environment in which they work. Our attention has been focused on characteristic patterns of decision distinguishing the Democratic and Republican campaigns. Describing these patterns has eased the task of differentiating marginal cases of Comprehensiveness from those of Incrementalism, and of separating both from decisions which were peripheral to the main directions of the campaigns and their characteristic patterns of decision.

To judge the impact of these patterns, we have suggested visible political results that would follow from them. These consequences range from staff morale and intraparty cohesion to the electoral behavior of American voters. Our major hypothesis was that weaknesses inherent in the model would lead to adverse political outcomes for campaigners attempting to be Comprehensive, while Incrementalism would yield commensurate benefits. The evidence of the 1964 campaigns gives strong support for this hypothesis. From our investigation, we conclude that the Republicans increased their already serious difficulties by aspiring to be Comprehensive in their decision-making and coordination. The Goldwater campaign, insofar as it was planned, was planned from a Comprehensive point of view. The effort to establish a Comprehensive style of organization created new problems without resolving those that existed. By contrast, the campaign of Lyndon Johnson was substantially Incremental in both its design and execution, and it reaped the expected rewards.

Many factors converged to produce the contrasting decision-making of the two campaigns, but the personalities of Barry Goldwater and Lyndon B. Johnson must be counted the most important. The beliefs and styles of these

two men had effects which were both immediate and indirect. Their reputa-
tions preceded them. Advisers sharing his belief in conservative certainties
were drawn to and accepted by Goldwater, while Johnson attracted and
recruited men of proven political experience who were undistracted by
intense ideological concerns. Thus the personal characteristics of the candidates had much to do with the kind of men who joined them, and these men
in turn dominated campaign decision-making. Goldwater's command revolved
around a small set of individuals—Denison Kitchel, William Baroody, Warren
Nutter, and Karl Hess—deeply committed to the conservative cause. These
close advisers were inclined to exclude the "practical politicians" from real
campaign leadership, and the Moley memorandum provided the necessary
justification. As a result, the top Goldwater leadership tended to be cut off
from the party's fund of experience in presidential campaign politics.

Lyndon Johnson, on the other hand, relied on a diverse and experienced
group of personal advisers and selected tested Democratic veterans to lead his
campaign. There were exceptions, of course; but men not versed in national
campaign politics, such as Bill Moyers or Lloyd Wright, were balanced by old
hands such as James Rowe, Lawrence O'Brien, and John Bailey. There was no
dearth of new ideas in Democratic counsels, but they had to pass demanding
tests of usage and practicality.

Influences flowing from the immediate political situation reinforced attitudes toward campaign policy-making already present in the personalities of
the candidates and their top advisers. Goldwater's "inner circle" felt that a
"silent vote" would emerge to bring victory. Presenting "a choice, not an
echo" presupposed dramatic tactics, dramatic issues, and dramatic changes in
campaign organization. Only Comprehensiveness seemed to promise that
these choices would be the right ones.

The appraisals by Democratic leaders of their campaign's favorable circumstances and triumphant progress were close to the mark. Indeed, many feared
the wrath of Johnson more than electoral defeat. They felt a thick cushion of
popular support. They had issue positions and campaign operations of proven
effectiveness. As far as substantive social programs were concerned, Lyndon
Johnson, as President, had taken positions on most of the major issues facing
the national community. These positions could be enlarged or modified, but
they could hardly be rejected or altogether replaced. This was true for the
entire four-year Democratic record. Johnson could not dissociate himself
from a Kennedy position without inviting the loss of supporters, a prospect
quite at odds with his desire to win additional votes while losing none. It is no

surprise that Incremental additions to what had been done before were pre-ferred to risky innovations.

The President was seeking a record-breaking majority, and the fact that innovations were tried in the use of television does not demonstrate the effects of a long lead upon Democratic willingness to take risks. Rather it indicates the success of a "nonprofessional," the Bernbach advertising agency, in convincing the President that additional votes were within his reach. The Democratic campaign situation may have made Incrementalism "easy," but ease alone does not explain its use.

What would have happened if widespread evidence had indicated a close election; if the polls had shown the public evenly divided between Goldwater and Johnson on key issues? How would the Democrats have made their decisions about television spots and publicity materials? Might not the Presi-dent have had a heightened desire to hold policy-making in his own hands, thus undermining the Incremental patterns that actually occurred?

We asked each of our Democratic respondents how their own decisions would have been different if the campaign had appeared close. Since most of these individuals had played important roles in the 1960 campaign, their answers had a foundation of experience. All agreed that the pressures would have been greater, but very few thought that they would have done things differently. While tensions might have been more oppressive, patterns of decisions would not have been substantially different. If anything, these patterns would have been more Incremental. Campaign experience and long familiarity with American party politics disposed these men to Incremental decision-making, even while they consciously admired the organizational neat-ness of the Comprehensive Ideal. Above all, the Democratic leaders gave few signs of being "true believers" in some *Weltanschauung* which promised social salvation and electoral victory.

In contrast, Goldwater's closest advisers were conservative ideologues. They accepted the basic premise of the Goldwater strategy—that there was a latent conservative majority within the electorate—as a matter of faith. It was never subjected to systematic testing, and when information was received that ques-tioned its validity, the Goldwater leaders constructed rationalizations or offered competing evidence, such as "taxi-cab polls," in order to preserve the purity of their faith. The defects of previous campaigns were identified by the Moley memorandum. The "inner circle" was predisposed to centralize au-thority in its own hands, and Moley's recommendations gave this impulse the sanction of an experienced campaigner. The validity of Moley's suggestions was taken to be demonstrated by Nixon's defeat in 1960 and reinforced by the events of the New Hampshire and California primaries.

Three things are clear: First, basic decisions about the substance and organization of Goldwater's campaign were not the result of a Comprehensive process, but many key leaders behaved as if they were, as faith substituted for investigation. Second, Goldwater decision-makers were committed to Comprehensiveness and tried deliberately to achieve it in campaign organization. Third, Incremental procedures of decision-making were frequently and explicitly rejected. Incrementalism in the organizational structure was denied by the insistence upon clear delegations of authority and the supremacy of the organization chart. An Incremental strategy of seeking the support of identifiable groups in the electorate was explicitly rejected when, as in Florida, Goldwater delineated those aspects of his position most likely to offend a given audience.

The Republican campaign was a test, not of Comprehensive decision-making, but of our hypothesis that efforts to introduce it would bring adverse political results. The Comprehensive aspirations of the Goldwater leaders were never achieved; yet they were abandoned only grudgingly. The Republican party proved basically unresponsive to commands from the top and unable to agree on the purpose of presenting a truly conservative candidate. It remained a diffuse, loosely-federated structure. The requirements of the Moley memorandum could not be met, and from the outset the campaign paid a very high price for the intense effort to put Moley's design into operation. Five critical weeks elapsed after the Republican convention before the remodeled National Committee was ready for action.

Added to the delay was the disruption and alienation caused by the Comprehensive reorganization of the Washington headquarters. In the minds of many who experienced the sweeping managerial decisions of Dean Burch and John Grenier, the disagreements and suspicions which had arisen during the primaries and the national convention were confirmed. All of this could not be overcome by the single attempt at the Hershey conference to reach minimal understandings with such leaders as Eisenhower and Romney. And the Hershey conference did not begin to bind up the wounds in local organizations first opened by the operations of the Draft Goldwater Committee.

A central difficulty with the Comprehensive model is that it offers little help when its grand design has broken down and sure knowledge is beyond the decision-maker's grasp. Goldwater's Comprehensive plan was designed to protect the purity of his conservatism, in the conviction that conservatism would triumph. It made no provisions for the fears of Goldwater's policies aroused by his opponents for the nomination and reinforced by the Democratic campaign. Denison Kitchel has told of going to bed every night worrying about "the bomb issue."[4] Wherever the candidate went, local party officials asked him to explain again, to *this* constituency, his stand on social security and nuclear war. Evidence from every side, including the professional Opinion Research Corporation in Princeton, revealed that these two issues were of primary concern to the voters. Every cue from the political environment showed that Goldwater had to modify his public image on these issues if he was to begin closing the gap that separated him from Johnson. In an effort to repair the damage, Goldwater made a futile attempt in speeches and statements to remold his image by "explaining" his true position. Actually, his severest critics were a group of his own lieutenants, who later complained that if he had only been faithful to his basic plan, and had not made changes in his style and position, things would have gone better.[5] This continuing dedication to a discredited Comprehensive plan hamstrung adaptive decision-making, and Goldwater's close advisers devoted a great deal of energy to fending off efforts of other subordinates to modify the campaign.[6]

It is true that Barry Goldwater's decision-making was vitally different from that called for by the model of the Comprehensive Ideal. It is also true that Goldwater and his advisers, by carefully examining the basic assumptions of his candidacy, could have been more Comprehensive. Such self-examination would have been completely out of character for Goldwater and his conservative followers, and there is no certainty that it would have produced a better campaign. The basic conditions of the Comprehensive model—an orderly world of sure knowledge—were not approximated. Given the circumstances of American politics, they could not be. Thus to argue from our findings that if only there had been a more articulate candidate, or more time, or more conservative Republicans, Comprehensiveness would have worked, is to argue against the entire thrust of our analysis. The Goldwater command came closest to the Comprehensive model in its plans for collective decision-making and coordination. The resulting organizational structure was not appropriate in the context of the American political process, nor did it fit the reality of the Republican Party.

The Democratic campaign provided a more complete test of Incrementalism, and we have argued that Incrementalism passed the test. Perhaps the most telling evidence was furnished indirectly when elements of Comprehensiveness were discovered among predominantly Incremental patterns. Presidential efforts to monopolize information and control, or to impose decisions from on high, were cases in point. But the most ambitious single instance involved the participation of Doyle Dane Bernbach in decisions about television advertising. Major segments of the agency's Comprehensive-type plan for publicity managed to survive the Incrementalism of the White House and National Committee. The agency achieved this by avoiding political "professionals" and by creating essentially a Comprehensive substructure within an overall Incremental process of decision.

The immediate political results were clear. The decision-making that led to the famous TV spots was accompanied by sharp and unreconciled internal dissension. When the first two spots were shown, the press reaction was critical, and the vice presidential candidate himself declared that a mistake had been made. The professionals finally succeeded in preventing the showing of one film. This much is known. We also know that the advertisements gained far more than the usual quota of secondary attention; but whether, as their proponents claimed, they also disrupted Goldwater's decisions and cost him public support is quite uncertain. Equally uncertain is the type of television publicity the Democrats would have chosen through a more Incremental process. In the absence of further evidence, we can only conclude that this partial attempt at Comprehensiveness had the disruptive consequences predicted by our analysis.

Incrementalism and the Democratic Order

We offer no final solutions to the problems of American political organization or policy-making. Yet the ubiquity of decision-making invites the application of our analysis to a wide range of political situations. Perhaps the most immediately relevant involve proposed reforms in the structure and policy-making of American parties. We have seen that "good organization" is one of the most common prescriptions for the ills and weaknesses in American party politics. Every leader is for it. Every candidate hopes that it will be achieved for his campaign. Our analysis carries the clear implication that good organization can indeed make a difference in political results, but in most cases precisely what such organization is or does may be grossly misunderstood. An organizational leader like Republican Chairman Ray Bliss may sanctify good organization in order to avoid destructive disagreement on policies. A concentration on the details of organization can provide an escape from more fundamental issues. American party leaders have known this for a long time, and we cannot overlook the functional utility of this device.

Yet it carries the dangers of deception. For organization is another way of referring to how decisions are related and coordinated. It is a structure of collective decision-making, and each of our models prescribes specifically what this structure should be. Thus organization is not just a neutral pattern or activity. It maps the process of decision-making, and one map will produce different kinds of decisions than another. But in 1964, Goldwater's organization aggravated disagreements and dissent. Inherent in its structure were policy responses to domestic and international problems whose very clarity created discord. What is more, the early triumphs of the Goldwater "steamroller" blurred the real story of grassroots Republican enthusiasm for the Senator's candidacy and gave a misleading impression that such an organization could mobilize a national majority under the Goldwater banner.

In the opening chapters we reviewed the conceptions of party structure and policy-making held by working politicians. There was little doubt that politicians still see Comprehensiveness as the ideal toward which party organization should move. Even academic scholars who have given us major pluralistic interpretations of power and politics in the United States seem often to see political party improvements only in terms of decision-making becoming more centrally coordinated and exhaustively "rational."[7] It may be recalled that the argument for Comprehensive organization rests on the assumed ability of central decision-makers to specify goals, reason out the best solutions, and thus provide optimum coordination of effort. Comprehensive problem-solving seeks criteria with which to fix relations among a set of decisions so that conflicts within the set are minimized. Finding these criteria is the key element which makes the resulting coordination "reasoned."[8] Ordinarily, of course, democratic politics are the scene of disagreements over what these criteria should be. Thus Comprehensive organization presents, in exaggerated form, all the problems of individual decision-making when there is disagreement and uncertainty about ends, means, and consequences. When there is conflict over which coordinating criteria are most desirable, any criterion used must be arbitrary.

Our argument for the superiority of Incrementalism in presidential campaigns applies equally to party policy-making and organization in general. We do not deny that Comprehensive forms can work—and work well—in situations of high information and consensus. But it is very hard to find such situations in local or state party politics, and they appear to be virtually nonexistent at the national level. The vast majority of party situations in the United States do not luxuriate in consensus and complete knowledge. They also do not exhibit Comprehensive organization. Patterns of Incrementalism, however, are quite evident in much of the fragmentation, competition, bargaining, and accommodation that have marked party life in America. This is not to say that the Incremental model exists wherever some of its characteristics are found. No single analytic model is likely to encompass the multiplicity of decision-making problems confronted by American parties. Nevertheless, our analysis of Incrementalism in the presidential campaign of Lyndon B. Johnson associates us with investigators who have found it working effectively in such other realms of politics and government as foreign policy-making,[9] national budgeting,[10] the judiciary,[11] and party organization itself.[12] In each instance, the process of decision-making takes a particular form from the environment of law and usage within which it is operating; but each shares basic Incremental characteristics.

Given the variability of party organizations in the United States, we cannot argue flatly against the wisdom of more "discipline" or "central coordination" at particular points in the party structure. Yet the utility of Incrementalism in campaign decision-making does not support the American Political Science Association report, *Toward A More Responsible Two-Party System*, published in 1950.[13] At this late date, it is hardly necessary to review the many arguments for and against this distinguished recommendation for major party reform.[14] But certain aspects of that recommendation were tested by the Goldwater campaign of 1964, and decision-making theory provides an excellent framework for discussion of the results.

The Goldwater leaders chose a conservative doctrine as the "coordinating criterion" for the decisions of their campaign. In the best Comprehensive fashion, they sought to clarify their goals and then rationally to elaborate these goals in the innumerable decisions of campaign implementation. This led to intensified conflict and the loss of support among Republican decision-makers of different persuasions. Tactical modifications to meet changing conditions of the campaign were extremely difficult, and adherence to this criterion was accompanied by serious misperceptions of what campaign conditions really were.

For Goldwater and his key lieutenants, the national election was a means for achieving a conservative political order. They neglected the fact that men often take the same political positions and perform the same political acts for different reasons. The politician, by deemphasizing goal conflicts, is thus able to mobilize individuals with diverse purposes to support common positions and engage in common actions. Whatever their motivations, such acts are politically beneficial to the candidate and the party. Decisions are politically costly when they engender value conflicts which spill over to destroy the agreement needed to perform the specific political acts of the campaign.[15] In 1964 it was apparent that such conflicts are minimized through an Incremental approach to campaign strategy and organization.

The functions of political parties are not limited to the recruitment of candidates, the clarification of issues, and the representation of public opinions on alternatives of policy. Parties also serve an integrative function for the political system. They aggregate "interests," and thus, in complex societies, form a variety of majorities supporting different programs and candidates. Ideally, with an Incremental two-party system in the United States, both parties would so vigorously compromise, bargain, and adjust, to achieve public approval for the specific elements in their policy-candidate "packages," that substantial policy majorities would be represented whichever party won the presidency.[16]

The argument for party responsibility and discipline, however, is toward more coherent national party positions, clarification of interparty policy alternatives, choice between such alternatives by the active partisans in the national convention, and enforced adherence of all partisans to the majority choice of positions as well as of candidates. In areas of controversy, this cannot fail to stimulate conflict and raise all the difficulties of majority expression uncovered by Kenneth Arrow and others. It also does not bode well for the party that tries it first, as the experience of Senator Goldwater demonstrates.

In many ways our analysis is particularly important for the minority party in American politics, which may find the promises of Comprehensiveness irresistibly tempting. As loss follows loss, arguments such as those voiced by Goldwater conservatives find willing listeners. But they promise an illusion. In his study of American oppositions, Robert A. Dahl has shown that while cleavages may, on occasion, be extremely sharp in the United States, they are not highly related to broad socioeconomic groupings or to each other. Americans are not cast into "exclusive camps," available for mobilization.[17]

This basic distribution of political attitudes has consequences for the make-up of American parties and implications for strategy:

Unless attitudes are highly polarized, it is impossible to divide a population into two like-minded collections of people. No matter what criterion is used for dividing people, as long as there are only two categories or collections, then within each category there will be many conflicting views. Given the existence of a two-party system, it follows inevitably that . . . each of the two parties can hope to win only by constructing an electoral coalition made up of people whose views coincide on some questions but diverge on others.[18]

To these factors must be added the decentralized structure of government in the United States and the accompanying fragmentation of power. For the opposition party that succumbs to the appeal of Comprehensiveness, the result of ideological purity and unyielding alternatives can only be losses among many population groups and an increasing proportion of members "low in political skills, realism, and effectiveness."[19] This is the melancholy reality that we found powerfully illustrated in Goldwater's presidential campaign. Indeed, Goldwater's decision-making came remarkably close to the "noncooperative collective action" and "rationalistic problem solving" that Dahl poses as a hypothetically "extreme" system of political opposition. The strategic implications for the candidates and policy arguments which the minority party must advance to achieve even temporary victory are emphasized by V. O. Key's analysis of the 1952 election:

> The entire episode throws light on the qualities that a minority must possess if it is to serve its purpose. A minority led by radical conservatives probably would have had great difficulty in winning in 1952. This is not to say that a serviceable minority must be identical with the majority; it must be different. It must be different enough in the appropriate aspect to arouse hope that it can cope satisfactorily with those problems on which the majority has flunked. It must not, though, so threaten accepted policies and practices that it arouses widespread anxieties. The circumstances of 1952 made the Republican party for the nonce a usable minority—in a country normally Democratic.[20]

The Incremental model of decision-making and coordination does not resolve the inherent difficulties of a minority party, nor does it remake the character of the American party system. But it holds the promise not merely of discovering political majorities but of building them. The policy values of geographic and functional interests are pulled together through the activities of many Incremental decision-makers. These diverse political leaders make many appeals, and an even greater number of adjustments, in the course of gathering support for themselves or their candidates. Following an Incremental strategy, they readily incorporate new issues into the party's position at their level.

Similar patterns occur at all levels, thus integrating local concerns into the larger "platform" of the party, making the campaign a complex appeal to many different interests, an instrument for probing weaknesses of the opposition. The resulting patterns of decision come remarkably close to those Anthony Downs attributes to rational parties operating under conditions of uncertainty.[21] At the national level, especially, the "fit" of the heterogeneous situations and decisions is seldom neat or painless. But the intensive interaction between the representatives of various groups and interests produces a surprising amount of coordination or consistency among party decisions.[22] A key element is the high incidence of "feedback" in Incrementalism, with each decision-maker concentrating on his own area of concern and expertise, and adapting to others to achieve results.

At first glance, it might be supposed that this disjointed process would be a veritable hodge-podge of careless choices and sloppy administration. There are no grounds for this supposition in either the Incremental model or the empirical evidence. The individual decision-maker shows no lack of dedication, precision, or concern for details. He has a great deal at stake, and he wants very much to make the "right" decisions. It is also important not to regard American politics as a real-life representation of the Incremental model. We found many elements of Incrementalism in the 1964 Democratic campaign, but we also found that politicians did not appreciate the advantages of their own styles of decisions. Even such a determined Incrementalist as Lyndon B. Johnson exhibited sporadic yearnings after Comprehensiveness.

It should also be clear that praise for Incremental campaign decision-making, on theoretical grounds, does not mean that we admire every operation and detail of the 1964 Johnson campaign or that we would hold it up as a model to be emulated by future candidates. Presidential campaigns can do more to elevate the level of political discussion than did Lyndon Johnson's and still be Incremental.

Finally, we would commend the Incremental style to the attention of those who seek remedies for the nagging defects of the American democratic system. Minority groups, including migrant laborers, Indians, and many Negroes, suffer serious deprivations and are scarcely represented in the mechanisms of policy. "Irrational controversy" is a feature of the political landscape.[23] For these and other ills, the application of Incrementalism should provoke and multiply political interaction. Indignant protests, diverse solutions, and calls for support would be heard from many quarters. These would focus on sharp divergences from such norms as due process, equal opportunity, or restrained debate. Costs would be calculated. Resources and power would be estimated and reestimated. Linkages of interdependency would generate countless discussions, none conclusive. And out of this maneuvering, negotiating, and bargaining would emerge partial, often decentralized, remedies. These would become immediate precedents for further remedies, until the demands for action subsided—to be replaced by others. How many protests, how many discussions, how many bargains, and how many remedies depend upon the intensity of the conflict and how closely the Incrementalism approaches its model.

Perfection is never achieved; the conceptual apparatus of Incrementalism makes no provision for it. As the model condition is approached, however, fewer dissents are submerged, and major deviations from widely shared standards become less frequent. There are no certainties and no final solutions. Social policy builds up through a series of shifting majorities, facilitating responses to each constituent element of policies and programs. While the process is involuted, one of the most demanding characteristics of Robert Dahl's model of "Polyarchal Democracy"—each citizen's ability to "insert his preferred alternative(s) among those scheduled for voting,"[24]—is approximated as Incrementalism grows.

Obviously, the prescription of Incremental decision-making for American political leaders presupposes a pluralist interpretation of the American political system. In brief, this interpretation holds that political decisions are arrived at in America through a complex process of bargaining and compromise between groups and their spokesmen; that each group may dominate decisions in its own sphere of influence (as a board of directors dominates the decisions of an individual corporation); but that no single group, interest, or elite is able to dominate the entire political process. In the phrase of sociologist Arnold M. Rose, it is a "multi-influence" process.[25] The creative role of the politician is to serve as broker between these diverse interests and to lead in formulating temporary policy agreements which change as new groups or elites combine with one another, or enlist the support of more general public opinion, to press for policy modifications.

Students of American society are far from unanimous in accepting the pluralist interpretation. The most influential dissents have been entered by sociologists Floyd Hunter[26] and C. Wright Mills.[27] The Hunter-Mills interpretation holds that voters and the leaders they elect exert little, if any, influence upon the outcome of really significant policy issues. In this view, Congress is totally subordinate to the Executive branch and is left to worry over secondary issues. Meanwhile questions of war or peace and the direction of national affairs are determined by a self-conscious, even conspiratorial, power elite with official positions at the top of great corporations, in command of the military forces, and heading the departments of the federal executive.

It is a striking fact of contemporary American political activity that extremists of both left and right have accepted versions of this thesis. Students marching upon the Oakland Army Induction Center and groups of Minutemen drilling in the hills of Orange County[28] are alike convinced that some insidious conspiracy has captured the seats of the mighty, denying the majority of Americans access to the instruments of political decision-making. The antiwar demonstrators and the Minutemen would disagree totally as to the purposes of the presumed conspiracy and would disagree to a certain extent concerning the targets of their wrath. But they would agree that some action is needed now, or will be needed soon, that is outside the accepted rules governing democratic political action. Their claim that the structure of democratic politics is a transparent fraud will find increasing acceptance if events demonstrate that strongly held preferences cannot find a place on the agenda for political consideration.

The unequal distribution of political influence among American citizens is a reality which cannot be denied. But to acknowledge this inequality is not the same as to depict a closed system manipulated by a conspiratorial elite. Nor does the recognition of inequality include a prediction that those possessing power will of necessity act in a manner calculated to deny real influence and access to the less powerful. V.O. Key comments:

> ... the critical element for the health of a democratic order consists in the beliefs, standards, and competence of those who constitute the influentials, the opinion-leaders, the political activists in the order. That group ... refuses to define itself with any great clarity in the American system; yet analysis after analysis points to its existence.[29]

Our own analysis delineates the success of Incremental decision-making on the part of Lyndon B. Johnson in 1964 and the dissent and friction which resulted when Barry Goldwater and his associates attempted to impose Comprehensive solutions upon his Republican fellow-partisans. A presidential election does not encompass the entire American political process, yet it is a basic component. In a formal sense, a presidential election should reveal the most "multi-influenced" aspect of that process, for differences of social position, education, and income are eliminated in the voting booth: each voter casts but one vote. This of course begs the question of the control of devices for influencing the individual voter; and many of Goldwater's supporters are no doubt convinced that the same "conspiracy" which prevented the nomination of a conservative candidate for 30 years was activated to prevent his election, through a systematic misrepresentation of his nature and policies in the mass media.[30]

Given the nature of the American electorate, however, and the fragmented two-party system, a presidential candidate will have the greatest success if he attempts to build an electoral majority by including the attitudes of as much of the electorate as possible within the span of his calculations. He can do this only by remaining open to signals from groups within the electorate as well as to every element of his organization. His campaign must remain fluid, imprecise, and Incremental.

After election, a president may find little help for his governmental burdens in the apparatus of his campaign.[31] Yet politics do not stop at the White House, and the president's decision-making will benefit if he remains open to the same kinds of signals, and establishes policies which may be modified by the process of bargaining and mutual adjustment which is the hallmark of Incrementalism.[32] In particular, he should be ever aware of the vulnerability of complex organizations to "information pathologies"[33] and resist the temptation of feeling that Comprehensive decisions can be made on the basis of the knowledge accumulated at a given time. When Incremental decision-making becomes self-conscious, embedded in "beliefs and standards of the influentials," the health of the democratic order will receive new protection. Access of diverse groups to the process of decision will become more certain, and the actual operations of the political process will more nearly conform to the pluralist model.

We have provided abundant evidence that Incrementalism, as practiced by American political leaders, does not result from a conscious choice between decision-making methods. Lyndon Johnson's Incremental methods were developed from long political experience; they seemed an extension of the instincts of *homo politicus*. As Majority Leader of the United States Senate, Johnson was dealing with other Senators, who were his equals in custom and the Constitution. The only path to accomplishment was the Incremental route of bargaining and mutual adjustment. As President, however, Johnson commanded the resources of knowledge and influence which made Comprehensive decisions seem both possible and attractive. We have described the failure of Johnson's effort to "dictate a consensus" to the Democratic National Convention concerning the treatment of the Mississippi Freedom Democratic Party. Although the policy seemed a reasoned compromise to Johnson, the principals in the dispute had not participated in making this Comprehensive decision. Their opposition threatened unfavorable political consequences, and the President was forced to involve the principals in an Incremental process of redeciding the issue.

Yet President Johnson's attraction for the authoritative statements of goals and policies from the top became more pronounced after the election. Opposition to these in the realm of domestic policy was muted for many months. Opposition in the realm of foreign policy began quietly and rose to a crescendo. By then, the President did not acknowledge "opposition." Instead, he spoke disdainfully of "dissent."

Writing in October 1967, military expert Hanson W. Baldwin attributed what he considered to be the failures of President Johnson's Vietnamese policy to the practice of "consensus politics"—the desire not to alarm the electorate by involving it in the decision.[34] Others have seen a failure of Incrementalism writ large in the many "small steps" through which the United States commitment in Vietnam was gradually increased. They saw in this type of decision-making a tendency to foresake large solutions for minor remedies, to march blindly if slowly toward disaster. Better, say these critics, for the policy-makers to have evaluated all the consequences in terms of the "great" national values or goals before deciding to act. We find nothing persuasive in this call for Comprehensiveness. Writing shortly after Baldwin, Richard H. Rovere showed the impenetrable nature of these consequences and the innumerable considerations to be resolved before the great goals can be identified.[35]

In our view, Baldwin's analysis depicts not a fulfillment of Incrementalism but the same tendency toward secrecy and personal control that Lyndon Johnson exhibited in his campaign. This constitutes a deviation from, not an adherence to, the Incremental model. It represents the same kind of " 'closed' politics" which Roger Hilsman found so detrimental to the Bay of Pigs decision.[36] Whatever other evaluations may be made of these decisions, in every case they resulted in sharpened internal dissent. War policy obviously cannot be made in a public forum; neither can campaign strategy. The two are not identical, but we suggest that Incrementalism provides ample justification for the inclusion of critics—of "rival advocates"—in decision-making wherever there are situations of uncertainty and disagreement. Patterns of decision in which alternative views are not heard, or are simply castigated, do not give the electorate even the illusion of participation. And it is the belief in the possibility of participation that insures legitimacy for democratic regimes.

This book, then, is a case for Incremental decision-making in American politics. We have used the 1964 presidential campaign to test the theoretical capacity of such decision-making to produce favorable political results. We hope that our analysis has suggested productive ways of looking at political strategy and organization, and that it will, in the Incremental tradition, stimulate future studies of questions we have not asked and answers we do not suspect.

Notes on Chapter 14

[1] *The Intelligence of Democracy* (New York: Free Press, 1965), Chs. 9-13.

[2] Lindblom, p. 151.

[3] Lindblom, esp. Chs. 9 and 10.

[4] Theodore H. White, *The Making of the President 1964* (New York: Atheneum, 1965), p. 330.

[5] This point has been expressed in various ways. The presumed attraction of Ronald Reagan's campaign speech, for example, was that it sounded like "the old Goldwater." Stephen Shadegg, *What Happened to Goldwater?* (New York: Holt, 1965), p. 253.

[6] See above, pp. 120-125; and Shadegg, pp. 221-241.

[7] Lindblom, *The Intelligence of Democracy*, esp. pp. 303 ff.

[8] Lindblom, Ch. 12.

[9] Roger Hilsman, "The Foreign-Policy Consensus," *Journal of Conflict Resolution*, 3 (December 1959), pp. 361-382; and, *To Move A Nation* (Garden City, New York: Doubleday, 1967), esp. Ch. 35.

[10] Aaron Wildavsky, *The Politics of the Budgetary Process* (Boston: Little, Brown, 1964); and Aaron Wildavsky and Arthur Hammond, "Comprehensive versus Incremental Budgeting in the Department of Agriculture," *Administrative Science Quarterly* (December 1965), pp. 321-346.

[11] Martin Shapiro, "Stability and Change in Judicial Decision-Making: Incrementalism or Stare Decisis?," *Law in Transition*, 2 (Summer 1965), pp. 134-157.

[12] Lindblom, *The Intelligence of Democracy*, Ch. 19.

[13] (New York: Rinehart, 1950).

[14] Stephen K. Bailey, *The Condition of Our National Political Parties* (New York: Fund for the Republic, 1959); Julius Turner, "Responsible Parties: A Dissent from the Floor," *American Political Science Review*, 45 (March 1951), 143-149; and J. Roland Pennock, "Responsiveness, Responsibility, and Majority Rule," *American Political Science Review,* 46 (September 1952).

[15] A particularly succinct discussion of the political costs (and benefits) of decision-making is found in Aaron Wildavsky, "The Political Economy of Efficiency," *The Public Interest*, 8 (Summer 1967), esp. pp. 45-48.

[16] Lindblom, *The Intelligence of Democracy*, p. 327.

[17] Robert A. Dahl, ed., *Political Oppositions in Western Democracies,* (New Haven, Conn.: Yale University Press, 1966), p. 58.

[18] Dahl, p. 59.

[19] Dahl, p. 61.

[20] V. O. Key, Jr. (with the assistance of Milton C. Cummings, Jr.), *The Responsible Electorate* (Cambridge, Mass.: Harvard University Press, 1966), pp. 78-79.

[21] *An Economic Theory of Democracy* (New York: Harper, 1957), Ch. 7.

[22] "In a set decisions are consistent with one another if there is no way to alter any decision(s) in such a way as to benefit one person and harm no one." This "Pareto Optimum" definition is found in Lindblom, *The Intelligence of Democracy*, p. 193.

[23]Dahl, ed., *Political Oppositions in Western Democracies*, pp. 64-68.

[24]Robert A. Dahl, *A Preface to Democratic Theory* (Chicago: University of Chicago Press, 1956), pp. 70 ff.

[25]Arnold M. Rose, *The Power Structure* (New York: Oxford University Press, 1967) *passim*. The leading pluralist among political scientists is Robert A. Dahl, cited above.

[26]Floyd Hunter, *Community Power Structure* (Chapel Hill: University of North Carolina Press, 1953); *Top Leadership, U.S.A.* (Chapel Hill: University of North Carolina Press, 1959).

[27]C. Wright Mills, *The Power Elite* (New York: Oxford University Press, 1956).

[28]The selection of these two examples from the State of California is not intended to suggest that extremist political activity is unique to that state, or even that it is more prevalent there than in other areas.

[29]V. O. Key, *Public Opinion and American Democracy* (New York: Knopf, 1961), p. 558. For a careful documentation of the existence of a "national upper class" and the reasons for describing it as a "governing class," see G. William Domhoff, *Who Rules America?* (Englewood Cliffs, N.J.: Prentice-Hall, 1967).

[30]For a documented account of the more notable lapses of journalistic objectivity, see Lionel Lokos, *Hysteria 1964: The Fear Campaign Against Barry Goldwater* (New Rochelle, N.Y.: Arlington House, 1967). Mr. Lokos is overlooking much relevant evidence, however, when he concludes (p. 180) that the conservative voters are yet to be mobilized.

[31]Norton E. Long, "After the Voting Is Over," *Midwest Journal of Political Science*, 6 (May 1962), 183-200.

[32]This is spelled out by Roger Hilsman, *To Move A Nation*, pp. 548 ff.

[33]The phrase is Harold L. Wilensky's. See his *Organizational Intelligence: Knowledge and Policy in Government and Industry* (New York: Basic Books, 1967).

[34]Hanson W. Baldwin, "A Vietnam Balance Sheet," *The Reporter* (October 19, 1967), pp. 14 ff.

[35]Richard H. Rovere, "Reflections: Half Out of Our Tree," *The New Yorker* (October 28, 1967), pp. 60 ff. After a painful and sobering discussion, Rovere does reach a conclusion: "I haven't a clue as to how we can get out (of Vietnam) . . . But out is where I want us to be, and I don't know what a man can do except say what he thinks and feels." This follows his inability to resolve conflicting goals and consequences.

[36]Hilsman, *To Move a Nation*, p. 550.

Index